INDIVIDUALIZING INSTRUCTION

Roger Hiemstra
Burton Sisco

INDIVIDUALIZING INSTRUCTION

Making Learning Personal, Empowering, and Successful

Jossey-Bass Publishers

San Francisco • Oxford • 1990

INDIVIDUALIZING INSTRUCTION
Making Learning Personal, Empowering, and Successful
  by Roger Hiemstra and Burton Sisco

Copyright © 1990 by: Jossey-Bass Inc., Publishers
                       350 Sansome Street
                       San Francisco, California 94104
                                    &
                       Jossey-Bass Limited
                       Headington Hill Hall
                       Oxford OX3 0BW

Library of Congress Cataloging-in-Publication Data

Hiemstra, Roger.
    Individualizing instruction : making learning personal,
empowering, and successful / Roger Hiemstra, Burton Sisco.
        p.   cm.—(The Jossey-Bass higher education
series)
    Includes bibliographical references.
    ISBN 1-55542-255-1
    1. Individualized instruction.   2. Adult education.   3. Learning.
I. Sisco, Burton, date.   II. Title.   III. Series.
LB1031.H54   1990
374'.1394—dc20   90-34309
                                                     CIP

Manufactured in the United States of America

The paper in this book meets the guidelines for
permanence and durability of the Committee on
Production Guidelines for Book Longevity of the
Council on Library Resources.

JACKET DESIGN BY WILLI BAUM

FIRST EDITION

Code 9061

The Jossey-Bass
Higher Education Series

Consulting Editor
Adult and Continuing Education

ALAN B. KNOX
University of Wisconsin, Madison

Contents

6.   Six Steps to Individualizing Instruction   77

7.   Assessing What Learners Know and Need to Know   94

8.   The Importance and Use of Learning Contracts   104

9.   Evaluating Learners, the Learning Process,
     and Yourself   121

**Part Three: Achieving Success in
Individualizing Instruction**   133

10. Adapting the Process to Nontraditional and
     Informal Settings   135

11. Responding to the Needs of Special Audiences   150

12. Realizing the Potential of a Personalized Approach   167

     Resources for Individualizing Instruction   179

     A.   A Guide to Practical Applications   181

     B.   Research and Theory   229

     References   261

     Name Index   293

     Subject Index   299

Preface

Instructing adults can be one of the most gratifying experiences in life, and it is something enjoyed by countless men and women from all walks of life. The motivation to teach adults is seldom economic considerations or a desire for personal gain. Most instructors teach out of a genuine interest in helping mature people succeed and grow.

At the same time, many instructors and trainers feel considerable anxiety about how best to teach adults. Some of the more perceptive among them realize that teaching adults is different from teaching children in that (1) adult learners are extremely diverse, as a result of the varying levels of education and experience they possess; and (2) when given the opportunity, they prefer to be in charge of their own learning. The problem facing most adult instructors is finding reliable information that takes into account adult diversity and experience and integrates this information into a proven system for teaching adults.

Individualizing Instruction: Making Learning Personal, Empowering, and Successful details a comprehensive teaching and learning process that ensures instructional success. The individualizing process is designed to be flexible, practical, and applicable in a variety of settings, ranging from literacy instruction to training in the corporate world.

When we refer to individualizing instruction, however, we are not using the term in its earlier sense. Thus, it is not a matter of programmed instruction or teaching machines. Nor is it the same as individualized education, where learners use specially designed teaching-learning units or modules for the mastery of self-selected goals. Certainly, there are some similarities, but we are actually advocating a use of the term more akin to Carl Rogers's (1983) call for self-initiated learning, responsible participation in a learning process, and self-evaluation within a "freedom-to-learn" climate. As Miller and Hotes write, "Individualized instruction . . . emphasizes individual responsibility for efforts in performance" (1982, p. 20).

A number of books offer assistance on teaching adults, but none of them describes an effective instructional process that capitalizes on the adult's unique individual qualities and ability to accept personal responsibility; thus, teachers are forced to draw on many sources for ideas and guidance. In this book, the reader will learn how to plan, organize, and implement an individualizing process for adults. Particular attention is devoted to areas rarely covered in other sources, such as recognizing how different learning settings require that adjustments be made in the instructional process, capitalizing on the adult learner's need to accept personal responsibility, and working effectively with various adult populations.

We have set the following goals for *Individualizing Instruction*:

1. To help you instill greater confidence in your adult learners as they work toward achieving their potential
2. To remove the mystery and lower the anxiety often associated with the instructional transaction
3. To increase the satisfaction that you and your learners can gain from engaging in instructional endeavors together
4. To make teaching more gratifying and exhilarating
5. To provide you with a practical and consistent way to organize instruction so that learners will assume greater responsibility for their own learning

6. To enable you to demonstrate to colleagues the value and importance of incorporating flexibility into their own teaching

Background

This book is based on more than thirty years of combined experience at working—in various instructional capacities and locations—with adults. We have taught at several postsecondary institutions in a variety of credit and noncredit settings, including semester-long graduate courses, intensive summer sessions, short-term training workshops, concentrated weekend experiences, and distance education programs. We hasten to add that probably 99 percent of the learners with whom we have worked have been twenty-five years or older, so we do not have much experience with younger people or undergraduate students. Fortunately, we have taught many students from diverse cultural and social backgrounds and believe that our understanding of instructional processes has been enhanced by these experiences.

The individualizing process has been tested and retested in various settings and with many types of adult learners, including nonreaders, older adults, graduate students, business and industry trainees, journeyman and apprentice instructors, workers in various health fields, and many others. The process has its roots in adult education scholarship and our own beliefs about the learning potential of each person, it grows out of our actual experiences with learners, and it has undergone a constant process of evaluation.

Most aspects of the process have been tried by us at least three times. Whenever some aspect of the process is still being developed or has been brought to our attention primarily through the literature, we include appropriate references for your review or assessment. Thus, we have written this book so that we can share our experiences with others who would like to improve their teaching and want the satisfaction of helping adults take responsibility for their own learning. At the same time, we will be most grateful to hear from instructors who encounter difficulties in using the process or who discover ways to elaborate on our ideas. We believe that it is only through ongoing dialogue and the exchange of ideas that the individualizing instructional process can be further improved.

Overview of the Contents

This book deals with an individualizing instructional process for instructors or trainers who wish to work with or develop self-directed adult learners. It provides information about the process and its underlying assumptions; it discusses how the process works, how it can best be maintained, and what roles learners should play in it. Throughout the book, we summarize the various research findings that undergird the process and that contributed to its evolution.

We believe there are at least nine questions that an instructor of adults will want to ask in evaluating the individualizing process:

- What are some instructional techniques that are effective in individualizing instruction?
- What are the situations, audiences, and kinds of content conducive to individualizing instruction?
- How is individual ownership of learning experiences best promoted?
- How can the individualizing of instruction be established?
- How can what the learner knows and needs to know be determined?
- How can learning contracts be used to enhance individualized instruction?
- How can the individualizing of instruction and learning be evaluated?
- How can instruction be individualized in nontraditional learning settings?
- How can instruction be individualized for various audiences?

Chapter One provides insight into why an individualizing instructional process has considerable potential for adult learners, while Chapter Two presents background information about adults and adulthood and describes the importance of facilitating adult learning. The nine questions just listed serve as focal points for the nine subsequent chapters, that is, Chapters Three through Eleven. A concluding chapter discusses ways to ensure success when using the individualizing process. We believe that the material presented here will provide you with a comprehensive guide to facilitating and individualizing adult instruction.

The book is divided into three parts. Part One, consisting of five chapters, will help you decide when it is appropriate to use individualizing approaches in your instructional efforts. As noted above, the first chapter provides an introduction to individualizing instruction as a procedure for enhancing a learner's potential. We point out that it is crucial for adults to be involved in deciding what they will learn, how they will learn it, and how their learning will be evaluated. Not only is this enlarged role for learners consistent with findings in educational and training literature over the past twenty years, but it is also supported by considerable research on self-directed learning preferences. In Chapter One, as in all other chapters, we use vignettes to establish a setting for the subsequent discussion. Important points are italicized at the beginning of various paragraphs throughout the book.

The second chapter presents background information on adulthood and describes various mental, physical, emotional, and social characteristics of adults. Some understanding of these characteristics is obviously necessary if we are to succeed as adult educators.

Chapter Three sets out to answer the first of the nine questions: What are some instructional techniques that are effective in individualizing instruction? Our six-step individualizing process model is introduced in this chapter.

In Chapter Four we respond to the second question: What are the situations, audiences, and kinds of content conducive to individualizing instruction? In other words, how can you know when it is appropriate to use an individualizing process as opposed to some other approach?

Chapter Five, which concludes Part One, looks at the learner's responsibility in any learning endeavor. It provides an answer to question three: How is individual ownership of learning experiences best promoted?

Part Two describes some of the fundamentals that you must

master if you plan to individualize your instructional efforts. Thus, in Chapter Six we discuss how the individualizing of instruction can be established, and we describe what happens during each of the six steps in the individualizing process. In general, we use traditional or formal educational settings in our example discussing how the process is implemented. The reader eager to understand how the individualizing process works may wish to read this chapter first and then move back to earlier chapters for background information or forward to Chapters Ten and Eleven for more information on the use of the process in varying settings or with various audiences.

Chapters Seven, Eight, and Nine provide information on some basic tools that an instructor can employ to make the individualizing process as effective as possible. Chapter Seven focuses on the importance of assessing learning needs and provides answers to another guiding question: How can what the learner knows and needs to know be determined?

Chapter Eight describes a crucial tool in facilitating individualized learning activities, namely, the learning contract. This chapter focuses on how learning contracts can be used by learners to guide their personal learning endeavors.

In Chapter Nine, which concludes Part Two, we consider the question of how the individualizing of instruction and learning can be evaluated, discussing various techniques and approaches.

Part Three provides insight into how to use and be successful with the individualizing process in different settings and with various audiences. Chapter Ten addresses the question, How can instruction be individualized in nontraditional settings? The chapter includes discussion of the impact that technology is having on adult instruction.

Chapter Eleven answers the question, How can instruction be individualized for various audiences—for example, adults with special needs and older adult learners?

The final chapter, Chapter Twelve, shows how instructors can achieve success through the individualizing instructional process. Ideas are presented on how to promote success, what to do when things go wrong, and how to prevent problems from occurring.

A resource section providing supplemental material on various topics concludes the book. The section is divided into two parts. Resource A, "A Guide to Practical Applications," is intended for the reader who is looking for materials or examples that can be adapted for immediate use with learners. It contains nine individual units. They address common concerns about the individualizing process and describe various needs assessment techniques, sample evaluation forms, and specific learning activity ideas. Resource B, "Research and Theory," presents more advanced information, which is based on current research into adult teaching and learning. It covers such topics as self-directed learning, learning styles, the physical learning environment, and needs assessment. This part will be of greatest interest to the reader who already has considerable understanding of the individualizing process or who wishes to pursue research or additional reading on some aspect of individualizing instruction.

We conclude this preface with the same message we use to end our workshops on instructing adults and our formal graduate courses on instructional methods and techniques. We can provide only a matrix of ideas and approaches, from which you must extract, synthesize, and adapt those elements that fit your personality, preferences, and predilections. In all of this we wish you much success, and we will be pleased to receive your reactions to our approach, as well as your suggestions for improving the instruction of adults.

Acknowledgments

Writing a book is an arduous task, even when two friends and colleagues do the writing together. Add to this the nearly two thousand miles that separated us for long periods of time, and the task becomes even more difficult. We owe much to numerous unnamed individuals who shaped our thinking and offered stimulation and encouragement when the process seemed endless. Without their assistance, the book would not have been possible.

We owe a lasting debt to several leaders in the field of adult education whose persistence and imagination have left an indelible mark on our lives. The pioneering work of Cyril Houle, Malcolm

Knowles, Howard McClusky, and Allen Tough in understanding how adults learn, under what conditions such learning occurs, and how people use various community resources for learning has influenced us beyond measure. Their work laid the foundation upon which this book is written.

To our countless students who challenged and inspired us to improve our instruction and to find a way of nurturing the potential in all of us, thank you. At the same time, we apologize for our frequent experimentation with new techniques and ideas, trusting that you realize that we did so in our quest to be the best instructors we could be.

Thanks are due to Lynn Luckow of Jossey-Bass for his patience and understanding, to Alan Knox at the University of Wisconsin, whose comments on early drafts proved to be invaluable in helping us organize the book in a more intelligible manner, and to other early readers who provided useful suggestions.

Finally, to our wives, Janet Hiemstra and Ellen Sisco, and our children, Nancy and David Hiemstra and Geoffrey and Jessica Sisco, who supported us through the best and worst of times, we want to express our gratitude. We are indebted to them for their constant patience and understanding. As a small token of our appreciation, we lovingly dedicate this book to all of them.

July 1990   Roger Hiemstra
                                                 Syracuse, New York

                                                 Burton Sisco
                                                 Laramie, Wyoming

The Authors

Roger Hiemstra is professor of adult education and co-director of a Kellogg Foundation–sponsored project at Syracuse University focusing on adult education history, adult education resources, and the impact of technology on adult learners. He received his B.S. degree in agricultural economics from Michigan State University (1964), his M.S. degree in extension education from Iowa State University (1967), and his Ph.D. degree in adult community education from the University of Michigan (1970). He was a Mott Intern in the community education program in Flint, Michigan, for a year.

Hiemstra served from 1964 to 1967 as county extension agent for the Iowa Cooperative Extension Service, where he first began working with adults as learners. From 1970 to 1976, he taught adult education at the University of Nebraska. He has since served as professor and department chair of adult education at both Iowa State University (from 1976 to 1980) and Syracuse University (since 1980).

His longtime interest in community adult education led him to write *The Educative Community* (1972, updated in 1985). His interest in adults' potential to assume the primary responsibility for their own learning was the impetus for *Lifelong Learning* (1976), and a coauthored book, *Self-Direction in Adult Learning: Perspectives on Theory, Research, and Practice* (forthcoming, with R. Brockett).

He has also served as editor of *Lifelong Learning: The Adult Years* and of the *Adult Education Quarterly*. He teaches courses on the community and the adult educator, international adult education, professional writing and publishing, program planning, self-directed learning, and teaching methods and techniques.

Burton Sisco is assistant professor of adult education at the University of Wyoming. He received his B.A. degree in history from the University of Vermont (1973), his M.Ed. degree in teacher education, also from the University of Vermont (1977), and his Ed.D. degree in adult education from Syracuse University (1981).

Sisco first worked with adult learners as a Kellogg Foundation intern at the Community College of Vermont (1976–77). After completing his doctoral studies, he was a research associate on a National Institute of Education research project investigating the learning efforts of rural, undereducated adults (1979–1981) and, at the same time, worked as an administrator in the Division of Continuing Education at the University of Vermont and taught adult education courses at Saint Michael's College in Winooski, Vermont. From 1983 to 1985, he was assistant professor of adult education at Syracuse University.

Sisco's primary research interests are adult cognition, self-directed learning, teaching effectiveness, and the historical foundations of adult education, and he teaches courses in these fields, among others. He currently serves on the steering committee of the Adult Education Research Conference of North America and has held numerous leadership positions with the American Association for Adult and Continuing Education (AAACE). He is editor of the *MPAEA* [Mountain Plains Adult Education Association] *Journal of Adult Education* and book review editor of *Adult Literacy and Basic Education* and has served on the editorial board of the *Adult Education Quarterly*.

INDIVIDUALIZING
INSTRUCTION

PART ONE

A PERSONALIZED APPROACH TO ADULT INSTRUCTION

Individualizing the instructional process does not work equally well in all situations. Moreover, you will have to decide how to adapt the process to a particular setting, whether to emphasize certain elements at one time and other elements at another, and whether to use only portions of the process with certain audiences. Part One of this book is designed to help you determine under what circumstances you should try individualizing some of your instructional or training efforts.

We discuss several elements in the five chapters that make up Part One: (1) the role that adult learners, themselves, can play in any instructional process; (2) the notion that an instructor or trainer is really a facilitator or manager of the process; (3) the need for instructors to understand the emotional, physical, mental, and social characteristics that make each learner unique; (4) when it is most appropriate to use individualizing approaches; and (5) the learner's responsibility in an individualized setting. We also present some of the philosophical underpinnings of our approach.

In Chapter One we very briefly describe our six-step model to provide you with an introduction to the major components of the individualizing process. Chapter Three provides a somewhat more detailed description of each step. If you already have had some experiences instructing adults, you may be familiar with many of the

1

components in the process that we describe. In fact, in building our instructional process, we have borrowed from many of the approaches to working with adults described in the literature over the past two decades. What makes our approach worth examining, we believe, is its comprehensiveness. Thus, we discuss a large number of topics that are crucial to instruction, ranging from what to do during the first few hours with learners to how to manage the physical environment so that it will stimulate rather than inhibit learning.

In this part, as in Parts Two and Three, each chapter begins with a vignette that establishes a context for the material to be presented. Although we use fictitious names, all the vignettes represent situations that either we or some of our students have experienced. For example, Joe Daniels in Chapter One experiences a fairly negative classroom environment when he attempts to reenter the educational environment after a long absence. The Joe Daniels story was patterned very closely after the experience that one of our graduate assistants had when he first went back to school.

We are afraid there are many teachers or trainers "out there" similar to the one he encountered. These are usually well-intentioned people who are striving to be good teachers. However, they subject adults to ridicule, they emphasize attendance charts, they lock classroom doors so that people arriving late cannot enter, they give boring lectures, they employ speed or timed tests, they grade on a curve with a guaranteed percentage of failures, and they employ a host of other methods tied primarily to didactic or socratic models of teaching. Such models obviously have considerable utility and will be used for many, many years to come, but we believe they often do not "fit" very well with the needs or expectations of adult learners.

The reader may wonder why we initially present a rather negative view of teaching. Unfortunately, that view matches reality in too many cases. But we also know something about the positive side of teaching and learning, and we believe that the chapters in Part One will convince you it is worthwhile to analyze our individualizing process and adapt aspects of it to your own teaching or training efforts.

1

How Adult Learning and Achievement Can Be Enhanced

Joe Daniels [fictitious names have been used here and throughout the book], forty-three years of age, had been working on the production line in the local tool and die factory for twenty-five years. There had been rumors for the past few years that many of the production workers would be replaced by robotic machines. Joe and his friend Barney were talking about these looming changes at the local watering hole one day after work. Barney said, "If we don't do something soon about these robots and computers taking over everything, we will be out of a job!"

Later that evening, Joe was talking to his wife, Helen, about these changes. Their conversation eventually focused on what Joe could do to improve his job skills. Helen mentioned the nearby community college that she thought had worker-retraining programs. Joe decided to find out what was available.

The next day, as soon as his shift ended at 3 P.M., he drove out to the college. Eventually he found the career counseling center and described his situation to the receptionist. He then found himself in conversation with a vocational education specialist and

3

was encouraged to enroll in an introductory course on computer science scheduled to begin the next week.

When Joe entered the classroom the following Tuesday afternoon, he was a little late because he had encountered some difficulties finding a parking space. The teacher gave him a mild tongue lashing for not being on time. Then, when Joe looked around, he discovered that he was one of the oldest people there— his graying temples were clear evidence of that.

The instructor continued his discussion of the course requirements and the importance of keeping up with all the reading assignments. He then asked each person to look at the person in the chair to the right and then to the left. He exclaimed, "The chances are very high that at least one of the people you looked at will fail this course—and, remember, two people looked at you, too."

The instructor then began two hours of continuous lecturing about the textbook he had authored and how important it was for each learner to memorize its contents. When Joe raised his hand to ask a question about a word he did not understand, the instructor said, "Why is it that the gray-haired ones in my class always are the first ones to not understand something?" Joe began to wonder if he had made a mistake in going back to school.

Why an Individualizing Strategy for Adult Learners?

The explosion of books and articles, research, and program development related to adult learners has been phenomenal during the past decade. Many organizations have discovered that people such as Joe are potential clients for education or training, even though not all teachers have a good understanding of adults as learners. Evans (1985) views this recognition of adult learning potential as part of what he calls the posteducation society. This recognition affects institutions of higher learning, business and industry, private entrepreneurs, and society as a whole in various ways.

Various North American authors have written about adult learners. For example, Apps (1981) talks about adults such as Joe who are returning to college campuses. Cross (1981) synthesizes what is known about adults as learners. Daloz (1986) discusses teaching and mentoring, and Smith (1982) offers suggestions for helping adults learn. Authors from other parts of the world, such as Griffin (1983) and Jarvis (1985), have also focused attention on adults as learners.

The actual process of instructing adults has received inadequate attention in the literature. Certainly, considerable attention has been given to the andragogical process, an instructional approach that has assumed increasing importance over the past twenty years. Knowles (1980; Knowles & Associates, 1984) has been the primary initiator in North America of the literature on andragogy, which he refers to as a system of concepts related to instruction. Savicevic (1981) provides a useful review of andragogy as it is employed in several European countries.

A parallel area of interest has been the growing body of knowledge about self-direction in learning. Making use of Tough's (1979) seminal work on adults' learning projects, various researchers have demonstrated that mature learners frequently prefer to be in charge of their own learning with only minimal direction from an instructor, trainer, or other resource. Both these areas of study have prompted a change in the role of the instructor from that of content giver to learning manager, facilitator, and resource locator. It is this changing role and our belief in the need to individualize instruction whenever possible that we address in this book.

Linking the instructional process with learner inputs, involvement, and decision making is crucial. The potential of humans as learners is greatest when instructors systematically provide opportunities for them to make decisions regarding the learning process. The instructional process that we describe in this book builds on the notion of individual decision making, the need for instructors to help learners become more self-directed, and the respect that we have for the untapped potential of adults.

This approach asks learners to determine their personal

needs and build appropriate learning situations to meet those needs. It accomplishes these goals without imposing too many external controls or instructor-directed biases. Sometimes learner needs and subsequent goals are known early or can be determined quickly. At other times such needs and goals may be preset by an employer, stem from a specific content area requirement such as a college credit course, or arise out of some personal situation. There also are instances when the learner needs some time or discussion with colleagues before specific learning needs and goals surface.

In Chapter Three we briefly describe a process that we use for individualizing instruction in such a way that learner inputs, involvement, and decision making are facilitated. This process includes six steps: (1) preplanning activities prior to meeting learners, (2) creating a positive learning environment, (3) developing instructional plans, (4) identifying appropriate learning activities, (5) implementing and monitoring the instructional plan, and (6) evaluating individual learner outcomes.

The individualizing process is based on the belief that all people are capable of self-directed involvement in, personal commitment to, and responsibility for learning. More specifically, we believe that they are able to make choices regarding instructional approaches, educational resources, and evaluation techniques. You may find the experience of adapting all or some portions of the individualizing process to be a wrenching one. It may mean giving up some of your beliefs about instructor or trainer roles. Personality and institutional constraints may need examination and change. It may require you to reexamine your former teacher role models. Frequently, many of our role models were traditional instructors who used an approach quite contrary to the individualizing one. Thus, it may take some time before you feel comfortable with the changes required by the latter approach. If your experience was similar to ours, it most certainly will mean a reexamination of your own philosophy about instruction.

We also need to note that some learners, perhaps the more timid ones, those who prefer prescribed learning, or those with little educational experience, will have considerable initial difficulty in a setting where individualization is stressed. However, we have found that most such learners eventually thrive on the process, and initial confusion or problems with such activities as needs assessment or designing learning contracts are soon diminished.

Educational Changes

The increasing number of adults involved each year in training or educational endeavors is a worldwide phenomenon. Although there are similarities in types of learning activities, there also are some unique differences across countries or cultural boundaries. For example, developing countries frequently use education for adults to improve literacy, to upgrade occupational competencies, and to promote community development. Some societies use adult learning for political indoctrination in addition to nationwide literacy or development programs. The developed world often uses adult education and training for the same purposes but also uses them to promote personal satisfaction, personal improvement, coping skills, and civic responsibility.

Various societal forces have stimulated the need for educational change. Although the many social changes taking place today affect people throughout the world, within the United States at least four forces have stimulated increased interest by adults in learning. The first of these includes the ever increasing rapidity of social change, the constancy of technological advance, and the expanding awareness of global conditions. These trends have resulted in a continuous need for new skills and increased knowledge. A related need is the continuing struggle to maintain high levels of literacy. Kozol (1985) has helped to focus attention on this problem. As a result, large numbers of adults have enrolled in adult basic education, Laubach Literacy International or Literacy Volunteers of America programs, and high school completion courses.

A second major force is the job obsolescence experienced by many adults. The educational response has been midcareer counseling, retraining for displaced workers, and complete career shifts, often through extensive back-to-school commitments.

The third force focusing societal attention on adult learners is the undeniable fact that the American population is a steadily aging one. Increased longevity, a slowing birth rate, and the huge number of babies born after World War II have created a population aging faster than ever before in our history. This provides a potentially large pool of older adults interested in learning opportunities.

A fourth force is the changing life-styles that now permeate American society. Single-parent families, families in which both spouses work, experiments with new family arrangements, and efforts to enhance individual development represent only some of the changes in life-styles. Self-study, participation in a variety of conferences or workshops, increasing private adult education opportunities, and involvement in encounter groups have been some of the educational responses.

Societal changes have affected a variety of organizations charged with delivering educational services to adults. Various organizations and institutions have begun to experience their own changes because of increasing demands by adult learners. There is every reason to expect that such impacts and changes will continue for some time and actually cause new learning forms to evolve. We believe that an individualizing process can potentially assist instructors and trainers as they attempt to respond to such changing situations.

Theories About Adult Instruction and Learning

This section could be titled our philosophy of and theory about adult instruction and learning. We base some of our beliefs on research findings while others have been derived from personal observations. Still others represent our assumptions and values about how a particular technique should be used with learners. Such beliefs and assumptions have evolved over time and will, no doubt, continue to change in the future. You may wish to match your own beliefs with those that follow to determine what changes might be required as you experiment with elements of the individualizing approach.

Essentialism to Eclecticism. We begin our discussion by describing some dominant philosophies of education in the United States. Essentialism, for example, has been a pervasive force in American education for much of the country's history. Its goal has been to transmit cultural essentials as a means of shaping the knowledge and values of the individual. The emphasis has been on content mastery, with instructors primarily serving as transmitters of knowledge. Essentialists believe that schools make up one of our society's most important institutions and that the mission of schools is to pass current knowledge on to individuals in their formative years.

Progressive scholars such as John Dewey (1938, 1956) had a considerable impact on educational philosophy. Dewey believed that education was a continuous process of reconstructing experiences and that learners were capable of active roles in the learning process. He also felt that an instructor's role was to guide the process of learning and that the school is a social institution that should both reflect and alter culture.

There have been various interpretations of Dewey's and other educational philosophers' positions. For example, American educators of young people in the past twenty-five years have vacillated between "open schools" and "back to the basics." Adult educators, too, have based a variety of programs on such essentialism beliefs as Americanization efforts, adult vocational training, and adult basic education.

Liberalism is another philosophical approach that has had a tremendous impact on education in the Western world (Elias & Merriam, 1980). Based on classical Greek philosophy, liberal education became a foundation for early Christian approaches to education, as well as a predominant force in early American schooling efforts. Similar approaches have been developed or used in several other countries. This emphasis on developing each individual's intellectual powers by exposure to classical thinkers was a basis for many of the early adult education efforts in the United States, such as the Great Books movement. Thus, the stage was set for considerable debate between the essentialists and those who believed in liberal education for adults.

There actually are many current differences among educators of adults regarding the adult as learner. Some feel that the role of adult education is to develop participants into mature individuals who will contribute to society in positive ways. Other educators believe that the aim is to liberate or free the individual mind. Still others believe that the education of adults implies keeping them abreast of institutional, occupational, or technological changes. There are also many educators who fall somewhere in between these various beliefs or who have been affected by behavioral, humanistic, or radical beliefs. In addition, people such as Cropley (1980), Gross (1977), Hiemstra (1976a), and McClusky (1974) have argued that learning must be lifelong in nature. Elias and Merriam (1980) provide a useful description of the various belief systems.

Consequently, many instructors or trainers of adults have become eclectic in their philosophical bases. They have chosen those aspects of various doctrines, philosophies, and approaches that fit a particular situation or an individual teacher's needs. One of us has described elsewhere how a person can use an eclectic approach to translate personal values and philosophical beliefs into a strategy for instructing adults (Hiemstra, 1988b).

We consider our own beliefs regarding instruction and learning to be very eclectic in that we have tapped various philosophies to build our own individualizing approach. For example, we have been heavily influenced by humanistic beliefs, and we therefore think that instructors should help learners take a larger role in the educational process and that instructors themselves should become facilitators. However, we also have had success in utilizing learning contracts, an instructional tool that is founded in behavioralist traditions. Similarly, there are times when instructors must use lectures to present basic information. We anticipate that you, too, will need to glean from the book that with which you feel comfortable, can master, and can incorporate into your own personal style or philosophical beliefs.

Enlarged Learner's Role. This eclectic derivation of approaches to instructing adults has resulted in the use of facilitator techniques in which learners are encouraged to take an active role in the entire learning process. This role, somewhat enlarged over that assumed by most learners during their K-12 education and even during their undergraduate years, includes participation in various activities, such as assessing individual learning needs, planning content emphases and even methodological approaches, and serving as a learning resource for others in the educational setting. The result of such an active role is that learners usually take personal responsibility for the learning efforts.

In addition, many researchers have demonstrated that mature individuals prefer self-directed learning (Brookfield, 1985; Knowles, 1975; Long & Associates, 1988). Kidd (1976), in describing the term *Mathetics* relative to the science of people's behavior while learning, discusses relevancy, relatedness, and responsibility in terms of individual needs. McClusky (1964), in talking about the relevance of psychological theory to the adult education field, suggested that the adult learner is both autonomous and independent. He concluded that learning activities should facilitate active participation, be problem centered in nature, and be highly meaningful to the adult condition.

There are several ways in which learners can greatly increase their self-directed skills and enhance learning based on preferences for personal control of decision making. We believe that there are at least nine instructional variables that learners can control in an individualizing process (Cooper, 1980; Hiemstra, 1988a). As Table 1 displays, the level of control or the sharing of control between a learner and facilitator varies from situation to situation.

Learners are encouraged to seek ways of tying learning activities to the practical realities of job, home, and community. In addition, learners have the freedom to select various written or mediated resources to enhance their grasp of the subject matter, especially after a learning experience is completed and subsequent needs arise.

Teacher as Facilitator. Another of our beliefs concerns the instructor's role in the learning process. The traditional role of instructors was to impart knowledge to receptive learners. However, the instructional process that we advocate requires the instructor to facilitate or manage the learning process itself, especially when mature, adult learners are involved. In other words, the learning process is more important than the content of the course or body of knowledge being covered.

Therefore, the instructor or trainer works to assist individual learners in taking responsibility for their learning. This does not mean that you as an instructor may simply ignore subject matter.

Table 1. Learner Control of Instructional Variables.

Variable	*Learner Control Possibilities*
Needs Identification	Various techniques are available to assist learners in identifying learning needs associated with a study area's contents. Rediagnosis of needs throughout a learning endeavor also should be possible.
Content Area and Purpose	The specificity of topics and purpose for the learning process should be controlled by the learner. A learning plan or contract can be a useful tool, and a facilitator can assist with any refinement activities as needed or desired throughout the learning process.
Expected Outcomes	The nature of desired or expected outcomes should be controlled by the learner. Such outcomes typically relate to needs and purposes. The facilitator provides advice and concrete suggestions as needed.
Evaluation and Validation	Learners should select those evaluation or validation methods that suit personal learning styles and preferences. Facilitators serve as evaluators as needed.
Methods of Documentation	Learners should choose those methods for documenting and demonstrating accomplishments that have long-term uses, such as diaries, logs, journals, scholarly papers, or physical products.
Appropriateness of Learning Experiences	Learners should select those learning experiences best suited to their individual situations or needs. Facilitators can obtain feedback on the appropriateness of various experiences.
Variety of Learning Resources	A variety of potential learning resources permits learners to choose as needs and interests dictate. Facilitators work to locate and make available such resources.
Adequacy of Learning Environment	Learners should select those components of the learning environment that best meet their needs. Facilitators promote an environment that will foster excitement, intellectual curiosity, and involvement.
Pace of Learning	Learners should select a pace best suited to their particular needs or life situations. The facilitator and learner may need to negotiate a pace or completion date for learning activities.

Source: Adapted from Hiemstra, 1988a.

Frequently, you will need to maintain control to varying degrees over key concepts or topics studied because of your institution's expectations or because your learners may have limited initial awareness of these concepts or topics. For example, an instructor in a continuing education session for nurses may possess the most recent information about a new technique and must present it as directly, quickly, and effectively as possible. A university professor has a responsibility to both university and learner to see that the promotion of ownership by learners does not result in a focus on some subject quite different from that initially proposed. A business trainer may be working with executives in sessions that are quite costly in terms of the time involved, and the trainer must therefore be concerned about efficiency and effectiveness.

What, then, is the operational mix for the instructor, trainer, or leader between an expert (instructor-directed) role and a facilitator (learner-directed) role? There is no easy answer to such a question because much will depend on the situation, the particular content areas, the unique mixture of learners, and the instructor's personality. In addition, people frequently bring to the initial learning periods their own expectations about the instructor's role.

The individualizing process will often require you to weather some initial learner confusion, anxiety, or suspicion. It has even been our experience that occasional hostility or uncooperativeness must be overcome. In other words, an investment of time is required to build a "community of learners," where you become a specialist in the learning process and evolve a personal role appropriate to that process. In such a setting content expertise often will be secondary to your skill in learning management and developing a community spirit that allows learners, your expertise, and available learning resources to come together.

Success with such an approach also will depend on your own attitude. In other words, an instructor in a facilitator role will need to believe in the overall potential of promoting self-direction in learning, accept learner input, criticism, and independence, and seek out a wide range of learning resources. Changing your approach or attitudes toward instruction generally requires dedication, hard work, practice, and time.

Stimulating the Learner to Learn. An important variable in
facilitation lies in your success at providing the stimulus for
learners to become excited about a subject area, so that they want
to learn about it and are willing to dig into available resources. This
will entail your helping learners locate a variety of resources and
discover their own ability to use such resources. We suggest that the
development in individuals of a positive attitude about learning
and the relevancy of the subject matter to personal needs may be
more important than mastery of the actual subject matter.

Research evidence supports this notion that the facilitative
approach to instruction does in fact promote a positive attitude
toward the learning activity itself. Cole and Glass (1977), Pine
(1980), and Verdros and Pankowski (1980) have studied the effect of
personal involvement by adults in assessing needs, determining instructional approaches, and carrying out instructional activities. In
general, such researchers have found that individualized involvement usually does not increase or decrease content mastery. However, those having ownership of the process almost always have a
more positive attitude toward the content, instructional process,
and facilitator, as well as a greater desire to study the content further
after the formal learning experience has ended.

We also have had considerable success with learning contracts as a mechanism to further interest in a topic, stimulate people
to learn, and help them individualize their learning efforts. Contracts actually are excellent tools for instructors, too, in that they
permit different criteria to be used in judging issues such as the
progress of each learner as the situation may dictate. They also serve
as a good planning tool by assisting learners to think through issues
such as goals, objectives, resources, timelines, outcomes, and evaluation. Knowles (1986) presents some useful examples of how contracts can be used, and we provide more detail on our own uses of
the contract in Chapter Eight.

Related to the issues of promoting positive learning attitudes
and individualizing planning efforts is the issue of self-confidence
and self-initiative on the part of learners. Even though considerable
research has shown that many adults prefer to be self-directed, it has
been our observation that the moment some adults enter any type
of formal classroom or training setting they revert to prior spoon-

feeding expectations. In other words, the adult in a typical classroom where chairs or desks are in rows and a "teacher" is situated in the front initially expects to be provided all the necessary information. The instructor's role thus needs to become one of encouraging learners to become self-directed, make various personal learning decisions, and take responsibility for their own actions.

A final point concerns how the instructor relates to learners. It has been our experience that the best way of stimulating people to become interested in the subject matter, involved in the instructional process, and positive about learning is to treat them as individuals and not just as members of a group.

Why Individualizing Instruction Makes a Difference

"In response to . . . forces, the form and content of teaching in higher education shifted markedly in the 1960s" (Trent & Cohen, 1973, p. 997). This shift has continued and was perhaps even more noticeable in the seventies and eighties. There is no reason to believe that it will not continue into the twenty-first century. The need to adapt to or keep up with change, the existence of more leisure time, more education at younger ages, and just plain more acceptability from society for participation in lifelong learning are some of the important reasons for this trend.

One reason we are promoting our individualizing process is the growing recognition that adults often require or at least desire nontraditional instructional styles and uses of instructors' expertise. The forces mentioned earlier have accented this expectation.

What, then, should be the instructor's role in promoting individualized learning for adults? We begin an answer to that question by elaborating on Jarvis's (1985) three broad approaches to instruction, "didactic, socratic and facilitative" (p. 94). As one of us has noted elsewhere (Hiemstra, 1988b, p. 105), the three approaches necessitate quite different roles for learners:

1.   Didactic—the instructor controls most of the direction and content through a lecture format. Learners are expected to acquire and retain knowledge primarily through memorization.

2. Socratic—the instructor uses questions to take the
    learner through a prepared and logical sequence
    of content acquisition. Learners are expected to
    respond to the questions.
3. Facilitative—the instructor creates an educational
    environment in which learning can occur. A var-
    iety of instructional techniques can be used.
    Learners are expected to assume increasing re-
    sponsibility for specific content determination
    and acquisition.

*The individualizing instructional process is based primarily
on the facilitative model.* The idea that the instructor is an expert
who dispenses knowledge to learners is fundamental to the first two
models. Learners are seen as receptacles for knowledge rather than
as mature people who can assume responsibility for their own educational experiences. This is not meant to suggest that techniques
such as lecturing, socratic questioning and discussion, and standardized testing procedures cannot be used in an individualizing
approach. They can, and we discuss the use of such techniques in
later chapters. As a matter of fact, many learners will deliberately
choose such techniques or procedures for part of their personal
learning plan. What we advocate is that the successful instructor of
adults use facilitation techniques and serve as a manager of the
various learning transactions rather than simply provide expert
information.

This manager role is different from the authoritarian role in
which the instructor assumes an expert hat and expects that learners
will be able to demonstrate they know everything they have been
told or have read in some assigned books. Some critics of an individualizing approach point out that autocratic teaching styles are
not the issue because there is certain material learners must acquire
to obtain a certain grade, move on to the next level, or demonstrate
a specified competency. Some critics, too, may suggest that regardless of the delivery style, it is possible to involve learners through
group discussion, creative projects, and application problems.
However, our point is that being a facilitator implies something
more than helping learners acquire certain information or become

involved in group discussion. It includes being able to help learners take responsibility for their own learning.

There are several specific roles that the instructor must undertake in any facilitative model where individualization is an intended educational goal. If you desire to promote positive feelings among learners, while at the same time managing a learning process that will untap the potential of each participant, you must be willing to carry out a number of tasks and functions.

1. As in more traditional approaches, there will be many instances in which you must serve as a content resource for learners. Instructors usually have considerably more expertise and knowledge about the subject than do learners, and learners will expect this expertise to be shared in various ways. However, using content specialists in areas outside your expertise may be necessary to meet all learning needs.

2. You must take responsibility for managing a process of assessing learner needs rather than presupposing what all those needs might be. The uniqueness of each set of learners necessitates such a role.

3. Once you have uncovered the needs or at least have arrived at some initial understanding of the needs, you will have to arrange and employ the resources necessary for your learners to accomplish their personal goals. In some instances this will require finding or creating new resources, obtaining knowledge or expertise on new areas of relevance to the learning experience, and making outside experts available.

4. We have found it important to use a wide variety of instructional techniques and devices to maintain learner interest or to present certain types of information. This may seem contrary to our view that each individual must take personal responsibility for learning. But making various techniques and devices available gives learners more control by giving them a wider range of choices. In addition, making various techniques and devices available gives learners more control because they can then make individual choices.

5. You also need to be aware of techniques for stimulating and motivating learners so that all can reach their potential. Wlodkowski (1985) presents many strategies for motivating adults.

6. Another role is helping your learners develop positive learning attitudes and positive feelings about their ability to be independent. Such attitudes and feelings will vary from learner to learner, with some people having acquired negative feelings about their abilities or past learning experiences. Thus, at times you will need to become a cheerleader or encourager and be willing to spend time helping insecure learners increase their confidence.

7. A very difficult task when learners are using various resources and taking quite different approaches to the achievement of goals is to determine whether learners are reflecting on what they have learned. As will be detailed in later chapters, you can help learners accomplish personal reflection through techniques such as small-group discussions, personal interactive journals, theory logs, and statements of personal philosophy.

8. A final role has to do with evaluation of learner progress. You need to evaluate learner achievements in various ways, ranging from more traditional testing or critiquing of written materials to less traditional techniques such as personal interviews with learners. It also is important to stimulate various types of self-evaluation by learners.

It is not an easy task for the instructor or trainer of adults to incorporate all eight of these steps into a personal repertoire of instructional skills. Often, adults in a formal classroom setting or in a training situation will be initially discouraged by unfamiliar instructional techniques or attempts to place responsibility for decision making back on them. Expecting directive instructional approaches based on remembered instructional models, they may become intimidated by the individualizing approach.

As a matter of fact, some adult learners greatly prefer traditional lecture techniques, and initially give a low rating to self-directed learning possibilities or those requiring considerable self-discipline (Cross, 1981). Unfortunately, used just by itself, a lecture format with standardized testing procedures may not meet the many needs of mature learners, although, as Centra (1979) notes, there are instances in which such techniques as lecturing can be used as springboards for discussion and further inquiry.

Finally, many instructors and trainers who are faced with large numbers of adult learners may have some initial difficulties in adapting their own instructional styles to the process advocated in this book. Obviously, no one style or approach can be completely adopted by others. Adaptation, experiment, fitting various techniques to one's personality, and some plain old trial and error will be required. However, it is our expectation that you will have more success with adult learners if you use the material presented here to examine your current instructional style, philosophy, and beliefs and make whatever adaptations you deem appropriate for your own situation.

2

Learners in Adulthood: Why They're Not Just Big Kids

Sally Rogers, a high school English teacher, was asked by the adult education coordinator to teach an evening course. The title of the course was Writing for Fun and Profit. Sally agreed, thinking that she could adapt most of what she used in her eleventh-grade writing course. She quickly found that she was mistaken. For example, most of the illustrations in the text focused on teenagers and their problems. She also discovered that a favorite technique she used with her eleventh graders, that of having the students find a current event in the newspaper and then write a short essay on it, was objected to by the adults. They wanted to write about things that were important to them rather than on current events. Sally then realized that she would need to understand much more about how adults learn and develop, and adjust her teaching approaches accordingly.

There is little doubt that, as a society, we are becoming more adult oriented. If we take a moment and look about us, we can quickly see images of such change in the media, in politics, in the workplace, and certainly on college and university campuses. As one example of this increasing adult orientation, many campuses now offer student services for the older learner. These services range from the usual counseling and advising programs to organized day-care centers and support groups for women. There have also been noticeable changes in courses such as the one that Sally Rogers was asked to teach. Many courses are now offered in the later afternoon and evening and on weekends.

Despite these changes, and the types of societal changes out-lined in Chapter One, however, most higher education institutions as well as most other organizations that instruct or train adults, continue to hold on to many old practices. Substantial alterations must occur in these various organizations if they are to serve the varied needs of the adult learner.

Adults as learners are not simply "big kids." Consequently, you must understand some of the differences between adults and young people as preparation for thinking about the instructional suggestions provided in this book. Adults differ from younger peo-ple in that they have more experience, have multiple responsibil-ities, and must use time in an efficient manner. Adults also are complex beings, and, as Draves (1984) has noted, "they bring to the learning situation a combined set of emotional, physical, mental, and social characteristics that makes each one of [them] unique" (p. 7). It is necessary to understand something about such complex-ities if we are to be successful in working with the adult learner and in using an individualizing approach to instruction.

Mental Characteristics

The debate over adult mental ability or intelligence may be traced to the beginning of the present century. Evidence collected during World War I suggested that intellectual ability reached its peak at about the age of seventeen or eighteen and then rapidly declined. Further studies using IQ tests tended to confirm this con-clusion and helped cement the notion that "you can't teach old dogs new tricks."

The first significant work on adult intelligence to begin to refute these claims was published by Thorndike in 1928. Using a series of laboratory tests, Thorndike concluded that although learning ability reached its peak somewhere between twenty and twenty-five years of age, adults could continue to learn and intelligence did not decline significantly until about age fifty. This rather optimistic view evolved despite the fact that many of his experiments included factors that support a negative picture of learning and aging. As Darkenwald and Merriam (1982) have noted, "His studies were cross-sectional, testing a young cohort against an older cohort, most of the results were based on timed and/or motor tasks, and the tasks selected were not particularly meaningful to the participants (learning to write with the left hand or memorizing an artificial language, for example)" (p. 105). Still, for the first time, educators who worked with adults had positive evidence about the intellectual functioning of people as they got older.

This more optimistic view of adult intelligence was tempered a few years later by the results of a study conducted by Jones and Conrad (1933). In this rather ingenious study, the researchers administered the Army Alpha test to residents of selected New Hampshire villages who had been invited to attend a motion picture showing free of charge. During intermission, the researchers had the residents complete the tests; those individuals who did not attend the movie were visited in their homes and invited to take part in the study. After analyzing the data, the researchers concluded that intelligence peaked at about twenty-one and then gradually declined. They found that there was a decline "which is much more gradual than the curve of growth, but which by the age of fifty-five involves a recession to the fourteen-year level" (Weisenburg, Roe, & McBride, 1936, p. 23). One of the most intriguing aspects of the Jones and Conrad study was how the researchers chose to interpret the performance of the different age groups on the various subtests. For example, scores on the information and vocabulary subtests did not reveal any age-related decline. However, deficits were noted on such subtests as numerical completions. On the basis of these findings, Jones and Conrad concluded that the information and vocabulary tests were the least valid indicators of intelligence but that tests emphasizing speed—for example, the numerical completion test—were a major factor in the measure of intelligence (Kidd, 1973). This conclusion put adults at a major disadvantage as compared to younger subjects.

Categorizing subjects according to age groups or cohorts and then comparing them on an equal footing were also considered acceptable practices during the early years of intelligence research. Fortunately, researchers have since realized that these assumptions are fallacious and, in fact, give younger subjects a decided advantage. For example, the assumption that all subjects are the same regardless of age has been shown to be erroneous (Botwinick, 1978; Schaie, Labouvie, & Buech, 1973). What researchers of fifty and sixty years ago failed to account for is that conditions change. They believed that all subjects—young and old—could be considered equal in every respect, despite the fact that younger subjects had considerably more formal schooling than older ones.

Assessing the actual learning ability of adults is no easy task. As may already be apparent, the task of assessing learning ability is not as simple or straightforward as was originally thought. In addition to the problems noted above, there are other complexities that confound the situation even further. For example, learning ability may be thought of as potential, as actual measured performance, as power to learn, or as speed of learning (Long, 1983).

Learning is usually associated with some change in performance. Although it may be desirable to link learning potential with performance, there is no way at present to measure potential independently of performance. Yet, many of the early studies did not distinguish between these variables. For example, Thorndike's work was heavily biased in the direction of ability or potential, when in reality he was dealing with evidence based on performance.

Once researchers realized that the study and analysis of adult intelligence were far more complex than originally thought, a very different picture began to emerge. Lorge (1963) conducted a replication of Jones and Conrad's original study; adjusting for the penalty that age places on timed tests where completion speed is a factor, he concluded that there was no intellectual decline with age. Lorge went on to say that his correction was not really a correction for age but for slowness, remoteness from schooling, disuse of practice with school functions, and lack of motivation.

The differentiation of fluid intelligence and crystallized intelligence helped promote a greater understanding of adult abilities and limitations. Additional attempts to describe adult mental ability were made by Cattell (1963), and these were further tested and refined by Cattell and Horn (Cattell, 1968; Horn & Cattell, 1966a, 1966b; Horn, 1967). They identified two distinct kinds of intelligence—fluid intelligence and crystallized intelligence—that helped account for improved performance by adults on verbal tests and declining performance on visual and reaction measures. Their theory is based on the premise that cohesion in intelligence is produced by the interaction of two contrasting but interacting influences: neurophysiology and acculturation (Knox, 1977; Schaie & Willis, 1986).

Fluid intelligence, which is thought to be primarily innate, plays a role in all types of problem solving. It is what Wechsler (1958) called "native mental ability" and determines how well an individual perceives complex relations, uses short-term memory, forms concepts, and engages in abstract reasoning. Fluid intelligence is relatively formless and seems to be independent of experience and education. Some examples of fluid intelligence include rote memory, common word analogies, and verbal reasoning.

Crystallized intelligence consists of acquired abilities such as verbal comprehension, numerical skills, and inductive reasoning. It is based on formal schooling experiences and everyday cultural or societal influences. Thus, crystallized intelligence appears to be culturally based and is best applied to bodies of information such as school subjects (Long, 1983). Some examples of crystallized intelligence include general information, word lists, reading comprehension, vocabulary tests, and how much knowledge the individual extracts from the social and physical environment.

Taken together, these two types of intelligence cover most of the learning tasks that confront adults. According to Knox (1977), "They constitute the global capacity to learn, reason, and solve problems that most people refer to as intelligence. Fluid and crystallized intelligence are complementary in that some learning tasks can be mastered mainly by exercising either fluid or crystallized intelligence" (p. 420).

Researchers investigating fluid and crystallized intelligence have discovered some interesting links between maturation and performance. Both fluid and crystallized intelligence increase during childhood and into adolescence. However, fluid intelligence tends to reach its peak during adolescence and then decline rapidly during adulthood. Crystallized intelligence, in contrast, continues to increase gradually throughout adulthood. Cunningham, Clayton, and Overton (1975) found that when untimed tests were given, the scores related to crystallized intelligence were the same in the fifties as in the twenties or even higher. Figure 1 summarizes fluid and crystallized intelligence patterns in relation to age.

What does all this mean? According to Knox (1977), as fluid intelligence declines and crystallized intelligence increases in adulthood, general learning ability remains relatively stable. Thus, as people continue to grow older, they increasingly compensate for the loss of fluid intelligence by relying more heavily on crystallized intelligence. In short, they substitute wisdom for brilliance.

In more practical terms, the distinction between fluid and crystallized intelligence helps explain the changes in intellectual performance over the life span. Since fluid intelligence is genetically based and less dependent on education or life experience, it

Figure 1. Fluid and Crystallized Intelligence Patterns with Age.

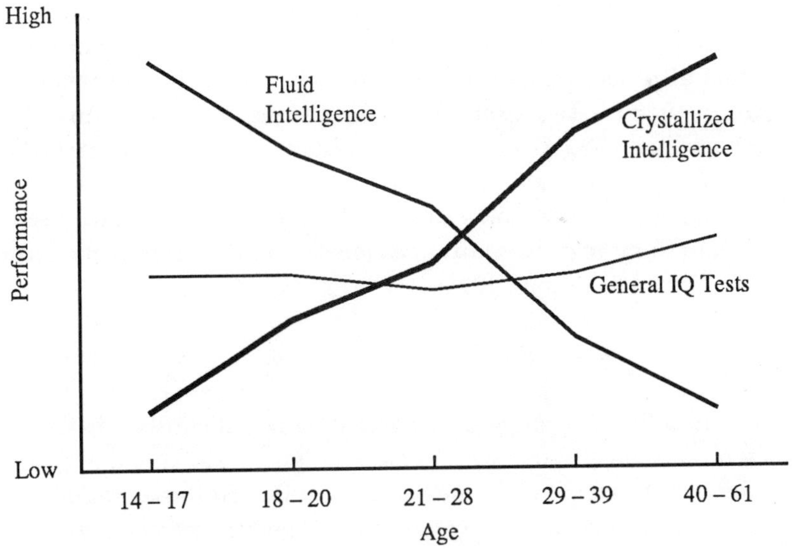

Source: Horn (in Goulet and Baltes, 1970).

makes sense that performance would decline on some standardized tests as an individual ages. Some subtests of the Wechsler Adult Intelligence Scale (Wechsler, 1958) are correlated with fluid intelligence. Crystallized intelligence, however, increases with age, and other subtests of the Wechsler scale are correlated with it. This type of intelligence is dependent on experience, accumulated knowledge, and the relationship between an individual and the social environment. As Darkenwald and Merriam (1982) observe, "The decrease in fluid and the increase in crystallized intelligence serve as equalizers with the end effect of a fairly stable overall IQ measure throughout adulthood" (p. 107).

Researchers who investigate the intellectual functioning of adults throughout the life span are painting an increasingly rosy picture of such functioning. As we have seen, adults can maintain or even increase their intellectual performance well into later life. Schaie and Willis (1986) sum up this mounting evidence by observing, "If you keep your health and engage your mind with the problems and activities of the world around you, chances are good that you will experience little if any decline in intellectual performance in your lifetime. That's the promise of research in the area of adult intelligence" (p. 318).

There are other factors related to age trends in learning ability that also help explain performance change during adulthood; these include physical condition, social class, and personality. At the same time, these factors are often mistakenly applied to learning trends over the life span and, therefore, are not separated out. For example, social class and extent of formal education have been shown to be more consistently associated with learning ability than is age (Fozard & Nuttall, 1971).

Physical Characteristics

Nowhere is change in adulthood more evident than in those factors associated with physical growth and development. We can readily see these changes in ourselves as well as in those around us. Telltale signs such as graying hair, slowed body movement, and the addition of eyeglasses and hearing aids are all associated with growing older. For many years, these signs were taken pejoratively; something to avoid at all costs. It was not unusual to find many older people putting on their eyeglasses or hearing aids only in the company of loved ones. Growing old in American society has, until recently, been viewed as a curse or deadly affliction.

Fortunately, there has been a change in attitude during the past twenty years. Television programs now portray the adult years in a realistic and accurate manner. Comedy shows like the "Cosby Show" include segments with older people in grandparent roles. Movies made for television have dealt with death, dying, and Alzheimer's disease. Even advertisers, once fascinated with the fountain of youth, have started to become more balanced in their portrayal of adulthood (Hiemstra, Goodman, Middlemiss, Vosko, & Ziegler, 1983). But it is perhaps in politics that we have seen the most dramatic shift in the public's view of adulthood. It is not unusual today to find elected officials well into their seventies or eighties who hold enormous power. If such changes continue, adulthood will be viewed in an increasingly optimistic way.

A variety of physical changes have a significant bearing on the learning performance of adults. With aging there are sensory changes that result from deterioration of the sensory apparatus itself or deterioration in the central nervous system. Both are susceptible to disease. The two most dominant sensory processes that we use are our eyes and ears, and both exhibit marked changes over the life span. Some years ago, Kidd (1973) spoke to this point: "Probably . . . [the] best index of the soundness of the human animal is the health and capacity of the eye. There are more substantial changes associated with aging of the eye than in almost any other characteristic" (p. 62). Growth in the function of the eye is very rapid in early childhood but then begins to slow during adolescence. This is followed by a gradual decline until the beginning of the fourth decade of life. A sharp decline then occurs and continues until age fifty-five. After that, the rate of change becomes more moderate.

In addition to a marked change in visual acuity during adulthood, there is also a change in the amount of illumination required. Research evidence suggests that, after age fifty, the amount of illumination becomes a critical factor. For example, a fifty-year-old learner is likely to need twice as much illumination as a twenty-year-old learner (Cross, 1981).

The gradual deterioration of eyesight illustrates how the effects of aging need not interfere with the learning process. Without a doubt, if left unheeded, these changes will have a detrimental effect on learning performance. However, with the use of corrective eyewear and environments that can be adjusted for light intensity, normal and effective learning performance can be expected throughout adulthood.

Hearing, like vision, is susceptible to significant changes over the life span. Loss of hearing is the result of changes in the sensory apparatus itself, that is, the neural processes involved in the transmission of sound become impaired. In most people, hearing acuity increases to about age fifteen and then gradually declines until about age sixty-five. Thereafter, there is a sharp decline in hearing ability. Older people are also susceptible to a significant loss of hearing at the highest frequencies (beyond 10,000 cycles per second) as well as at the lowest register of 125 cycles per second or less (Kidd, 1973).

Cross (1981) suggests that of all the physical impairments that accompany aging, loss of hearing may be the most difficult to overcome because it isolates the individual and is not usually visible to others. She goes on to say that the psychological damage may be greater than the actual physical affliction. Often, a spouse or loved one can be instrumental in helping an adult recognize the importance of correcting for hearing loss. If this can be accomplished, corrective equipment, such as hearing aids, can return hearing performance to near normal conditions. In addition, the size of hearing aid equipment has been reduced to a point where the devices are hardly noticeable. Some can even be embedded in the ear canal or in the stem of eyewear.

There are other physiological changes that also affect adult performance. They seem to be less significant than vision and hearing but do have an effect. The most obvious is reaction time. Quite simply, as people grow older, they slow down and, on the average, perceive, think, and act more slowly than younger learners. At least that is what timed tests have demonstrated. However, there is mounting evidence that the importance of speed of learning is overemphasized in most learning settings to the detriment of learners of all ages.

Another factor that exercises some effect on adult performance is physical health. With advancing age there is a shift from acute illnesses (such as infections or accidents) to chronic illnesses (such as arthritis or circulatory problems) (Knox, 1977). What this means is that as people grow older, they are more likely to contract long-term diseases. This obviously can have a dramatic effect on learning performance and offers another explanation for the variation of performance over the life span.

What steps can be taken to deal with these physiological factors so that the learning performance of adults can be enhanced? Obviously, knowing something about the normal physical changes that accompany adulthood is a good starting place. However, there are some concrete steps instructors of adults can take to expedite this process even more. In later chapters, we go into great detail along these lines.

Emotional Characteristics

Emotional factors also play a significant part in the learning enterprise, especially for adults. How people view education and learning is often tied directly to the kinds of experiences they had as students in their younger years. For example, if an individual found school to be a positive and rewarding experience, he or she will probably maintain this favorable attitude throughout adulthood. If, on the other hand, an individual found school to be a negative and painful experience, then these same feelings often remain during the aging process. The end result may be the difference between a lifetime of active learning versus one of isolated provincialism.

Adults do not have fewer emotional experiences than children. They are just better at hiding their feelings. In describing a motivational model for adults, Cross (1981), pinpoints self-evaluation and attitudes toward education as two of the most important elements in understanding how and why adults participate in learning activities. She points out that those persons who lack confidence in their abilities as learners are unlikely to volunteer in learning situations that might present a threat to their self-esteem. A similar situation also exists in regard to attitudes toward education. Thus, it is highly unlikely that an adult who had bad educational experiences as a youngster would return voluntarily to the scene of a former embarrassment.

Recent research into adult participation has yielded some interesting findings as to what causes a person to enroll or not enroll in a learning activity. Rather than focus on what motivated a person to enroll in an evening course at the local community college, researchers have attempted to determine what obstacles or barriers prevented participation.

These obstacles or barriers can be organized according to three categories: situational, institutional, and dispositional (Cross, 1981). In a class such as that taught by Sally Rogers and described at the beginning of the chapter, it would not be unusual for several students to face one or more obstructions. Situational barriers are obstructions that arise from the circumstances of a person's life at any given time. Lack of money for tuition because the car broke down the week before classes started is one example. Lack of child care for a single parent would be another. Institutional barriers consist of all those policies and procedures that prevent or discourage an adult from participating in educational activities. Inflexible course schedules, full-time fees for part-time study, and administrative offices that are open only during the day would be examples of this kind of barrier. Dispositional barriers include attitudes and perceptions about oneself as a learner. Many older people, for example, feel that they are too old to learn. Another example would be the adult learner who breaks out in a cold sweat every time at the very thought of taking a math test.

These various barriers make it much more difficult for the adult learner to participate in an educational activity than it is for the younger person whose primary occupation is that of student. Joe Daniels, Sally Rogers's students, and most other adult learners must juggle all sorts of roles, responsibilities, and expectations in order to participate in the first place. If any one of these barriers proves to be insurmountable, then the results will be predictable.

When participants are asked to indicate which barriers are most important or significant, situational and institutional barriers are cited more frequently than dispositional ones. Participants frequently single out factors such as time, money, or unresponsive institutional practices. However, this situation is often misleading. The real importance of dispositional barriers is probably underestimated in that it is far more acceptable to say we are too busy to participate in learning activities or that they cost too much than it is to say we are too old to learn or lack the ability. Because of this, you should be alert for hidden signs that reveal the true feelings of the individual learner.

Social Characteristics

There is little doubt that the life of an adult is much more varied and demanding than that of the child or adolescent. Adults are expected to be responsible for their actions, provide for themselves and their loved ones, and contribute to the welfare of the community. Society expects, even demands this. These "social roles," as Havighurst (1972) called them, are part of everyday life but can be easily overlooked in the context of education.

It is important for an instructor to find answers to two questions: What does it mean to be an adult? and What does being an adult have to do with being a learner? An understanding of certain social characteristics of adults is obviously important to the success of the instructional transactions in educational settings. The first question—What does it mean to be an adult?—can be examined in a number of ways. We might say that an adult is a person who has come of age and thus enjoys certain rights and responsibilities, such as voting or military service. We might also say that an adult is one who has accumulated a potpourri of experiences, both good and bad. Another definition might emphasize the notion of independence and autonomy, while still another might focus on the characteristics of maturity and wisdom.

Regardless of how one defines an adult, two social characteristics stand out as significant in the context of teaching and learning: experience and diversity. Adults come from a variety of backgrounds, occupations, and locations and have an assortment of experiences:

> John Chamberland spent considerable time in the
> diplomatic corps while Joe Daniels, whom you met in

Chapter One, has spent his adult life working in a local tool and die factory. Both feel the need to learn how computers work and, as a result, are drawn to the same community college course. John has two advanced degrees, is comfortable with academic settings, and wants to use the computer to manage his personal finances. Joe, in contrast, fears that his company will soon introduce computer-assisted robots and hopes the course will help him in terms of job security. He is not comfortable with academic settings, having dropped out of high school. He later successfully completed the General Educational Development (GED) exam primarily through independent study in a learning resource center in the company's training unit.

Unless the instructor of the computer course can overcome some of his negative stereotypes about older learners and provide a means whereby differences in background and experience are integrated into the learning environment, Joe and perhaps even John may simply drop the course.

There are other social factors that should be considered when instructing adults. Smith (1982) has identified four essential characteristics that adult learners exhibit. First, they have multiple roles and responsibilities, and this results in a different orientation to learning from that of children or adolescents. Second, adults have accumulated many different life experiences, and these result in preferences for certain kinds of learning modes, environments, and styles. Third, adults pass through a number of physical, psychological, and social phases during their lives. The periods of transition from one phase to another provide for the analysis and rearrangement of prior experience. Fourth, adults experience anxiety and ambivalence in their orientation to learning. For example, negative schooling experiences earlier in life may inhibit their attempts to become more autonomous and self-directing.

These four characteristics, according to Smith, create the conditions under which adults learn. In other words, adults learn best when they feel the need to learn and when they have some control over what is to be learned. Adults use their experiences as resources in learning and look for meaningful relationships between new knowledge or information and prior experience. The motivation to learn is often related to the individual's developmental changes and life tasks. For example, a young couple receiving the pleasant news that they are going to have a baby will typically want to learn more about parenting and how to handle newborn babies. Finally, adults generally learn best in supportive environments where differences in personality, background, and learning styles are recognized and accepted.

Similarly, Knowles (1984) has identified several key characteristics about adult learners as a result of his work on andragogy. His findings, which have been supported by research, form a solid foundation for working with adults. They are as follows (p. 31):

1. Adults are motivated to learn as they experience needs and interests learning will satisfy; therefore, these are the appropriate starting points for organizing such activities.
2. Adults' orientation to learning is life centered; therefore, the appropriate units for organizing adult learning are life situations, not subjects.
3. Experience is the richest resource for adults' learning; therefore, the core methodology of adult education is the analysis of experience.
4. Adults have a deep need to be self-directing; therefore, the role of the instructor is to engage in a process of mutual inquiry with them rather than to transmit personal expert knowledge and then evaluate their acquisition of it.
5. Individual differences among people increase with age; therefore, adult education must make optimal provision for differences in style, time, place, and pace of learning.

The foregoing discussion has illustrated some of the differences between adults and children or adolescents. The real problem comes when we ask the second question—What does being adult have to do with being a learner?—because it is often difficult to explain the relationship between the two concepts. Some instructors see learners as "generic" students, whatever their age, and they are content to instruct adults in a manner that is inconsistent with what we know about adulthood.

Thus, there is need for congruence between what it means to be an adult and what it means to be a learner. Successful instructors of adults realize this and look for ways of integrating the individual circumstances, abilities, and experiences of adults into their learning activities. Effective instructors find out about their participants through such techniques as informal conversations, needs assessments, and collaborative discussion groups. They spend time helping participants create positive relationships with the learning content, other participants, and the instructors themselves.

Adults bring a wealth of experience, both helpful and unhelpful, to the learning environment. Arriving at an awareness of each participant as a distinct and developing individual is an important first step in your role as instructor. Treating each individual as you yourself would expect to be treated is of vital importance. Creating an atmosphere where participants can feel good about themselves, about those around them, and about you as the instructor can help establish a spirit of mutual inquiry.

Through a more fundamental understanding of adults as learners, you can help them to realize their own unique potential. By creating supportive and challenging settings, you will assist learners in planning, implementing, and evaluating their own learning. And, in the process, you will actually further the goals of individualizing instruction.

3

Working Individually with Adults: Strategies and Techniques

Frank had just completed a stimulating weekend teaching a course on human development and aging. He was tired, but nevertheless began to reflect on the weekend's experiences and how well his use of various techniques seemed to have been received. The weekend had consisted of a Friday evening session, followed by a seven-hour block on Saturday.

Frank's preplanning had involved deciding what needed to be covered and how best to approach each task, given the available time. From his previous experiences, he had recognized the desirability of using at least three special techniques to maintain learner interest and involvement. These included a minilecture on life transitions, which was followed by small-group discussion; use of an outside resource on issues in aging via a teleconferencing link; and a gaming and simulation device that simulated developmental changes over the life span. General group discussion and individual counseling sessions made up the remainder of the weekend course.

An evaluation conducted midway on the weekend and another one at the end provided Frank with

positive feedback on his efforts. Before he dozed off, he
reflected on the changes he had made in his instructional methods over the past two years.

There is nothing more gratifying than seeing your techniques work and watching a group of adult learners grow and develop. They are often highly motivated, possess a sincere desire to
learn, and bring special qualities to the instructional situation. As
Frank experienced, facilitating instructional activities with adults
typically is very fulfilling. We believe that adults can be exemplary
learners and deserve the best kind of instruction available.

Numerous writers have addressed the subject of instruction,
although most have concentrated on children and adolescents (for
example, Highet, 1976; Joyce & Weil, 1972; Postman & Weingartner,
1969). There is also a fair amount of material directed toward the
college student (see Eble, 1983; Ericksen, 1984; McKeachie, 1965). Unfortunately, however, there has not been much written specifically
about instructing adults, and many people apparently believe that
instructing adults is the same as instructing children. In contrast, we
think that there are some crucial differences. This chapter explores
various aspects of instruction and looks at instructional techniques
that have proved to be effective in working with adults.

What Is Good Instruction?

The question of what good instruction is has been debated
for years. We all usually know when we have experienced good
instruction and when we have experienced bad instruction. Although it is probably easier to describe poor instruction, good instruction is something all of us prize and value. Granting that good
instruction is important, how are we to measure it?

One of the problems here is that nearly everyone holds an
opinion about the subject. Given this, criterion standards that are
reasonable and fair to the instructor, learner, and any institution
involved are difficult to obtain. Measurements are often conflicting
and problematic. For example, they can range from objective-based
checklists that are referenced against statistical norms to subjective
assessments by colleagues or administrators interpreted against

qualitative reference points that may or may not be useful guides for evaluating instructional performance (Ericksen, 1984).

Effective instructors of adults are those who help learners become more self-sustaining, more intellectually curious, and more capable of learning by themselves. What constitutes effective instruction of adults, how does instruction of adults and young people differ, and how can adult learners be empowered to realize their own learning potential are important questions for which we have been seeking answers during the past several years.

Apps (1981) has studied the qualities of exemplary instructors such as Frank. He was particularly interested in the common ingredients that contribute to effective instruction, especially with adult learners. Apps found that exemplary instructors tend to consistently follow nine instructional principles (pp. 145–146):

1. Learn to know your students.
2. Use the students' experiences as class content.
3. When possible, tie theory to practice.
4. Provide a climate conducive to learning.
5. Offer a variety of formats.
6. Offer a variety of techniques.
7. Provide students feedback on their progress.
8. Help students acquire resources.
9. Be available to students for out-of-class contacts.

We, too, have arrived at certain beliefs about instructing adults as a result of our own study and experiences. We believe that successful instructors of adults are those who continue to learn themselves. They constantly integrate new knowledge and information into their classes. They tend to be learner advocates who believe in human dignity and potential. They understand how to assess their own skills for teaching adults, perhaps through using something like Rossman's (1982) self-assessment inventory. They are adept at creating teachable moments for their learners. They are dramatic when appropriate, they are humorous when the situation dictates, and, above all else, they avoid humiliating learners. Most important, good instructors are never content with the way things are but instead see changes as allies. Finally, they strive to link individual needs, interests, and experience with the learning content.

To be an effective instructor is to be a good and earnest servant of the traditions of the past, the uncertainties of the present, and the opportunities of the future. We readily admit that there is no one best way to instruct others, just as there is no one best way to live. Yet there are certain ideals to which all good instructors should aspire. The following list, which is based on the work of Kidd (1973), summarizes these ideals:

1. Thou shalt never try to make another human being exactly like thyself; one is enough.
2. Thou shalt never judge a person's need, or refuse your consideration, solely because of the trouble caused by the individual.
3. Thou shalt not blame heredity nor the environment in general; people can surmount their environments.
4. Thou shalt never give a person up as hopeless or cast the individual out.
5. Thou shalt try to help everyone become, on the one hand, sensitive and compassionate, and also tough-minded.
6. Thou shalt not steal from any the rightful responsibilities for determining their own conduct and the consequences thereof.
7. Thou shalt honor anyone engaged in the pursuit of learning and serve well and extend the discipline of knowledge and skill about learning that is our common heritage.
8. Thou shalt have no universal remedies or expect miracles.
9. Thou shalt cherish a sense of humor, which may save you from becoming shocked, depressed, or complacent.
10. Thou shalt remember the sacredness and dignity of thy calling and, at the same time, "Thou shalt not take thyself too damned seriously."

Early in this chapter we talked about the gratification that comes from working with adult learners who are growing and developing. We believe that almost everyone who has worked with adults in an instructional setting will readily attest to this fact. Adults are usually highly motivated, have specific goals in mind, and become deeply involved in the task of learning. In fact, beginning instructors may find such enthusiasm disconcerting at first. However, we have found working with highly motivated and excited learners very satisfying. The problem often is to recognize the specific cause for a person's enthusiasm and then find ways of capitalizing on it.

One of the biggest challenges facing the instructor of adults is to keep in mind that adults are not simply overgrown children. Typically, adults have had a variety of experiences that distinguish them from younger people. They also have different styles of learning. We acknowledge that many instructional approaches work equally well for children and for adults. However, if an instructor continues to teach in a manner that fails to take into account the mental, physical, emotional, and social factors that constitute adulthood (see Chapter Two), then the difficulties of instructing adults will be needlessly magnified.

Linking Instruction with Learning

Certain ways of instructing adults are more appropriate than others, and one important step is linking instruction directly to learning activities. It may sound overly simplistic to make such a statement, but in fact this kind of linkage is sometimes not made or even seen. Many instructors simply assume that the responsibility for learning rests primarily with the learner. Most of us were educated under a system in which the teacher told us what to learn and how to learn it and then evaluated us according to how well we parroted the information back. The unfortunate consequence of such a situation is that little attention is given to how meaningful the material is, the individual's motivation for learning, and the instructor's personality or communicative ability. We believe that these are all important factors that contribute to effective instruction and learning.

Few will argue that the ultimate quality of instruction must be defined in terms of what happens to learners. However, measures of instruction are oversimplified if they limit attention to how well the instructor presents information. They must also take into account the degree to which the instructor influences learners in terms of their motivation and values, problem-solving abilities, capacity to think independently, and so on. As Ericksen (1984) suggests, "A valid appraisal of teaching must be anchored to what happens to the individual student because, in essence, teaching is the interaction between two persons: the instructor and the learner" (p. 4).

Instructional Planning

The linking of instruction with learning is made easier if an instructor has a good grasp of the many and varied instructional modes and methods available to adult educators. An instructor typically is responsible for selecting, arranging, implementing, and evaluating those learning activities that will assist learners in attaining desired goals and objectives. In subsequent chapters we discuss some exceptions to this rule, when the learning is mainly self-directed. Generally, though, basic decisions about how learning will occur and under what conditions are part of the instructional planning process.

There are many instructional options available to assist the instructor of adults in putting learning decisions into action. These options range from individual methods such as independent study to group methods such as workshops or seminars. In all cases, the instructor must be both flexible and responsive in working with individuals. To develop this flexibility and responsiveness, an instructor must have some knowledge of the general nature of instruction and then be able to determine which instructional strategy is most appropriate in a given situation.

Instructional Strategies. There are several instructional elements common to most learning situations. Using as his basis Gagne's work on conditions required for learning, Dickinson (1973) suggests that there are nine such elements necessary for effective instruction. These elements, listed below (only very slightly adapted from Dickinson, 1973), are usually put into practice as a series of verbal strategies or directions given to learners by an instructor. The events may not always occur in the following order, although they typically do (pp. 65–66):

1. Gaining and controlling attention: By means of statements or gestures, the instructor directs the learner's attention to the material that is to be learned.
2. Informing the learner of expected outcomes: The instructor tells the learners what their performance should be like when the learning is completed.
3. Stimulating recall of relevant prerequisites: Before learning new material, learners are given verbal directions so they will recall the material learned previously that is relevant to the new material.
4. Presenting the new material: The instructor presents the new object, skill, or printed material that is to be learned.
5. Offering guidance for learning: The instructor attempts to facilitate the learning process by providing guidance in the form of questions or directions to the learner.
6. Providing feedback: The instructor informs the learners or structures the situation so they can find out for themselves whether or not their performance is correct.
7. Appraising performance: At the end of a sequence of instruction, the learner is given an opportunity to appraise personal performance against some external standard.
8. Making provision for transferability: The instructor provides a variety of experiences, examples, and problems so that the learner can transfer the material to a variety of different settings.
9. Ensuring retention: The instructor attempts to ensure that new material will be retained by providing the learner with a number of opportunities for practice and by relating it to previously learned material.

In working with a group of children or youth, the instructor must provide nearly all such instructional elements. However, in an adult group, there is greater variety of knowledge and experience so that some of the instructional activities, particularly the latter ones, can be undertaken by the individual learners. As Dickinson points out, "A group of adult learners can be quite adept at providing feedback, appraising performance, and providing transferability, and the instructor's function then becomes that of creating a situation in which the learners are able to assume more and more of the components of instruction" (1973, p. 67).

An additional consideration for the instructor of adults is the particular instructional strategy to be used. Selection of a particular strategy will depend on the learners' characteristics, the nature of the learning situation, and the instructor's personality, among other things. However, there are two general types of instructional strategies: closed and open.

In a closed strategy, the instructor controls all aspects of the learning situation. Learners are expected to be relatively passive, follow the instructor's directions, and listen intently so that they receive the information given. This type of strategy generally fits within the didactic model and even, to a certain extent, within the socratic model, both described in Chapter One.

In an open strategy, the instructor follows the facilitative model more closely by providing various types of assistance to learners. In this model, learners are expected to assume an active role in determining and directing their learning. As noted in Chapter One, the facilitative model undergirds the individualizing approach.

An effective instructor is one who is able to select and use a variety of strategies depending on the situation. Thus, we are not suggesting that there is only one correct strategy. A particular instructional element, model, or strategy may work well with one group of adults, but another group may require a different approach. For example, a closed strategy might be appropriate for a group of adults with low literacy skills who initially need a great deal of structure and guidance. In contrast, an open, flexible strategy might be more appropriate if the group consists of physicians or lawyers participating in a seminar on ethical practice. The key is for instructors to avoid relying on one instructional strategy or approach at all times and to be prepared to make adjustments as warranted.

The general strategy selected for a given situation provides some guidance to the instructor in apportioning responsibility for carrying out the nine instructional elements described earlier. If the situation is open, then learners normally will assume more responsibility for carrying out the various elements. Conversely, if the situation is closed, then the instructor will assume increased responsibility for executing the elements.

Instructional Procedures. A wide variety of instructional procedures are available to the adult educator. According to Verner (1964), distinctions can be made among three different types of instructional procedures:

1. Methods. Methods refer to the ways in which a group of participants are organized for the purpose of conducting an educational activity. There are individual methods such as independent study, correspondence study, internships or apprenticeships, and computer-assisted instruction, as well as group methods such as classes, seminars, workshops, and institutes.

2. Techniques. These are the ways in which instructors can establish a relationship between themselves, the learners, and the learning task(s). Techniques may be classified according to their main purpose or function, such as imparting knowledge (the lecture or speech), teaching a skill (demonstration or simulation), changing attitudes (role playing or group discussion), and encouraging creativity (brainstorming or self-analysis and reflection).

3. Devices. These are instructional aids that extend or increase the effectiveness of methods and techniques but do not teach by themselves, although this distinction has become somewhat blurred as a result of the sophistication of much of today's instructional technology. Devices may be classified by the function they perform in the instructional setting. For example, they can have an illustrative function (overhead transparency or film), an environmental function (seating arrangements), a manipulative function (tools or equipment), and so on.

One of the most important tasks facing the instructor of adults is selecting the instructional procedure that will yield the desired learning results. A competent choice of procedures depends on a number of factors, including knowledge of the instructional process, an understanding of the characteristics of participants, and a reasoned appraisal of the strengths and weaknesses of the available methods, techniques, and devices. At the same time, there is no perfect procedure that will work with all learners every time. A procedure that works well with one group might be inappropriate for another. A procedure that works well one week may yield different results the following week with the same group. To use educational procedures effectively requires patience, sensitivity, and flexibility on the part of the instructor.

In many respects, an individualizing approach requires more advanced planning than the traditional teacher-directed approach. Thus, an organizational structure for participatory planning must be devised, various materials must be prepared, and a good deal of anticipatory thinking regarding what should be expected in terms of learner involvement must take place. We realize that this process may cause some initial consternation for the instructor who has not previously used an open instructional strategy, but we believe that the end product will be well worth the time invested.

Finally, we noted earlier the range of techniques available to the instructor of adults. The most commonly used technique is the lecture, but we believe that there is no reason to always use the lecture as the primary mode of instruction, just as there is no reason for relying exclusively on some other technique such as group discussion. The choice of a given technique depends on your instructional philosophy, your prior experiences or training, and the goals and objectives you have. The best instruction results from the use of a combination of techniques, selected after careful evaluation of the individuals with whom you are working.

Any number of techniques may be used in our individualizing process, depending on the situation. For example, in a three-credit graduate course we typically use as many as fifteen or twenty techniques. These range from minilectures to small-group discussions, from films to dialogues, from huddle groups to demonstrations, and from simulations to role playing. We also believe that variety helps to stimulate and motivate learners. In each case, we try to link the technique to the educational purposes and strengths of the learners.

Model for Individualizing Instruction

Obviously there is a need to put all these planning elements together in some way. In the individualizing process, this means laying out a general plan that is consistent and flexible and also provides a coherent way for promoting effective instruction. The model presented below is aimed primarily at learners in a group setting. In subsequent chapters, we will describe how the individualizing process is designed, implemented, and used in other kinds of settings.

Our process consists of six specific steps as depicted in Figure 2. Each step involves ongoing planning, analyzing, and decision making by the instructor. This six-step process should be used flexibly as a guide or framework upon which to build. It has been shown to work equally well in formal and informal settings. The hallmarks of the model are facilitation, cooperation, participation, and learner satisfaction.

Step One. Activities Prior to the First Session. There are many activities to plan and many decisions to be made prior to the first meeting. Typically, instructors start by developing a rationale statement that describes why learners should be interested in the learning experience, how it will help them professionally, and what

Figure 2. Individualizing Instructional Process Model.

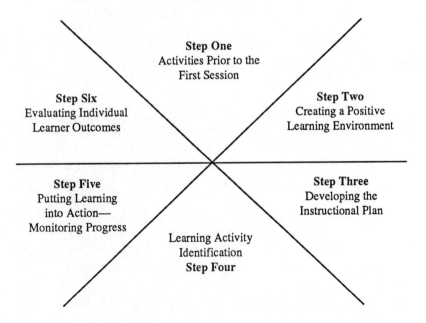

Step One
Activities Prior to the
First Session

Step Six
Evaluating Individual
Learner Outcomes

Step Two
Creating a Positive
Learning Environment

Step Five
Putting Learning
into Action—
Monitoring Progress

Step Three
Developing the
Instructional Plan

Learning Activity
Identification
Step Four

the instructional process will be. Additional activities include determining suggested learning competencies and requirements, identifying necessary support materials such as books, articles, and audiotapes, and securing needed learning resources. We also recommend the preparation of a workbook or study guide of supplemental materials that will include any necessary syllabus information, descriptions of learning activities, bibliographical citations, learning contracts, and any special readings or other material.

Step Two. Creating a Positive Learning Environment. Once the learning experience is under way, there are several activities that will help in creating a good learning environment. These include paying attention to the physical environment of the room, arranging for bathroom and coffee breaks, and building an informal learning situation in which adults are made to feel comfortable with the instructional process. The importance of creating what we call the three R's is stressed and modeled at this point: Relationships with each other (achieved by using icebreakers); Relationship with the instructor (achieved by using icebreakers or personal introductions); and Relationship with the contents of the learning experience (achieved by reviewing the workbook and other related materials).

Step Three. Developing the Instructional Plan. This step is crucial to the overall success of our individualizing process. It involves spending time on such matters as suggested learning topics, activities, and objectives. A needs assessment process is introduced and completed individually and collectively so that the best use can be made of varying levels of experience and competence. Once this process is completed, the instructor then uses the information to develop a learning plan that lays out the topics to be studied, in what sequence, and through what kinds of instructional techniques.

Step Four. Learning Activity Identification. This step involves the identification of various learning activities, techniques, and approaches that learners might use in developing and executing their learning contracts. It is here that the various foundational assumptions—what Knowles (1980) would refer to as andragogical elements—such as setting objectives, establishing time lines, planning for evaluation, initiating problem-centered learning, applying it immediately, and emphasizing personal experience are put into operation. We also emphasize the potential of self-directed learning here. Several techniques are often utilized, including the interactive reading log, the theory log, and the personalized journal, to aid learners in their personal growth, synthesis of knowledge, and reflection on their newly acquired knowledge.

Step Five. Putting Learning into Action—Monitoring Progress. Once the learning plan has been established, the next step is putting it all into action. This is accomplished through various techniques, including minilectures, small- and large-group discussions, case studies, role playing, individual learning projects, and the like. As the learning unfolds, we stress the importance of formative evaluation, which enables both learners and the instructor to monitor group and individual progress so that feedback can be exchanged and adjustments can be made as the situation warrants.

Step Six. Evaluating Individual Learner Outcomes. In a sense, the ultimate test of the individualizing process is the success of each learner in terms of outcomes. Because individuals are unique and their experiential bases different, the importance of matching desired learning objectives to mastery cannot be overstated. By using learning contracts, learners are able to specify what it is they want to learn, how they will learn it, what form or product the learning will result in, and how they will know when they have acquired the desired proficiency. Thus, evaluation becomes a process of development and mastery and a means of ensuring that quality learning and critical thinking take place, rather than of handing out rewards or punishments.

Throughout the six-step process, the underlying intent is to promote good educational practice by creating an instructional system that takes into account individual differences, experiences, and learning needs. The instructor's role becomes one of managing and facilitating the learning process. We believe that optimum learning is the result of careful interactive planning between the instructor and the individual learners. The individualizing process is designed to enable this to occur.

The ultimate challenge for any instructor is to find ways to ensure success in learning. Content mastery is important, but so is the process that enables mastery to occur. Understanding the instructional process, helping participants realize their potential, being supportive and flexible when the need arises, and varying methods so that active learning can occur are all ingredients for instructional success. In subsequent chapters, we will offer specific methods that you can use to become a more effective instructor of adults. A beginning question is, When do I individualize instruction? This will be taken up in the next chapter.

4

Assimilating
a Personalized Approach
into Your Instruction

Cheryl Brown, a community college instructor, was talking with a colleague about teaching older learners. Her colleague of seventeen years was taken aback by the increasing number of older learners at the college and how they seemed to be so different from their younger counterparts. She told Cheryl, "I don't know about you, but the adults in my classes can be a pain at times. They seem almost too intent on learning and expect me to meet their various needs. They are often impatient with my teaching examples; one even challenged me in class, noting that I had my facts wrong. I've always been a good instructor, so why am I having problems all of a sudden?"

Cheryl tried to comfort her colleague by noting that she too had experienced problems teaching older learners in the past. She described how a workshop on teaching adults and further reading on the subject had helped her to better understand the adult learner and how the instructional process could be revised so as to teach them more effectively. Cheryl offered to help her colleague learn more about instructing adults noting, "I can really relate to your problem. Adults are won-

derful learners, but they must be approached differently from the traditional students we have been so
accustomed to. One good place to begin is to think
about how you can use the experience that each adult
learner brings to your class. Remember, adults usually
are experience rich and theory poor, so finding ways
to build upon their experience will likely bring
greater success. It works for me and if you like, I'd be
happy to show you how I do it." Cheryl's colleague
nodded affirmatively.

One of the most important tasks for any instructor is to organize and deliver information that will be responsive to the needs
of learners and will help them attain desired or necessary competencies. This statement may seem rather obvious, but too often instructors such as Cheryl's colleague fail to consider the varied needs
of their learners. When working with adult learners, an instructor
must recognize that while they may in fact be theory poor, they
bring many rich experiences to the instructional situation, and they
normally have a myriad of reasons for choosing to learn. Thus, the
importance of implementing an instructional approach that takes
into account varied learner needs and experiences cannot be
overstated.

Most instructors teach the way they were taught, as was probably the case with Cheryl's colleague. This usually means assuming
an authoritarian role and taking responsibility for all decisions regarding what will be learned, how it will be learned, and how it will
be evaluated. While this approach certainly has some value for situations in which a high degree of structure and control is necessary,
our work with adult learners suggests that an individualizing approach is more effective than an authoritarian one because it capitalizes on learners' innate capacities for self-direction. But you may
ask, How do I make the transition from a teacher-directed instructional approach to an individualized one? How can I successfully
employ an individualizing approach? What kinds of audiences are
more likely to thrive in such a setting? What kinds of topics or
content areas appear most conducive to individualizing instruction?
In this chapter we explore the answers to such questions.

Overcoming Resistance

It would be naive of us to expect every reader to embrace our individualizing instructional approach without some degree of hesitancy, confusion, or skepticism. After all, most of us were initially trained to believe that instruction was largely a one-way street. Nearly everywhere we turn even today, we can find instructors who insist on controlling all aspects of the teaching and learning process. Both of us remember our own uncertainty regarding our roles as instructors. Should we be content experts and transmitters of that content only, or should we find ways to facilitate learning in others? Through active experimentation, enormous patience on the part of the many adult learners with whom we have worked, and an openness toward improving our own instruction, we have developed an instructional process that works especially well with adults.

The true test of this process will be how well you assimilate the various parts of it into your own instructional efforts. The transition may not be easy since a good deal of "unlearning" will need to take place before the process becomes part of your own instructional repertoire. All we ask is that you be open to the potential of organizing instruction differently and give our approach an honest try. As a means of "easing" you into the individualizing approach, we will discuss some of the typical problems that we and others have encountered when initially using the process.

The negative response of certain learners may cause you to question whether the individualizing approach really works. For example, some of our learners have found this approach to be too permissive and loose. This reaction was probably to be expected, since most of these learners had been accustomed to a more teacher-directed approach. But we had not anticipated this response, and it initially left us with some serious doubts about the individualizing process. In fact, we wondered if the research on self-directed learning (some of which we had conducted ourselves) and adult development had been in error.

We came to understand that this reaction is normal in some people. As we carried out our own formative evaluations, examined the evaluation feedback from learners at the conclusion of learning experiences, and reflected on the responses of those who exhibited resistant behavior, we realized that they often had more rigid personalities and learning styles than the other participants. Thus, their reaction was not necessarily directed at the individualizing instructional process as much as it was directed at the very idea of change.

To help those individuals more likely to resist change, we suggest you try the following. First, be aware that some people are going to perceive your instructional role in a conventional or teacher-directed manner. This means that you will be expected to tell them exactly what they should learn, how they should learn it, and how they will be evaluated.

We suggest that you confront this expectation during your first encounter with the learners. Tell them something about yourself and about your view of the role of education. You could mention those findings from the self-directed learning literature that suggest that adults, when given the opportunity, prefer to direct their own learning. Or, as you gain experience in facilitating individualized instruction, you could describe how this has influenced your own teaching to a point where you now organize it very differently. You may need to discuss with various learners certain aspects of the individualizing process and how it emphasizes collaboration and shared responsibility for teaching and learning.

When first meeting with a class, we also explain that our role will at times be that of content-transmitter, at other times that of facilitator of learning, and at still other times that of manager of resources. We emphasize our commitment to helping learners meet their individual needs. Finally, we provide a great deal of encouragement and support while the learners become "comfortable" with the individualizing process.

Second, try the individualizing process or aspects of the process that you are interested in at least three times. We believe this is necessary to test the relative merits of this approach and to evaluate it thoroughly. The first time you use it, the process will be new to both you and the learners. The second time it will be new to the learners but not to yourself, and the third time it will be fairly routine so that you can critically assess the process and its impact. Additionally, some learners will have experienced the process already and can serve as role models for new people. They can thus help you implement the individualizing process with greater ease.

Some colleagues may question your use of the individualizing instructional process and challenge its efficacy. The plain truth is that some instructors are threatened by the idea of giving learners a role in the instructional process. They often have conventional ideas about what an instructor should and should not do. Although it is easy to become personally threatened by this reaction, we believe that the best defense is offense. We have found that most colleagues are at least willing to discuss their views of instruction. We recommend that you do so in a neutral location over coffee or tea. There, you can start a dialogue about your views of instruction much as you would do when first introducing the individualizing process to a group of new learners. Though you may not convince everyone, at least your colleagues will have a better idea of what you are doing.

Another effective approach is to invite colleagues to observe your classes and evaluate what you are doing. Try to establish a mutually convenient time for such observations and stress your desire to receive feedback about your teaching. Often, this strategy eases tensions and helps convince colleagues of the value of this new instructional approach. Sometimes, former critics become avid supporters.

Certain bureaucratic hurdles may interfere with the use of the individualizing instructional process. While these hurdles or barriers are sometimes only sources of irritation, they should certainly not be overlooked or ignored. The key is to understand the nature of the agency's or institution's policies and follow them according to the spirit rather than the letter of the law. For example, certain institutions have a standardized syllabus format that must be followed. If this is the case, go ahead and follow the prescribed format but add additional material through attachments or appendixes. Our experience suggests that this compromise usually satisfies the needs of both the institution and the learners.

Other problems can arise if you decide to use learning contracts. Learning contracts enable learners to designate what it is they intend to learn, what strategies they will use to accomplish their learning goals, what evidence will be used to demonstrate that they have achieved these goals, and how the learning will be evaluated. Often, learners indicate what grade or performance level they are working toward as part of the contract. We use an evaluation scheme that results in a pass or incomplete score. If the learner has not completed all contracted activities by the end of the term, we will grant an incomplete or award a provisional grade that may be changed at a later time.

However, some institutions discourage such practices and make it nearly impossible to employ them. If your institution is one of these, you may have to make some modifications to the practice we follow or find a way that permits you to use at least some elements of the learning contract. While most institutions tend to follow conventional instructional practices that can impede the individualizing approach, change often is possible, but only through creative problem solving on your part and confidence that the process will work.

Personalizing Your Instructional Approach

Moving toward a more personalized way of organizing your instruction is much easier than you might think. While you may feel some initial hesitancy and trepidation, you will find that the rewards for adopting the individualizing process are substantial and well worth the effort. There are, however, a number of steps that you can take to ensure your success with this approach.

Above all else, be patient, flexible, and trusting in the abilities of yourself and the learners. It is not unusual to want fairly immediate results if you are trying a new approach to something. If the results are slow in coming, a typical response might be to abandon it. However, one of the consequences of such a response is that many good ideas are then never able to mature. Thus, we caution you about expecting too much too soon when you adopt the individualizing approach to instruction. Because the process involves a good deal of preplanning, challenges previous instructional experiences, and is often new to you and your learners, it will take time to realize the kind of benefits that will surely come. So our advice is simply to be as patient as possible with your learners and yourself.

Another item to consider is flexibility. If we could give every reader something, it would be an endless supply of flexibility. The individualizing process is by design a flexible way of organizing instruction. In fact, that is one of its best features. But some people may feel that the freedom thus provided is an invitation for learners to take advantage of the situation. And, at times, this could happen. Our experience, however, has consistently demonstrated that adults thrive in instructional settings where options are open and subject to individual choice. In our teaching, therefore, we encourage adults to take advantage of the freedom provided and select those learning activities that will lead to desired outcomes.

Yet no amount of patience and flexibility will be enough unless you have ultimate trust in your own and your learners' abilities. This may seem obvious, even trivial, but our experience suggests that the individualizing process works best when the instructor and learners become collaborators. For this kind of relationship to occur, however, it is essential that a climate of trust and honesty be established. A particularly good way of accomplishing this is through role modeling. For example, we often start each class meeting by saying, "Greetings, fellow learners." This helps establish a spirit of mutual inquiry and says to the learners that our roles are complementary. But this is only possible if you are comfortable in your role as an instructor and believe that the ultimate aim of education is to help learners reach their potential.

Giving frequent feedback to learners and receiving it from them are useful ways of promoting instructional success. One of the most important things that you can do to ensure instructional success is to give frequent feedback to your adult learners, so that they can know in a timely manner what kind of progress they are making. For example, on any written materials received from learners, we recommend that you give written feedback by the next class meeting if at all possible. This allows necessary corrections to be made quickly and lays foundations on which to build later learning. When this is not possible, tell learners exactly what the situation is and let them know when to expect your feedback.

In addition, we recommend soliciting frequent feedback from learners regarding the learning process and your methods of instruction. Among other things, this helps to pinpoint any

changes that need to be made in your approach. You will also be
better able to gauge your own instructional effectiveness. We feel
this is vitally important since it is far better to make adjustments
as the learning experience unfolds than to wait to the end when
improvements are impossible. In addition, by asking for frequent
feedback from the learners, you are helping to build greater trust
among everyone and demonstrating your commitment to learner
success.

It is desirable to use a variety of teaching techniques in the
individualizing process. One of the worst things any instructor can
do is use the same teaching technique over and over again, regardless of its effectiveness. For example, many instructors rely almost
exclusively on the lecture method without considering other techniques that could work even better in helping learners meet their
desired competencies. This is not to say that the lecture technique
is inherently bad, just that many instructors repeatedly use it at the
expense of other equally effective techniques.

To combat this problem, we recommend that you conduct an
"instructional audit" of your teaching units. This involves analyzing each lesson plan or activity and then choosing at least three
different instructional techniques to deliver the necessary content.
For example, for a group of learners who meet two hours in a row,
you might decide to use a minilecture, large-group discussion, and
a simulation exercise. By using several different techniques for delivering information, you are varying the presentation modes, providing learners with opportunities to participate, finding ways of
involving the learners in the teaching and learning process, and
breaking a long period into smaller units. We find this combination
works especially well with adults, who prefer being actively involved in the instructional transaction.

Recognize and use learner expertise in your instructional efforts. One of the characteristics that distinguishes adult learners is
the amount of expertise they possess. For example, it is not unusual
to find a significant number of experienced professionals in an
adult learning situation. In an industry seminar dealing with strategic planning, you might find several individuals who possess substantial administrative expertise but lack specific knowledge about
strategic planning. You can capitalize on their expertise by linking

the new information about strategic planning with any problems that participants might have in setting long-term goals. Providing illustrations that grow out of participants' experiences and asking for potential solutions to these problems are additional ways of connecting new information with the expertise at hand. By doing this, you are significantly increasing the odds that participants will retain the new information, and, more importantly, put it into action.

Recognize that the individualizing process will not work perfectly for all learners and that some will take much longer than others to adapt themselves to the process. As effective as we believe the individualizing process to be, we recognize that it will not work perfectly for all learners. There will be a few who will resist every effort to assume personal responsibility for learning, regardless of what you do. For whatever reason, these learners will demand that you supervise and direct them at all times. They will constantly test your patience and even cause you to question the efficacy of the individualizing process. For these learners, we suggest that you provide the kind of direction they demand while at the same time encouraging them to assume greater self-direction.

In fact, however, most adult learners eventually thrive on the individualizing process, although some will assimilate it faster than others. The reasons for this are not altogether clear or certain, but they generally have to do with conditioning; some learners find it more difficult to give up the idea that an instructor's proper role is to tell them what should be learned, how it should be learned, and how the learning will be evaluated. They have so internalized this view of instruction that it takes them a long time to accept an alternative system. In addition, we suspect that some people are less trusting than others and manifest this through various kinds of skeptical behavior. Rather than being concerned about this, you should anticipate it by providing numerous opportunities for learners to raise questions about the instructional process and associated activities. In future chapters, we will provide some specific suggestions for introducing the individualizing process and dealing effectively with learners who are initially resistant to it.

The individualizing process is a structured approach to helping adults assume greater responsibility for their learning. The individualizing process is not a laissez-faire approach to learning. In fact, the process has considerable structure built into it.

There is nothing inherently wrong with structure. Certainly, instruction of any kind should be carefully planned and organized. At the same time, there should be sufficient flexibility so that mature learners can indeed direct their own learning. The individualizing process works as well for those learners who need greater structure as for those who need less. By focusing attention on the individual needs of learners and devising personalized plans for meeting those needs, you can transform the whole meaning of learning from one of passive acceptance to one of personal empowerment.

Situations Appropriate for the Individualizing Process

The individualizing process can be used effectively in nearly every situation. We have used it with similar results in formal educational settings such as graduate or undergraduate study, in short courses or intensive workshops, in nontraditional formats such as distance learning, and in training sessions for business and industry. The nature of the educational experience, the time period in question, the frequency of meetings, and learners' expectations regarding specific educational intents may necessitate some adjustments to the individualizing process, but that is one of its strengths.

The individualizing process can be used in almost any setting. Instruction takes place in many different settings. The most frequent location is the formal classroom. There is nothing about this setting that prevents you from working individually with each learner. In many ways the classroom is an ideal location for personalizing instruction and helping learners achieve desired competencies. But the process will take time to fully implement. For example, you will need to do a good deal of preplanning in regard to the subject under study and how best to tap the existing talents of the adult learners. This will lead to analysis of the various human and material resources needed to present the content. You will also want to consider how to best assess the competency levels of the participants, as well as how you will introduce the individualizing process. All these decisions will be addressed in more detail in Chapter Six.

The individualizing process also works well in more intensive settings such as workshops, training seminars, retreats, and weekend courses. We have found that just because the time frame is accelerated, the kinds of decisions described in the preceding paragraph are not different from those required for more formal arrangements. In fact, such decisions are nearly identical. However, you will need to strike a balance between time constraints and content needs.

Individualizing instructional efforts have most often been associated with the many forms of nontraditional education. These include independent study, learning at a distance, and computer-based instruction. Nontraditional efforts readily lend themselves to an individualizing approach because of their inherent emphasis on the individual. There are, however, some issues to consider such as feedback, resource identification, and performance evaluation. Chapter Ten describes how the individualizing process is used in nontraditional settings.

One concern that requires some planning and adjustment in the individualizing process is group size. We have found that the process is easier to implement if there are twenty-five or fewer learners. Obviously, this is not always possible. But even in those instances in which you are faced with large numbers of learners, we recommend that you still utilize a needs assessment procedure to determine learner interest in various topics and to help develop a learning plan. You might do this after dividing participants into smaller groups (see Chapter Seven for more detail). You probably should think about where each small group will meet; some possibilities are in various sections of an auditorium, adjoining classrooms, or smaller breakout rooms. The size of the group can present problems when you begin to implement the individualizing process, but through anticipatory planning you can successfully deal with this issue.

The individualizing process works with most groups of adult learners. At the same time, however, you should carefully consider their special learning needs and expectations. You will find that, while most adults prefer to be in charge of their own learning, some will be suspicious of instructional efforts that run counter to their previous experience. This is especially true when you are working with people who have fairly traditional views and expectations about the roles of learners and instructors.

In fact, it is not unusual to find some adults who will balk at a process designed to give them a greater voice in determining what it is they will learn, how they will learn it, and how they will be evaluated. Through your initial efforts at explaining why an individualizing process will work with adults and your repeated efforts to convince the doubters, most people will become converts to the process. Usually by the fourth meeting of a semester-long course, for example, people are thriving on the process.

In contrast, highly self-directed learners may sometimes jump too quickly into the process, expecting immediate results. Thus, it is important to keep an eye on such learners and help them to be critical about their learning and open to alternative, less obvious approaches.

There are other adult groups that require special attention in being introduced to and in using the individualizing process—for example, persons with disabilities, the undereducated, multicultural learners, and senior citizens. In each case, the process can be adapted to the special needs and conditions of such learners (see Chapter Eleven).

Other adults who often have some initial difficulties in using the individualizing process are highly trained professionals such as lawyers, physicians, and chief executive officers. These people typically are well educated, affluent, and extremely busy. In many instances, they already possess self-directed learning skills, and thus one would expect them to be receptive to instruction that emphasizes individualization. However, such professionals usually are task oriented and frequently prefer structured, teacher-directed activities. Thus, some compromises between teacher-directed and individualized activities will be required.

Many instructors are concerned about the relationship between subject matter and instruction. They wonder, for example, if the emphasis should be solely on content or process or on some combination of the two. We believe that good instruction is a marriage between content and process. The individualizing process links mastery of subject matter with procedures that exploit the talents, capabilities, experiences, and characteristics of the adult learner.

However, there are certain instructional situations, such as laboratory-based subjects and content-memorization requirements, that necessitate more emphasis on content and less on process. In these cases, the instructor interested in individualization often assumes considerable responsibility for the content or uses a standard lecturing approach but at the same time institutes features of the individualizing process that seem appropriate. For example, the instructor can use certain needs assessment techniques to focus subsequent presentations of content on the specific interests of group members, or lectures can include techniques to encourage learners to share pertinent experiences. The main point is that adults generally do best in individualized instructional situations, a compelling reason for incorporating as many aspects of the process as possible.

5

Fostering
a Shared Responsibility
Between Instructor and Learner

As a surgeon, Dave Drummond is well known for his expertise in innovative heart surgery techniques. He pioneered the use of lasers in open heart surgery and was part of a team that developed an artificial heart that is being used by an increasing number of transplant surgeons. Surgeons from around the world contact Dave on a regular basis for his advice, and he is in heavy demand as a speaker at international meetings dealing with heart transplants.

Dave, however, has just participated in an exasperating continuing professional education workshop entitled New Developments in Cardiovascular Immunology. The workshop leader seemed to be well prepared for the session but failed to consider the composition of the group. Present were other leading surgeons and several immunologists who could have made valuable contributions to the workshop. Dave thought about his own presentations and how important it was to find out who was in the audience. He had come to realize that spending a few minutes at the beginning of a session to find out who was there and why they were there helped improve the experience noticeably. He even found comments to this effect on the workshop evaluations customarily made at the conclusion of each event. Dave wondered why this had not occurred in the current workshop and concluded that helping each learner take more responsibility for the overall learning experience through sharing their expertise would have made the session more satisfying.

As we noted in Chapter One, an important assumption undergirding the individualizing of instruction is that learners have the ability to take considerable responsibility for their own learning. This includes making choices about the learning approach, establishing evaluative criteria, and seeking appropriate resources. In our experience such decision making fosters those feelings of personal ownership that Dave had come to recognize as important. In this chapter we discuss methods of promoting individual ownership of learning experiences.

Promoting Personal Ownership

Most adults, when given the opportunity, prefer to control their own learning activities and projects. Considerable research on adults' learning projects in the past two decades led by Tough (1979) and substantiated by many others has shown that individuals can take considerable control of various learning tasks. For example, in interviewing people on their learning projects, researchers found that many of them had planned and carried out a variety of learning activities, including participation in traditional "courses," as a means of achieving a larger learning goal. (The resources section later in the book provides more information on this line of research.)

Knowles (1984) identifies several strategies for enhancing an individual's control over the learning process. They center on (1) selecting well-defined objectives, (2) making contractual agreements, (3) keeping objective records of behavioral changes, (4) being able to alter stimulus conditions, (5) narrowing the stimulus control, (6) using self-reinforcing operations, and (7) making gradual changes.

Pratt raises the caution that adults vary considerably in their readiness and ability to exert control over such tasks as "collaborative planning, management, and evaluation of education" (1988, p. 161). He suggests that the amount of support required by instructors or the ability of learners to accept responsibility is based on such variables as dependency, competence, commitment, and confidence.

Even with this cautionary note, we contend that individualizing the process will enable learners or trainees to build on such variables as those described above to the limit of their abilities. It has been our experience that individualizing instruction empowers each person to take action, find resources, figure out a comfortable learning pace, and plan the kind of learning that is most appropriate for meeting any particular, specialized needs.

Access routes to learning resources need to be varied to meet the different individual requirements for educational support. One way to fill this need is to provide a variety of learning resources. These include audiotapes and videotapes made available through resource centers or for personal loaning, reading materials in a library, a workbook or study guide that contains supplemental reading materials, and notations of various other resources in the community. Brockett and Hiemstra (forthcoming) provide the following scheme for organizing such resources:

- Individualized resources—resources used primarily by an individual learner with minimal guidance from some expert, including internships, gaming and simulation devices, and personal journals.
- Instructional resources—resources used within a formal setting, such as course materials, reading lists, and evaluation tools.
- Agency/group resources—resources used either in conjunction with formalized learning experiences or in some formal organization, such as visits to an agency, simulated discussion activities, and learning networks.
- Mentored resources—resources used within some formal or informal mentored experience, such as independent study mentoring, peer reviews, and learning partners.

- Mediated resources—resources that are used in conjunction with some audiovisual or electronic device, such as radio, television, audiotapes, tape/slide learning kits, and on-line computer conferencing systems.

There is a constant need to find or build resources, to plan for varied activities in the learning setting, and to encourage learners to find their own resources. We have found it necessary to add new materials to our learning resource collection on a continuous basis. Some learners may need help in learning how to gain access to and use various resources, so the availability of various resources and their relationship to potential areas of learning need to be clearly communicated. We provide lists of resources in our workbooks, facilitate discussion about resources in the learning setting, and provide feedback about potential resources when learners turn in first drafts of learning contracts. We also provide assistance to learners who need help in using libraries, electronic networks, or information data bases.

In addition, we provide materials and training to participants who will be utilizing special techniques to obtain needed information. For example, a learner who plans to interview agency administrators or adult learners can receive help with interviewing protocols. We also provide feedback to learners on the resources they use and ask them to evaluate resources so that we can make more informed recommendations to future learners. Several useful books are available to assist learners in choosing resources (Gross, 1977, 1982a, 1982b; Knowles, 1975; Smith & Cunningham, 1987). Knox (1980, 1986) and Smith (1982) urge collaborative learning in which learners use each other as educational resources.

Self-discipline and self-confidence are requirements for successful individualized study. A very important factor in successful individualized learning is confidence in one's ability to determine needs, set goals, find appropriate resources, and evaluate how well activities have met goals. Brundage and MacKeracher (1980) refer to this as the "self-seen-as-learner." In other words, promoting a learner's ability to learn is an important instructional goal. Knox (1986) raises a related question: "How do you help participants become more confident in their roles as learners? A strengthened sense of educational efficacy can motivate adults to venture and accept the risk entailed in trying to learn and change. Success experiences from mastery of increasingly difficult tasks can increase self-confidence" (p. 47).

In Wlodkowski's (1985) view, the relation between success and further promotion of self-confidence is directly tied to the competence that a person achieves in carrying out learning activities: "Competence allows confidence to develop, which leads to emotional support for efforts to master new skills and knowledge" (p. 56). Along with this outcome, we emphasize the need for self-discipline as a learning tool. We try not to burden a learner new to the individualizing process with an immediate emphasis on self-discipline, but rather attempt to model self-discipline in our instructional approach and then encourage the development of such discipline as learners become more advanced.

Success in promoting self-confidence and self-discipline will vary with each learner. Some learners will come to realize their own potential much more quickly than others. As mentioned before, the instructor needs patience and faith that an individualizing approach will eventually enable most learners to carry out self-directed activities with considerable success.

Instructors should serve as facilitators as well as emphasize the mastery of specific content areas in helping learners assume responsibility. Providing content expertise to learners while at the same time managing a learning experience is a complicated task, no matter what approach to instruction is being used: "Any teacher must discover how to balance encouragement, compassion, and support for students with rigorous evaluation and intellectual honesty, as well as—given the usual institutional context—issuing grades that affect the student's life chances . . . [this] notes a tension between the role of teacher as evaluator, screener, certifier, and the role of helping students" (Robertson & Grant, 1982, p. 346).

This mixture is further complicated when such tasks as evaluating and helping learners are carried out within an individualizing framework in which a facilitative process is intermingled with a certain amount of content acquisition. Caffarella (1988) even suggests that such a mixture presents an ethical dilemma, and Brockett (1988) notes that the potential for abuse exists in terms of promoting a nontraditional approach, such as an individualizing process that emphasizes "learner self-direction without adequately considering the actual needs of the population to be served" (p. 5).

Thus, it is not easy for an instructor to help learners take personal ownership for learning while at the same time satisfying those individual or institutional expectations that are rooted in traditional teaching practices. This approach requires a complex mixture of instructional activities: "The teacher-facilitator has some responsibility to give of self in terms of personal expertise and ability. This includes dealing with learners openly and honestly, letting them know what is expected of them and what they should be able to expect of the facilitator, and attempting to establish a climate of mutual respect . . . there are ways this responsibility can be carried out without jeopardizing individual learner growth or lessening the impact of the teacher with that expertise" (Hiemstra, 1988a, p. 102).

The instructor's attitude toward the ability of learners is very important when using an individualizing approach. Letting learners discover their own potential is a necessary cornerstone to success with the individualizing approach. However, some people will discover this potential much more slowly than others. There will be times when instructors, in promoting the notion of personal ownership, may have to accept poorer performance, at least initially, than their learners are in fact capable of.

> As an example, one learner we worked with had demonstrated an exceptional mastery of concepts in papers submitted for a beginning graduate course. Unfortunately, the papers were poorly written and contained many grammatical errors. Honest criticism, gentle nudging, a request for rewrites, and a lower grade than the student expected led eventually to a face-to-face conference where the belief in that potential could be shared. As a result, the student took steps to learn the principles of effective writing, worked hard to make improvements in subsequent courses, and eventually published articles prior to graduation from the doctoral degree program. The final dissertation was an excellent product, and thanks to an overall growth

in confidence, this person was able to obtain a top-level job upon graduation.

In our experience, such approaches pay off in many ways for most learners. In addition to the type of success described above, other important results include an enhanced capacity for self-reflection, greater confidence in personal learning abilities, and willingness to go that extra mile in educational endeavors. Wlodkowski (1985) details the importance of helping learners develop a positive attitude toward learning. Obviously, the promotion of personal ownership is possible within any instructional approach, but we believe that an individualizing process fosters this potential in all learners because it permits individuals to set their own rates of growth.

The instructor may need to play a counseling or mentoring role with some learners. Many adult learners will need some sort of counseling at certain points in their pursuit of new knowledge or skills. Miller (1986) notes that a variety of problems confront adults today: career changes, family role conflicts, changing family patterns, and various social and economic trends. If left unresolved, personal or family problems can serve as a barrier to learning or training efforts.

For example, special child-care needs may require a learner to leave the training session early each week. Another learner may reveal to you at some point during a learning experience that a marriage separation has created additional financial problems. A trainee might note that a loved one's illness has made future commitments to special training tenuous. A learner that you do not know well may come to you seeking advice about a career change. Chapter Two described various social, emotional, and other characteristics that you must consider when working with adult learners. Such characteristics or situations may fall somewhat outside the instructional role, but often are factors with which you must deal in some way if your individualizing efforts with learners are to be successful.

Goldberg (1980) reviewed many sources and suggested that there exists an increasing urgency for special knowledge and counseling techniques to solve the kinds of problems described above.

Dean (1988) offers several potential solutions to counseling problems and reviews recent literature to support the idea that many learners urgently need effective counseling. DiSilvestro (1981) supports this point of view. He and several colleagues describe the types of learners and programs in which adult counseling efforts will be most useful, although Knox (1981) cautions that many of us do not have appropriate training or preparation for formal counseling activities.

What then can we do as instructors if we have not had much formal counseling experience or training but are faced with learners who need our assistance in areas not directly related to the instructional activity? Brockett (1983) urges instructors to establish a helping, facilitating relationship with learners. He contends that there are at least three helping skills that each instructor can develop:

- Attending. Using this skill, you can let learners know that you are personally interested in them and their lives. This skill includes such functions as active listening, good eye contact, paying attention to nonverbal behavior, and promoting an atmosphere of relaxation.
- Responding. The ability to respond to needs expressed by learners includes such features as being empathetic, respecting others in nonjudgmental ways, being sincere or genuine, and making concrete suggestions about future actions, resources, or solutions to problems.
- Understanding. This skill involves establishing good rapport with learners so that the real meaning or urgency of problems can be understood. It includes such actions as constructive confrontation so that any incongruence in a person's actions can be pointed out; open, direct conversations so that the immediacy of problems can be discussed; and the willingness to let others know that you have had to deal with similar problems.

The individualizing approach described in this book provides a mechanism by which instructors can meet many of the counseling needs that may arise. Such instructional actions as establishing informal settings, paying attention to the physical environment, advising learners as they assess needs, guiding learners in their development of personal learning plans, and modeling lifelong learning skills all help to create a climate in which interpersonal relationships become possible. Obviously, the instructor must feel comfortable with the nature or depth of the interpersonal relationships that are established, and issues of objectivity in the evaluation role must be addressed. With some learners you will feel comfortable in assuming a close helping or even mentoring role; with others you will feel the need to keep some distance or will need to help them seek out professional advice of some sort. It has been our experience, though, that various counseling actions may be needed to enhance your instructional efforts and the ability of learners to assume personal responsibility.

Obstacles to Promoting Personal Responsibility

An instructor needs to be alert for personal, individual learner, or institutional problems that may affect the ability of certain learners to assume personal ownership for their learning efforts. For example, some individuals will have initial difficulty in accepting control of certain learning activities. Some colleagues may have difficulty understanding the individualizing approaches that you employ. Your sponsoring institution may actually have in place various barriers that inhibit use of individualizing instructional techniques. Instructors attempting to change from a more familiar socratic or didactic approach to the facilitative, individualizing approach may need to make such changes quite slowly until they reach a high level of comfort with or confidence in the procedures.

Occasionally, recalcitrant learners will abuse or take advantage of the freedom given to them by an instructor who uses an individualizing process. Are there some learners who will misuse the freedom provided by an individualizing process? The answer, unfortunately, is yes. Some individuals will try to do the very least possible in meeting your minimal expectations for a learning experience. Such learners have probably been unsuccessful in accepting personal responsibility for learning, and they waste their energies trying to figure out at what minimal level it is possible to work and still meet the basic requirements of the course or training session.

This difficulty in taking personal responsibility may stem from the belief that it is the instructor's role to direct all educational activities or, at the least, to prescribe the requirements for a learning experience. At times, the difficulty will be related to cultural expectations regarding the "teacher's" role—we have found this to be the case with some of the international students with whom we work. At other times it may be related to certain individuals' intellectual and ethical development, which causes them to expect that the instructor will be highly directive (Perry, 1970). Occasionally it appears that a particular learner may simply have either philosophical differences with us regarding our stress on individualization or a personal learning style that requires direction actions by an "authority" figure.

We have also worked with an occasional learner who overtly resisted the approaches we used, for reasons that were never quite clear. Such a learner is usually uncooperative in efforts to assess needs, refuses to complete a learning contract, or complains to other class members about the teaching approach. Such a person also can have a negative effect on the work of a small-group activity by being obtuse during group discussions or by refusing to carry out an equal share of the responsibilities required to complete some project.

We can only recommend that you confront such situations directly and that you take into account any knowledge you have about a particular group or individual. In addition to the counseling or advising requirements described in the previous section, commonsense responses based on your experience in dealing with adult learners are usually the best answer. This means that you simply work with this person on a human-to-human level by "demonstrating patience, respect for the dignity of each person, and by attempting to reach through individual to individual negotiation some sort of a compromise on the best way to proceed" (Hiemstra, 1988a, p. 122). Occasionally this will even entail asking the person to withdraw from the class or calling on some outside person to serve as an arbitrator to resolve remaining differences.

Individualizing the instructional process does not mean that every learner will be able to go off freely on some self-determined path. Most of us involved with facilitating adult learning have a responsibility to ourselves, to our teaching colleagues, and to some institutional base, as well as to the learner. This means that we must ensure that learners stay within certain boundaries, that they set reasonable goals but ones that stretch them, and that they learn to think critically.

Thus, this two-way relationship between an instructor and learner, often within some organizational framework, requires the formation of a learning partnership in which all participants work together for the enhancement of knowledge and skill. We have found that this partnership almost always greatly enhances the potential for personal growth and development.

Sometimes an instructor will work with learners who must be challenged to do better or to accept more personal responsibility. No matter what instructional approach you use, you will occasionally encounter learners who appear to be falling short of their potential. You may realize that a certain person is willing to settle for a minimal grade or performance level. You may even discover that a learner is leaning on others for basic information required to complete some assignment, to pass some test, or to achieve some level of proficiency.

On other occasions you might find yourself spending a great deal of time with a learner who seems to have difficulty accepting personal responsibility for completing planning activities, locating resources, or making decisions about the types of projects to be completed or turned in for evaluation. The learning style of such a person might require an outside "expert" to establish guidelines, or the person might have a low self-concept that inhibits active assumption of personal responsibility (Bonham, 1988a, 1988b).

Dealing with these situations on a case-by-case basis is the usual procedure. We tend to use one-on-one discussions with such people or ask more experienced learners to work with learners who are having difficulties with certain components of the individualizing process, such as completing learning contracts or carrying out needs assessment activities. We also provide quite specific models or guidelines for those needing special assistance in dealing with such components.

There is also the issue of the appropriate level of quality in regard to individual involvement, participation with others in group activities, and completed products. Brookfield (1988) urges us to think of the instructor of adults as a critical reactor to learning plans, initiatives, or actions. He believes that this role can include questioning original planning by learners, suggesting alternative learning activities, and challenging the evaluation or validation criteria chosen by people.

In keeping with our mainly humanistic philosophy that, in essence, gives considerable autonomy to each individual learner, we are willing to let a learner settle for a lower level of quality than what we believe is possible if that is the person's decision. However, we constantly urge each learner to strive for high quality, we attempt to provide fairly specific guidelines on what constitutes high quality for group participation or products to be completed, and we provide considerable feedback on all aspects of learning plans. We also provide opportunities for learners to renegotiate their learning contracts if they decide at a later date to upgrade their quality level.

Finally, we think that Brookfield (1987) is correct in urging those involved in the education of adults to give some attention to the development of critical thinking skills. There are a variety of learning activities that an instructor can use, such as brainstorming, interactive reading or writing experiences, study group experiences, and artistic experiences, to promote critical thinking. In subsequent chapters we describe such techniques in more detail.

PART TWO

HOW TO INDIVIDUALIZE
INSTRUCTIONAL EFFORTS

Now it is time to turn to some of the foundational aspects of the individualizing process. In Part One we discussed several instructional elements crucial to the decision to utilize individualizing approaches. On the assumption that you have now made the decision to adopt the process or some aspects of it for your own instructional or training needs, Part Two provides some fundamental information about how we individualize our instructional efforts.

Chapter Six describes the individualizing process. It focuses on the question of how the individualizing of instruction can be established. This is an important chapter to read and understand, because it describes how the basic individualizing process works in a formal classroom or training setting. We present a six-step model and describe corresponding activities or functions. We discuss the activities typically required prior to meeting your learners for the first time, how to create a positive learning environment, what is required in developing the instructional plan, how to identify various learning activities, and what kinds of institutional support are needed. A chart is provided to help you analyze the physical environment in which your instructional or training efforts take place.

In Chapter Seven, we provide information about the assessment of learners' needs and describe the importance of such information in subsequent design and planning efforts. This chapter speaks to the question of how we determine what the learner knows and needs to know within the individualizing process. We describe our methods for both individual and group needs assessment. We also describe some of the ongoing needs assessment activities that should be employed. A needs diagnostic tool is provided for your review, adoption, or adaptation.

Chapter Eight focuses on the question of how learning contracts can be used as a tool to enhance the individualizing process and describes the various ways in which we have employed them. A sample learning contract form is included. We also discuss several related issues, such as alternative approaches in contracting, how to deal with initial learner hesitancy or confusion regarding contracts, how contracts can be linked to grades, and whether or not contracts make a difference in the individualizing process.

The final chapter in Part Two discusses methods of evaluating individualized instruction and learning. It describes how evaluation of the learners, the instructional process, and yourself as instructor is crucial to the overall success that you and your learners or trainees will experience. Such topics as grading and testing, learner assessment techniques, and methods of evaluating your courses are explored. We include a model of a formative evaluation tool that we use midway through our courses.

6

Six Steps to Individualizing Instruction

As an adult basic education instructor, Sarah Roberts was familiar with the need to build self-confidence in her learners. She recalled that many came to the learning center with low self-esteem but also with a sincere desire to improve themselves. The learners were not always realistic about their personal goals or the time needed to accomplish them, so Sarah tried to set a tone of encouragement tempered with realistic expectations. She believed that small, incremental gains coupled with a great deal of positive feedback would lead to later success.

Sarah's views about the educational process were consistent with those of most other teachers at the learning center where she worked. She and her colleagues believed that the best way to instruct adults was through an individualizing process. This meant that they helped learners assume more responsibility for their own learning. Although many of the learners initially required a good deal of structure, the idea of individual control and accountability was constantly reinforced. Most of the students flowered under such conditions, and Sarah felt that the reason for this was related to the instructional process practiced at the center. Adult basic educators in other parts of the state must have agreed, since Sarah was in heavy demand as a consultant to help implement the individualizing approach in learning centers elsewhere.

In Chapter Three we introduced the instructional process model that included the six steps Sarah uses with her adult basic education students. The purpose of this chapter is to describe how the instruction of adults at any educational level can be individualized by means of these six steps. We will discuss various activities involved in preparing for and initiating individualized learning, such as planning, securing resources, developing various learning materials, and analyzing the physical learning environment. In addition, we make various recommendations regarding the instructor's role and the types of learning activities that should be considered, and we stress the importance of certain types of organizational or institutional support.

Activities Prior to Initial Meeting with Learners

As with any educational endeavor, in the individualizing process the instructor's activities do not begin during the initial contact with learners. The instructor must first develop an organizational structure for participatory planning, prepare various materials, and give considerable thought to the question of learner involvement. In many respects, more advanced planning is required in an individualized setting than in structured ones. Thus, the following sections detail various actions that usually take place in step one of our individualizing model.

Overall Planning. The planning required for individualizing instruction has some similarities with traditional curricular development activities. In other words, a variety of activities must take place in preparation for any course or training session, such as ordering books or other materials, preparing a syllabus or learning guide, and planning for presentations. However, when the individualizing approach is used, it is impossible to fully prepare for a course, training session, or workshop prior to meeting with the learners. Each group of learners will be different, new sets of needs will emerge, and the state of knowledge regarding the topics to be covered will constantly enlarge or change. The experience of facilitating such learning endeavors, especially if various evaluation steps are taken, will also result in later alterations.

Necessary competencies or requirements should be determined early in the planning phase. An instructor in most learning endeavors—for example, a formal graduate course, a training experience, or a short-term workshop, invariably must put on an institutional hat of some sort. By that we mean that the instructor is responsible for ensuring that the parameters of the educational experience are within the normal range of some sponsoring organization's catalogue description, curricular guide, or work plan. Even if you are serving as a private consultant and offering a learning experience of your own design, you will, no doubt, have some particular end goals in mind. The point is that if people sign up for a certain course or training experience or are sent to a particular workshop, they usually will anticipate the acquisition of certain kinds of knowledge and skills.

Obviously, if a training program syllabus has already been developed, a workshop has required a great deal of predesign work, or departmental faculty members have already determined the required skills for a course area, then defining competencies may mean nothing more than refining earlier work on the basis of an instructor's personal understanding and experience. If this is not the case—for example, when a new learning experience is being developed—then the instructor must go through a process of determining competencies. As we noted in Chapter Four, we believe that it is usually necessary to offer a course or workshop at least three times before all the required competencies will be determined. In addition, it is likely that any learning endeavor will need ongoing refinement as new knowledge becomes available.

We determine any necessary learning requirements by anticipating learners' expected proficiencies, estimating the amount of learning activity required for mastery, and thinking about what kind of learning experiences can be blended together. This latter function is based on our instructional philosophy, which stresses the blending of both theoretical and practical learning.

Another early function is that of finding, building, designing, and developing various materials to support learning. This function actually is a continuous one, with new materials constantly being developed and old ones being phased out. However, as noted earlier, individualizing instruction is predicated on a philosophy that places the instructor in the role of learning facilitator, resource provider, and encourager of self-directed learning. Thus, an important part of the instructional process is providing learners with a wide variety of learning materials. During our years as facilitators we have pulled together a very large array of films, videotapes, slides, audiotapes, overhead transparency slides, games, and simulation devices, to name only a few of the possible types of materials.

When you begin to think of yourself as a facilitator of learning, the need to obtain a variety of resources for learners increases, but you will not necessarily be highly knowledgeable about every area of need that is identified. Nevertheless, advance planning is always useful and can help ensure that certain materials and special resource people will be available.

It is important to prepare a workbook or study guide of supplemental materials related to the learning experience. This workbook or study guide should include syllabus information, organizational or workshop requirements, descriptions of learning activities, bibliographical citations, learning contract forms, and any special readings or other material. In most instances, we also provide material specific or supplemental to various learning activities. For example, in a miniworkshop on time management, the workbook contains numerous Gantt chart models and critical path analysis problems that allow learners to practice time estimations and calculations. In a graduate course on adult learning, the workbook contains the material necessary for conducting interviews of adults. For a training session via on-line computer conferencing, the study guide that participants receive ahead of time contains the information necessary for communicating with the university's mainframe computer.

There is an important advantage to creating your own work-

book or study guide. Such an endeavor facilitates advance planning and preparation for the learning experience in question. Obviously, however, not everything can be prepared in advance if you plan to use a needs assessment activity and direct some of the subsequent learnings to the specific needs of each group of learners.

In addition, developing a workbook or study guide is actually an ongoing and iterative process. We have found that we have to teach a course or workshop two or three times before we begin to feel comfortable or satisfied with the majority of the material included. In addition, we have found it necessary to constantly change, delete, or add to the material as our own knowledge of the subject matter evolves and as the literature in the field grows. Thus, although the workbook or study guide is a helpful instructional tool, it will require, like the other activities described in this section, constant attention and evaluation.

Creating a Positive Learning Environment

Once the learning experience is under way, there are several activities that help to establish a good learning climate. This section describes these activities, which form step two in the six-step model, and provides a picture of what typically happens during the first few hours that instructor and learners are together.

Initial Contact with Learners. In many learning experiences, actual content acquisition coincides with the start of the first session (Pratt, 1984). In these instances many instructors assume that each person is there with textbook in hand, an appropriate mental attitude in place, and pencil poised to receive the "gospel." The rest of the session is typically given over to a rapidly delivered lecture. Any mention of goals, expectations, and learning activities is made almost incidentally in between lecturing breaths of air. Very often a learner actually may be discouraged from or denied opportunities to engage in dialogue, seek understanding of learning goals, or ask questions.

In addition, the typical graduate student or training workshop participant with whom we work is a person between thirty-five and forty-five with considerable life and work experience. Thus, on the basis of our instructional experiences, we contend that the independent, self-directed learner—what we believe most adult learners are or can become—deserves and desires a different approach. It is particularly important for the instructor to set the correct tone during the first session—this is when learners form personal attitudes about the subject, the instructor, and the instructional process.

We believe that a proper room arrangement is an important element in successful instruction and learning. The resources section in the latter part of the book provides considerable information about the importance of the physical environment in promoting adult learning. For example, in a formal classroom, a training site, or an adult basic education learning center such as the one in which Sarah worked, a comfortable and appropriate setting for adults limits annoying distractions, takes into account special physical needs of the learners, and even enhances learners' ability to participate fully in the learning experience.

You may find it necessary to insist on certain rooms for your course or training session before it starts or find a different setting once the experience has begun if there are obvious comfort problems. It also occasionally may be necessary to request an extra room for breakout purposes, especially if you have large numbers in attendance. If another room is not available, a hallway, a personal office, a lounge, or a nearby restaurant table are all possibilities for small-group discussions.

Frequently, there may be nothing that can be done about the space assigned for a course or workshop. You then have to think about ways of making the most of the situation. If possible, for example, we move the chairs in a circle so that people can see each other. We also recommend that the instructor sit as a part of that circle to create a less formal situation. If the chairs are too uncomfortable, learners can be encouraged to bring their own chairs or cushions.

> John Deverone had a bad back caused by an injury he received while playing high school football. He had to use a chair that provided a straight up-and-down position when he sat down or he would be miserable

within minutes. This usually meant arriving early for meetings to hunt for such a chair.

When he finally reached the level of regional manager in his firm, he found it increasingly necessary to attend management training sessions and long organizational meetings. He finally purchased a back support device for fastening to chairs; this was a built-in lumbar support cushion that he carried with him to meetings. Although he often received strange looks from instructors or others in the sessions and meetings, the device enabled him to participate fully and without discomfort.

As another example of adjustments that can be made, assume that one of your courses or workshops is assigned to an auditorium. In many such sites the seats are bolted down, in semicircular or curved rows, and each row is on a level higher than the row in front of it. In such situations you should spend less time than usual standing up in front of the group and more time having learners work in small dyad or triad groups. You could also have learners move to chairs in the hall, to breakout rooms, or to groups of chairs and throw rugs brought into the auditorium and placed in any available level area.

Arranging comfortable rooms or functional areas will take considerable time both before and after a learning experience begins. It often means arriving at a room some thirty minutes early, carting in extra chairs or even folding tables, and spending many hours in a year's time rearranging chairs and then putting them back in place at the end of a session so overworked custodians or an instructor following you will not become annoyed. However, the results are worth it: Added physical comfort contributes to positive learning attitudes and experiences.

It is important to monitor the physical environment if learner involvement and responses are to be heightened. There is much that you as the instructor can do to attune yourself to learners' needs regarding the physical environment. For example, make sure that the temperature is within a normal comfort zone. In the summer this may mean opening windows or turning on air-conditioning. In the winter it may mean demanding that a room have more heat or encouraging all participants to bring sweaters or jackets. It may even mean requesting a different room if the level of comfort is so low that it impedes learning.

Lighting also is an important aspect of the physical environment. You should make sure that there is adequate lighting for normal activities and that the room can be darkened enough when various kinds of audiovisual aids are being used. Such attention is especially crucial when you are working with older learners who may have visual problems and thus need increased illumination.

The personal comfort level of learners needs to be monitored so that you can foster participation. This point has to do with arranging for lavatory and refreshment breaks. For example, if you have a workshop that meets for more than an hour at a time, we suggest that you plan a ten-to-fifteen minute break within approximately each ninety minutes of instruction. Some learners may prefer even more frequent breaks. During this period participants can grab a bite to eat, obtain a drink, go to the lavatory, have a smoke, or carry out brief but necessary discussions with the instructor or fellow learners.

Two subpoints need to be made here. Smoking is an important issue for some people. On the one hand, there may be regulations that ban smoking in the room, or certain individuals may be philosophically or medically opposed to smoking. On the other hand, if some people go for long periods without smoking, their ability to learn will be affected. You must be cognizant of all such views and as accommodating as possible. In addition, some organizations have specific regulations regarding whether or not food or drinks can be brought into the room. There will also be instances in which food or drink is not readily available. Therefore, we recommend that you work out arrangements with learners as to where food is to be eaten, whether coffee and other drinks are to be made available, and how certain breaks are to be used. Our experience has been that it is best to make such arrangements on a mutual consent basis in the first session. Table 2 presents a checklist of items for analyzing the appropriateness of a learning setting for adult learners.

Table 2. Analyzing the Physical Environment.

Sensory Concerns

____ Adequate lighting
____ Absence of glare
____ Lighting adequate for audiovisual devices
____ Attractive/appropriate colors and decorations
____ Adequate acoustics
____ Adequate sound amplification
____ Any noise to be reduced or eliminated
____ Temperature adequate for season of the year
____ Adequate ventilation or air-conditioning

Seating Concerns

____ Adjustable seats or alternative choices
____ Adequate cushioning if used for long periods
____ Can person's legs be crossed comfortably
____ Straight back and flat pan for people with back problems
____ Adequate sturdiness/size
____ Easily moved around
____ Seat height from floor adequate
____ Left-handed learner provided for

Furnishings Concerns

____ Adequate table or writing space
____ Can furnishing be rearranged for small-group work or sociopetal needs (so that all learners can see each other)
____ Table space available for refreshments/resources
____ If sitting at tables can the learners cross their legs
____ If learners sit at tables, can the tables be arranged in a square, circle, or U-shape
____ Absence of ragged or sharp edges on all furnishings
____ Adequate sturdiness for all furnishings
____ Can learners see each other adequately when seated

General Concerns

____ Adequate access/egress to and from site for learners
____ Adequate signage to direct learners to appropriate sites
____ Lavatory/cafeteria/refreshment machines nearby
____ Adequate parking nearby
____ Adequate lighting in parking area and building hallways
____ Space of appropriate shape and adequate size in learning site
____ Breakout rooms/areas available if needed
____ Does the learning site have flexibility and provide for learner movement if needed

It is crucial to help participants become acquainted with each other when building an informal learning situation. There are a number of techniques that we use in helping people become acquainted with, and begin to feel comfortable in, the learning set-

ting. If there is to be more than one session together, one of the first
tasks is to ask all participants to fill out one side of a five-by-seven-
inch (or larger) index card (we often do this as people are seating
themselves and waiting for others to arrive). We ask for such information as full name, address (both home and business if appropriate), phone numbers, past educational experiences, number of years
of working experience, learning expectations, and even user identification codes (userids) if the participants frequently use electronic
mail. We ask that the card be turned in after the session is completed. If there are no objections, a group roster listing participants'
addresses, telephone numbers, and userids can be provided at the
next session. We explain that there may be occasions when participants will want to contact each other outside of group meeting
times for the purpose of raising questions, studying together, or
working jointly on learning activities.

We then ask participants to turn their cards over, fold them
in half so that the personal information is inside, and thus make
"tent" cards that will stand up by themselves. They are then asked
to print in large block letters with a felt pen (several are circulated
around the room) their first name or a nickname. The name should
be put on both sides of the "tent" so that not only the person across
the room but also each person seated on either side in a circle formation can see the name. The instructor should make a tent card,
too (we prefer to use our first names rather than titles or last names
to help in the creation of an informal climate). Such name cards are
used for at least the first several group sessions to make it easier for
participants to learn one another's names.

The next activity is to have learners introduce themselves.
There are two techniques that we especially like to use (information
on other introduction techniques is provided in the resources section later in the book). The first is to have participants turn to their
closest partner or count off in twos and work in dyads. We mention
some questions that they could ask each other and then have them
spend approximately fifteen minutes becoming acquainted with
each other so that they can introduce their dyad partner to the rest
of the group. This provides a chance for two people to quickly
become familiar with each other and for others in the group to learn

something about all group members through the subsequent introductions.

If the group is not too large (perhaps not exceeding twelve to sixteen people), if we feel a real icebreaker is needed, or if several people in the group already know each other quite well, we ask partners to find out something rather unusual or special about each other to also report in the introductions. If there are uneven numbers, people can work in groups of three and simply take turns introducing one another, or the instructor can join a person in a dyad. This technique seems to be successful in breaking the ice, setting a tone of informality, helping to initiate the process of learning names, and promoting one of our three Rs—Relationships with others.

It is important to describe the instructional process to learners. We have found it very important to spend some time during the first hour or so talking about the instructional process that will be used in the course or workshop. The workbook of supplemental materials mentioned earlier contains a write-up that describes both the individualizing process and our personal instructional philosophies. Various examples can be given of how the process will be employed, how self-directed learning will be encouraged, and how the instructor's role as facilitator will evolve during the learning experience. Engaging in dialogues with participants and answering questions about individualizing the instruction and learning or about any learning requirements can continue until you feel that participants have a good understanding of your role as well as their own.

What the instructor is doing is investing initial time that will pay big dividends later in the learning experience. An instructor needs to spend most of the first two to three hours of a course in simply describing the instructional process and building relationships. Thus, it may appear that these first few hours are taken up mainly by activities outside the content parameters. However, if this time is employed correctly, learners and the instructor will be able to focus more directly on content during subsequent hours together.

Creating an Informal Learning Environment. In most traditional learning settings, the instructor is located at the front of the room and wears an invisible cloak of authority, while learners, as receptacles of the knowledge to be imparted, are kept a good arm's length away in rows of chairs. Obviously, this is somewhat overstated to make a point, but learners in such settings generally come to think that they must capture every word the instructor speaks. It is also not unusual for such learners to experience considerable anxiety about future evaluations or to spend a great deal of energy trying to figure out just what the instructor wants or expects.

An important key to the success of individualizing instruction is the establishment of an informal learning environment. In a setting where reliance on self and personal responsibility for learning are encouraged, an informal environment is necessary. For example, you need to pay special attention to the needs and interests of each learner. You need to use good human relationship skills, such as direct eye contact, active listening to learners, smiling, and humor. Even tools such as learning contracts can be used to foster a feeling of informality if learners are given opportunities to discuss openly their likes and dislikes regarding individualized planning through contracts. Taking initial time to create an informal setting will pay tremendous returns in the long run.

We also attempt to establish and promote friendships among learners. This is done through the getting-acquainted activities described earlier, by encouraging learners to engage in dialogues among themselves, and by suggesting that learners will be able to work together on various learning activities if they so desire. The intent is to promote relationships so learner-to-learner exchanges can be made freely outside actual meeting times.

The real intent in working at development of an informal environment is to establish early in the process that learners will have considerable control over their own learning. Such recognition of personal control means that an individual takes charge of understanding personal needs in relation to expected learning parameters, designing a series of learning activities that will guarantee the meeting of such needs, and carrying out evaluation functions to provide evidence that, in fact, goals are being met.

Developing the Instructional Plan

In contrast to more traditional teaching approaches in which instructors plan most, if not all, the activities for a course or workshop before it begins, step three in the individualizing process requires that some initial time be spent specifying what will be the major foci of the learning activities. Usually there will be certain topics that require emphasis. For example, if the course centers on planning and evaluating adult education programs and people have chosen to participate with that subject in mind, it would be inappropriate to spend much time discussing the history of adult education.

However, within a topic such as program planning, there are numerous subtopics on which time can be spent depending on what skills and needs that specific group of people brings to the learning environment. Thus, rather than prejudging what is best for that particular group of individuals and perhaps missing the mark for many, the instructor invests time in deciding exactly what should be studied.

There will be instances where for various reasons most of the hour-to-hour learning activities must be preplanned. However, we believe it is still important to involve learners in some sort of ownership-building process. Even if it is not possible for learners to have much say on specific activities, you can at least discuss with them such functions as how group discussions will be used, how individual activities can fit into group activities, and how learning experiences or evaluation activities will be designed.

It is important for instructors and learners to work out the learning plan together. Developing the learning plan together is crucial in terms of promoting feelings of personal ownership by learners. You obviously will need to develop an approach to this planning process that fits within your personal and any institutional philosophy under which you must teach, but this is how we approach planning activities.

Within the first few hours of a learning experience, we describe notions about building a group plan for the various learning activities. We discuss the value of investing some initial time in analyzing important individual and group needs, and we then engage participants in various individual and group needs assessment activities (these are described in Chapter Seven). We then explain that it is now the instructor's responsibility to build a tentative schedule of activities. We note that such a schedule must match both individual and group needs as much as possible, while at the same time meeting organizational and instructor expectations about the content to be covered.

After the needs assessment activities have been completed, we begin preparing for subsequent sessions. In a workshop, this might take place during a lunch break. In a graduate course that meets for three hours each week, this usually would take place between session one and two. Using the information obtained during the needs assessment activities as a basis, we make an initial effort at building a group plan for the remainder of the learning experience. We examine the various small-group reports (and even individual needs assessment forms if clarity is needed on some issues) and compile a majority report of needs. In a one-day training workshop, this would involve quickly prioritizing the major needs. In a formal course, it would involve making an early estimate of the amount of time to be spent on each topic. Even notes on the various resources that might be used can be developed.

Next we take a careful look at the competency requirements for the learning experience to see how closely the compiled needs information matches the overall intent of the course. The instructor must of course ensure that learners will finish the learning activities with the basic competencies necessary for mastery of the subject. In a shorter workshop, we typically will pull from a larger collection of transparencies and other resource materials those items that seem to match the identified needs. If it is a course that meets weekly, we begin detailing a plan of action and learning activities for the remaining sessions and pulling together learning resources that will supplement each group period.

Once the plan has been developed, it should be presented to learners for their feedback. In a graduate course, for example, learners are presented with the plan at the next session and asked to review it, modify it as necessary, and approve it. When a consensus has been reached, learners are encouraged to develop learning contracts based on the plan. For example, there will be some topics that may not be appropriate for certain individuals because they are already quite familiar with them. They may choose, therefore, to not participate when those topics are covered in class and can build alternative learning activities into their contract. Other topics may only be touched on in a general way during group sessions so that any participant desiring more in-depth material can describe in the contract how additional learnings will be obtained through special readings, interviews with knowledgeable people, or other learning activities outside class. Other topics may best be addressed by a learner through working with others, through some mechanism that allows several topics to be studied in depth, or through a term project. Obviously, in a shorter course or a one-day workshop, the activities described above must be condensed in many ways.

The instructor's role in all this analysis and feedback is to design a logical flow of events, to complete the acquisition of necessary resources if time permits, and to build in any maintenance or needs rediagnosis activities deemed necessary. Subsequent feedback to learners on their contracts or plans will be helpful once personal needs have been matched against topics to be studied during group sessions. Thus, in addition to addressing future topics through presentations to learners, the instructor truly becomes a learning process facilitator.

Identifying Learning Activities

The fourth step in the individualized learning process involves identifying various ways in which learners can increase knowledge and develop competencies related to their assessed needs and the learning content. The instructor should describe several learning activities in which participants can engage, some learning techniques they can use, and several experiences in or out of the formal setting that they might like to consider.

Such information can be brought to the attention of learners in various ways. Some of these ways should be described in the workbook or study guide. Some should be suggested early in a workshop or training session so that participants can give feedback. Others should be discussed during subsequent sessions if the time is available. Still others should be detailed in learning contracts completed by prior participants and, if the prior learners have no objections, such contracts can be made available to new learners so that they can gather ideas for their own use.

Learners should consider working together in small groups on some of the learning activities. The instructor can encourage development of critical thinking and reflection through such techniques as interactive reading or writing logs, critiques of written or mediated materials related to the learning experience, and the development of theory statements pertaining to materials they read. In our own instructional efforts, we often provide opportunities for learners to present information to each other by role playing, by leading a small-group discussion on a topic they have researched, or by giving a minilecture.

We also encourage learners to make use of the various educational resources that exist in their community. If time allows, interviews with agency administrators, brief internships in adult education organizations, and actual study efforts within some portion of a community can provide useful learning experiences. The Resources section of the book provides some specific recommendations on a variety of learning activity opportunities and ideas.

Putting Learning into Action

There are two additional steps in the individualizing model. In many respects, step five of the individualizing model parallels traditional instruction, although we employ more variety in terms of techniques and devices than many of our colleagues who do not use an individualizing process. This step involves carrying out our initial planning efforts and constantly monitoring the progress of learners. We use various instructional techniques aimed at keeping interest high both for us and for the learners—techniques such as lecturing, small- and large-group discussion, analysis of case studies, role playing, and debates. We use a variety of mediated resources, outside experts, and various kinds of games and simulation activities. We also employ some formative evaluation strategies to ensure that we are on target or to determine when certain adjustments should be made.

Evaluating Individual Learner Outcomes

The final step involves helping learners evaluate their efforts. We do some of this early in the process when we provide suggestions, assistance, or confirmation to learners related to their learning contract evaluation plans. We also provide evaluative feedback to them throughout the learning experience if they submit materials to use for our assessment. We also ask them to provide feedback to us in various ways during the course or training session. Chapter Nine provides more specific information on suggested evaluation activities.

To some, the six-step individualizing process will seem to be far outside the educational mainstream. This criticism will be more common when the learning takes place in formal settings and there is an organizational sponsor, such as a university or a corporation.

Consequently, an instructor or trainer will constantly need to fight what may seem like an uphill battle in obtaining the support necessary for the process to work. Arranging that extra breakout room, providing options to learners, and spending some initial time in a learning experience with activities such as introductions or needs assessment will seem strange and even educationally unsound to some of your colleagues.

Thus, you will need to work hard to obtain the institutional support necessary to the process. This will require you to spend some of your time explaining, justifying, convincing, and even defending your actions. It may mean that initially you may have to ask learners to send letters of support to high-level administrators or to discuss with others what they have learned through the individualizing process. You may even need to carry out evaluations that demonstrate the competencies and abilities obtained by your learners. The resources section of the book contains answers to questions typically asked about the individualizing process.

7

Assessing What Learners Know and Need to Know

Jeffrey Lockwood, a trainer for a large computer manufacturer, was thinking of offering a new noncredit workshop on stress management for employees. He had read about the need for such learning experiences in a recent trade journal, had completed an employee needs assessment that confirmed his suspicions, and had talked to the personnel director about the increasing number of employees who had been calling in sick in recent months. The personnel director thought that the stress associated with the company's large new government contract accounted for much of the increase in sick leave.

Jeffrey talked to his supervisor, Mary Lyons, about the results of his needs analysis. Mary wondered if such a workshop was really justified given the current strain on training personnel just to keep up with the workshops required for the new contract. Jeffrey showed her some of the figures he had compiled and also discussed the articles that he had read on the adverse effects of workplace stress. After further discussion of the potential impact on the whole organization if stress was not managed better, Mary agreed that they should begin conducting the workshop on a trial basis.

Assessing what learners know or need to know is an important feature of the individualizing approach. This is true for a wide range of educational settings, including both formal and informal situations and independent study possibilities. This chapter centers on formal classroom or training situations, but the notion of assessing needs as a prelude to planning learning activities is important in many other kinds of settings.

Individual Needs Assessment Techniques

The active involvement of learners in assessing those needs that will serve as a foundation for subsequent learning is crucial to success of the individualizing process. Utilizing needs as a basis for planning the content of instruction or training programs is an important part of the individualizing process. Not only did Jeffrey Lockwood obtain information about potential needs from the professional literature he read and from talking with the personnel director, he also actively involved the potential trainees in the process by means of his needs assessment survey.

A number of techniques can be used to assess learning needs at the individual level, ranging from survey forms to personal interviews. Each has its particular uses and limitations. One of us (Hiemstra, 1985a) has synthesized information about a variety of needs assessment techniques. A summary of this information is found in the resources portion of this book.

The first technique that we advocate for a formal setting asks the learner to give written responses to a needs assessment tool. A variety of forms or assessment devices are available that test some knowledge area or provide a pretest on various abilities (Knowles, 1975, 1984, 1986; Robinson, Athanasiou, & Head, 1969; Robinson & Shaver, 1969). Smith and Cunningham's (1987) source book contains a multitude of references on various topics, many of which include either assessment forms or materials from which assessment forms can be derived. Guglielmino (1977), Knowles (1975), and Oddi (1984) have developed instruments or forms that assess the ability to undertake self-directed learning activities.

Often it makes more sense to construct your own instrument than to use an existing one. This affords maximum flexibility and usually results in an instrument directly related to the learning experience as conceived by you or the sponsoring organization. Such an approach also permits modifications over time as changes in knowledge or in your learners dictate.

The construction of such a tool involves looking at desired competencies, requirements, and text or resource materials to identify terms, concepts, definitions, and other informational needs that appear to make up the probable parameters of the learning experience. It is important that you select those elements or topics of potential importance to the content area. Note, though, the deliberate use of the term *probable parameters* above. This step is where individualized instruction may begin to differ from more traditional approaches.

We employ the needs assessment instrument as a tool for facilitating participation by learners in selecting the actual content of the course. The format that we find most helpful is fairly simple and yet complex enough to stimulate thinking and searching on the part of the learner. It is adapted from Knowles's (1975) *Self-Directed Learning*; this book, along with one by Knowles and Associates (1984), also describes several other self-rating ideas or forms. Exhibit 1 provides a sample form based on a graduate course for adult education students entitled Program Planning and Evaluation in Adult Education. We use only four self-rating categories, "don't know," "low competence," "medium competence," and "high competence." We also have found that if more than fifteen categories or content areas are provided, people seem to have a difficult time carrying out the self-rating.

It has been our experience that the most useful needs assessment form is an evolving one. By that we mean that the form will probably change each time you prepare for a particular learning experience. Certainly the instructor learns a great deal about the content, what works and what does not, each time that the course or workshop is taught. In addition, the knowledge areas to be covered constantly change as a result of new research, literature, and organizational knowledge.

There are, however, two difficulties that we have experienced in using such a form. Sometimes learners have difficulty rating themselves and may have to utilize the "don't know" category for several of the potential content areas. Individual discussion with an instructor to clarify terms, to obtain some background information, or to help build some context, both when the form is filled out and when it issued as an aid in completing the learning contract, may be needed. The point is to help each learner make as honest an evaluation as possible.

Another problem involves the differences that are likely to exist from one person to the next when self-ratings are made. For instance, a set of skills rated high by one person may only be rated medium or low by another because of differences in backgrounds or levels of self-confidence when these people may in fact have identical levels of skills. In addition, it may be difficult for a learner to provide accurate assessments on all items because of a lack of experience with them or because considerable time has passed since a skill or knowledge area was addressed. Thus, the ranking each person is asked to make by going through the list a second time helps provide additional comparisons between people when the instruments are used for the group needs assessment process described in the next section. It also is important to encourage each person to add special or personal need items for either individual or group study.

If it is impossible to predesign an instrument, learners can be asked to list their expectations, suggest personal needs, and/or begin a process of designing learning objectives. In a workshop related to community education, for example, we use a gaming and simulation device in the first session as a means of making learners aware of what they do and do not know. In one of our graduate courses, a pretest of the knowledge most likely to be covered during the semester is administered to stimulate thinking about the possible range of topics to be covered. Personal interviews of learners or even the administering of standardized tests also can help both learner and instructor understand more about what is and is not known.

The purpose of these individual activities is to begin building personal ownership for learning and an acceptance of personal responsibility through a process involving self-recognition of strengths and weaknesses. Such activities move learners from a zone of comfort to one of some discomfort where they need to struggle

Exhibit 1. Needs Diagnosis Form.

NAME _____   DATE _____

Diagnostic Form

Program Planning and Evaluation in Adult Education

This form is designed to assist you in assessing your personal level of competence and need related to some of the content areas that can or will be covered in this course. This information will help you and me plan together a sequence of learning experiences that will build on and supplement current strengths, so as to develop as efficiently as possible many of the professional competencies that are required to work effectively in educational agencies and programs.

For each potential content area, please check the most relevant column indicating a self-rating. To assist in the decision regarding which column to check for each area, the information that is being sought in each of the four columns is indicated below.

DK – If you are uncertain regarding the relation between the listed area and your current level of need or competence and you would like or need to explore this relation further through discussion, reading, independent study, and so on.

LO – If your current competence related to the listed area is especially low but could be raised toward a desired level through specific learning experiences.

MD – If your past experiences have provided part of the desired competence and some learning experiences would develop the remainder.

HI – If your past experiences have substantially developed the listed area.

Self-Rate Your Competency

	DK	LO	MD	HI
1. Objectives – Ability to identify, select, and write various types of objectives for use in program planning.	☐	☐	☐	☐
2. Needs Assessment – Ability to conduct needs analysis as a basis for planning and setting agency or program goals.	☐	☐	☐	☐
3. Goal Analysis – Ability to analyze and set long- and short-range program goals.	☐☐	☐☐	☐☐	☐☐
4. Program-Planning Process – Ability to utilize a sequence of steps in planning and operating a program.				
5. Scheduling and Sequencing – Ability to bring together appropriate learners, mentors, materials, equipment, and facilities through good time management techniques.	☐	☐	☐	☐
6. Evaluation Planning – Ability to plan some evaluation strategies in conjunction with your program goals.	☐	☐	☐	☐

7. Evaluation Data Collection – Ability to construct usable instruments for data collection.

☐ ☐ ☐ ☐

8. Program-Planning Theory – Familiar with the various program planning models and related research findings.

☐ ☐ ☐ ☐

9. Methods and Material Selection – Able to select and use instructional methods, materials, and resources that are appropriate and related to the needs and abilities of individual learners.

☐ ☐ ☐ ☐

10. Advisory Councils – Understanding of the selection, training, and use of program-planning advisory councils.

☐ ☐ ☐ ☐

11. Evaluation Theory – Familiarity with the various approaches to and philosophies of evaluation.

☐ ☐ ☐ ☐

12. Terminology – Familiarity with various terms related to the technical procedures of planning programs.

☐ ☐ ☐ ☐

13. Organizational Constraints – Understanding of the organizational constraints and climate related to planning and evaluation.

☐ ☐ ☐ ☐

14. Literature Base – Familiarity with the theory, research, and literature related to program planning and evaluation.

☐ ☐ ☐ ☐

15. If you have additional needs, please describe them in the following section and self-rate your level of competency.

_____ ☐ ☐ ☐ ☐
_____ ☐ ☐ ☐ ☐
_____ ☐ ☐ ☐ ☐
_____ ☐ ☐ ☐ ☐
_____ ☐ ☐ ☐ ☐

Now that you have completed your self-ratings, please go back and numerically rank each LO that you checked according to the level of importance you would attach to it. Think of this in terms of the time that should be allotted in class for learning activities related to the content area. Thank you!

with new ideas, new concepts, or changing perceptions of personal abilities. By looking closely at their personal needs, individual learners will begin to see how the learning experiences can be used to fill in gaps or to enhance personal strengths.

Group Activities

Putting learners in touch with others is necessary in determining specific content areas or learning activities to be pursued during subsequent activities. It also helps facilitate our three Rs: Relationships with each other; Relationship with the instructor; and Relationship with the course content.

This at first may sound unnecessary in a process that stresses individualized instruction. However, something is definitely gained through the synergistic exchange of ideas and personal views regarding needs and content that should be covered in the learning activities. Discovering that others are both similar and dissimilar seems to help most individuals obtain a perspective on why certain topics may be important to cover in a particular learning experience even if they do not necessarily meet every person's immediately recognized needs.

A useful group technique is the discussion of those individual needs that come to light when participants complete a written diagnostic form. The technique that we utilize most often in our graduate courses involves the formation of small groups. This typically follows the completion of written diagnostic forms and comes at the end of our first meeting or during an early portion of the second session. If possible, we like to group together some people who have had experience with the individualizing process and some people who have not. Frequently, certain learners will be asked ahead of time to serve as leader for the groups.

We ask people to form groups of four to six people (we use some counting off technique, select group members ourselves if we have a rationale for doing so, or let learners form their own groups). If possible, we have extra rooms available or we use areas such as hallways, private offices, or staff lounges. We ask that a group leader be determined if one has not already been designated and that a group recorder also be selected.

The leader and group members are instructed to use the needs diagnosis form as a way of initiating discussion. They do this by going through and selecting the listed topics that will require the most attention in future group discussions and activities. This requires a tabulation of how each person has rated a topic on the form. This approach not only initiates discussion of the various topics but also facilitates a recognition of differences within the group and occasionally prompts a need for clarification from the instructor. We make ourselves available as a resource but attempt to keep somewhat a low profile during the process and typically act only to define terms or to describe the needs assessment activity. We want learners to struggle initially with the concepts, terms, or language, and we think that this begins the modeling of team building and conflict resolution, both of which are useful activities in an individualizing approach.

The groups work for twenty to forty minutes, discussing their individual rankings, tallying a group total on each item, and addressing new needs that surface from individual needs assessment forms or during the group discussions. At the end of the session, each group brings back a composite report that contains summary findings, describes other topics the group would like to see addressed, and provides suggestions relative to instructional techniques or learning resources. Unless there are unusual time constraints, each group makes an oral report of its findings to the rest of the class.

Learners are encouraged to keep their individual needs assessment forms for use in planning future personal inquiry activities and in filling out the subsequent learning contract, although if they have particular needs that they want to bring to the instructor's attention, their forms can be turned in along with the group report. We also encourage each group to determine if there are additional topics to the ones listed that will require some attention during future meetings. As noted above, each leader or recorder is asked to make a brief report to the larger group when the small-group discussions have ended so that everyone can see how similar or different their own rankings were and have an opportunity to seek clarification or to make other suggestions.

If the formation of small groups is not feasible or a group

report is not appropriate, another useful technique is to form learners into dyads or triads and ask them to discuss their perceptions of needs and the learning activities required to fill those needs. We have used this approach in training sessions where the time is short or when the content is fairly specifically prescribed. The discussion seems to help provide some clarification and initial awareness of how others view their personal needs and potential learning activities.

Ongoing Assessment

The assessment of needs requires attention throughout the learning process. The individual and group activities described in the preceding section take place for the most part during the first few hours that learners and facilitator are together. However, learners should be encouraged to analyze their needs throughout the experience. As new needs emerge or as needs determined earlier become either clearer or less relevant, we provide opportunities for learners to alter their learning activities through modifications in the learning contract. Obviously, there comes a point in any formal course or workshop at which it becomes impossible or impractical to change learning plans, especially if some sort of formal grade must be given, but the continuation of learning pursuits after a formal course has finished can provide very meaningful experiences.

In one of our semester courses, we attempt to complete the individual and group needs assessment activities within the first one or two sessions. We use the information gained to build a tentative learning plan or group track. We then communicate this information back to the learners in the next session to provide them with some understanding of what will be covered in the formal setting so that they can match their individual needs with planned group or in-class activities and know what to emphasize in their learning contracts.

Helping learners understand the value of assessing personal needs enhances their ability to carry out diagnosis efforts in subsequent learning experiences. Perhaps the ultimate compliment came during the evaluation activities after a course that we had taught together. One of the learners noted that after he had recognized that he could assess his own needs and then have the freedom to match his learning experiences with those needs, he was able to hone in more on what he was studying while at the same time feeling he had personal control over the nature of the thinking he did on the subject. We believe the individualizing instructional approach helps both learners and instructors achieve this kind of recognition of personal freedom and worth.

8

The Importance and Use of Learning Contracts

Myron Washington was talking with his colleague, Thelma Ramos, about a new instructional technique that he had heard about at a recent professional conference. The technique involved the use of learning contracts in the classroom, and Myron was curious to know if Thelma had ever used them in her teaching. Thelma said that she had been using them for a couple of years and felt that they were especially helpful in stimulating learners to take more responsibility for their own learning. Myron replied, "That's what the speaker was saying at the conference. I'm curious, though, how do you actually employ them? I don't think I understand how they are used. Maybe you could give me some tips and pointers." Thelma said she would be glad to and offered the following information:

During the first class meeting, she introduces the importance of self-directed learning and the need to find ways of nurturing this. She then describes learning contracts and suggests that they are a particularly useful tool for initiating self-directed learning. She hands out an illustrated example of a learning

contract to the class members and then answers any of
their questions. Thelma noted that most learners find
learning contracts somewhat disconcerting at first, but
that, once they overcome such anxiety, they tend to
want to use them again and again. Myron thanked
Thelma for the information and decided he would
incorporate contracts into his courses the next
semester.

Learning contracts as a tool for promoting self-directed adult
learning have received increased attention and use in recent years,
so it is not surprising that Myron heard about them at a conference
or that Thelma was already using them. In such institutions as New
York's Empire State College and the University of South Carolina,
as well as in many universities in various countries with nontraditional or adult education programs, learning contracts have been
used to help respond to the varying needs and backgrounds of adult
learners (Brockett & Hiemstra, 1985). In addition, individual instructors in a variety of settings have used learning contracts in
many ways (Knowles & Associates, 1984; Knowles, 1986).

Contracts often are associated with efforts to enhance self-
directed learning, as Thelma pointed out to Myron. Smith (1982)
and Smith and Haverkamp (1977) have developed a process called
"learning how to learn" in which self-directed learning competencies can be integrated into the design of formal courses and workshops with the expectation that greater self-direction will result.
This chapter discusses the learning contract and how it can be used
to promote self-directed learning and enhance the individualizing
of instructional efforts.

Learning Contracts Defined

*Learning contracts are very effective in helping adults indi-
vidualize their learning experiences.* According to Lindquist (1975),
learning contracts work especially well with adults since they help
satisfy at least four needs: "the logistical problems of working, mar-
ried adults; the strong motivation to learn what one needs or wants
to learn; the concern to develop intellectual skills and lifelong

learning habits; and the desire to individualize and personalize learning" (p. 76). Learning contracts have also been used successfully in a variety of adult education settings, ranging from basic literacy classes through graduate study (Bauer, 1985; Knowles, 1986; and Sisco, 1986, 1988).

Essentially, a learning contract is a written plan that describes what an individual will learn as a result of some specified learning activity. It serves as a tool for communicating learning intentions between the learner and instructor. Learning contracts can take many forms, and there are a number of terms used interchangeably in reference to them, such as learning plans, study plans, performance agreements, or self-development plans. We prefer the term *learning contract* because it is the one most commonly used today (Knowles, 1986).

A learning contract typically consists of five major elements that specify the following: (1) the knowledge, skills, attitudes, and values to be acquired by the learner (learning objectives); (2) how these objectives are to be accomplished by the learner (learning resources and strategies); (3) the target date(s) for completion; (4) what evidence will be presented to demonstrate that the objectives have been completed (evidence of accomplishment); and (5) how this evidence will be judged or validated (criteria and means for validating evidence) (Knowles, 1986). A key to successful development of a learning contract is to make the learning activities "specific enough for the student to proceed and yet sufficiently flexible to permit initiative and creativity" (Avakian, 1974, p. 54).

Learning contracts have a variety of uses in education or training settings. According to Caffarella (1983), they can (1) provide a means for dealing with the wide differences found among any group of learners, (2) enhance individual motivation for learning, (3) facilitate the development of mutual respect between the instructor and participants, (4) provide for a more individualizing instructional mode, and (5) foster the skills of self-directed learning. Learning contracts also offer an alternative way of structuring a learning experience by placing equal emphasis on the design of what will be taught (content plan) and how a body of content will be acquired by the learners (process plan) (Knowles, 1986).

Chickering (1977) and Wald (1978) testify to the crucial nature of the learning contract, particularly in postsecondary education settings. Chickering maintains that the power of the learning contract comes from its capacity to individualize learning activities, time, methods, and standards for evaluation. Wald believes that it captures more than any other academic process the creativity and potential of individualized instruction. Contracts also provide a means for addressing the particular strengths and weaknesses of each learner.

Studies by Caffarella (1982, 1983) and Kasworm (1982, 1983) have confirmed the effectiveness of learning contracts in formal adult education graduate study. Caffarella conducted studies using the learning contract as a means of fostering self-directed learning competence among graduate students enrolled in formal adult education courses. Kasworm studied the use of the learning contract in one of her graduate courses in adult education and concluded that it "was of value to the majority of the graduate students in their development of self-directed learning knowledge and skill" (1982, p. 127). Evidence from these studies indicated an increased competence for self-directed learning as a result of the learning contract. However, it should be pointed out that, in a later study, Caffarella and Caffarella (1986) concluded that while learning contracts do promote certain competencies for self-directed learning, it was impossible to suggest that contracts are a major tool in enhancing self-directed learning skills.

In still another study, Sisco (1988) investigated how instructors of adults promote and facilitate competence for self-directed learning through the use of teaching strategies. Using a modified self-reporting instrument based on the Self-Directed Learning Competencies Self Appraisal Form originally constructed by Caffarella and Caffarella (1986), Sisco found that the learning contract was mentioned most frequently as a strategy used by respondents to encourage and nurture self-directed learning in their students.

The use of the learning contract with adult learners is important in the establishment of personal ownership of and direction for learning. We have found the learning contract to be an indispensable tool in implementing our individualizing instructional process. It helps to emphasize the collaborative role that we believe is essential in working with adults and encourages personal ownership and direction. We are quick to caution, however, that the learning contract is only a tool and not an end in itself. But if used properly, it can help you attend to the diversity of learner needs, while at the same time providing a mechanism for learner accountability.

Using Learning Contracts in Individualizing Instruction

We view the learning contract as a key vehicle in helping adult learners accept personal responsibility for their learning. In keeping with this belief, we have incorporated the contract into our own graduate courses in adult education. While the majority of the comments in this section relate more directly to formal classroom settings, we will also describe how learning contracts can be used in a variety of other instructional settings. We have used contracting in weekend workshops (both credit and noncredit), in intensive training sessions for persons in business and industry, and in civic-oriented programs in our local communities.

As noted earlier, the contract provides a framework for indicating what is to be learned as a result of some specified activity. We make it known during the initial meeting with learners that they will have an opportunity to assess their needs and evaluate their competency levels, which will later be translated into individualized learning contracts. At this point, learners unfamiliar with our approach may be somewhat tense or anxious, so we spend some time discussing why we believe learning contracts are important. We also ask those learners with prior contracting experience to describe how they have used them. Once such discussion takes place and learners have had some time to think about the process, initial anxiety generally gives way to commitment to the use of contracts.

There are many possible formats that a contract can take. We prefer one that emphasizes learning objectives, learning resources, and evaluative plans. Knowles (1986) provides a sourcebook that illustrates a multitude of learning contract formats, organized according to the context in which the contracting is done: academic classroom courses, independent study, clinical courses, graduate assistantships, internships, continuing professional and management development, and total degree programs.

The format we use in our graduate courses was adapted from material originally developed by Knowles (1975); it is displayed in Exhibit 2. We ask learners to indicate the course number and title, their names, social security numbers, and the instructor's name. We assume that learners will want to contract for a grade of B or better since they are in graduate school and, in order to succeed at our respective universities, they must perform at least at that level. Thus, learners may elect to contract for a grade of either B or A, depending on their inclination, and may also include plus or minus signs if the grading system permits it.

The rest of our learning contract is divided into five columns on which each learner is asked to indicate (1) what is to be learned (learning objectives), (2) how these objectives are to be accomplished (resources and strategies), (3) the target date for their completion, (4) what evidence will be presented to demonstrate that the objectives have been accomplished (evidence), and (5) how this evidence will be validated (verification by judges).

In completing a contract, participants may use the learning objectives provided by the instructor, develop their own, or use some combination of both. We provide learners with a list of learning objectives that give guidance and direction to the learning experience. At the same time, however, we make it clear to learners that within the parameters of the course content they may establish objectives that are more in line with their personal needs and interests. We also encourage learners to think critically about their learning and at the same time to tie their objectives to the practical needs of a current or future job.

The learning strategies and resources describe how learners will go about accomplishing each objective. Learning resources may be either human resources or support materials of various types. For example, a human resource would be an adult education agency administrator selected for an interview. Support materials would include books and articles, films, videotapes, and slide/tape learning kits. Learning strategies refer to the tools or techniques used in accomplishing each objective. Examples would include carrying out an internship within some agency, writing a research report, taking a field trip, or completing a literature review. Critical reflection about some topic could be accomplished through an in-

Exhibit 2. Learning Contract Form.

LEARNING CONTRACT FOR COURSE # _____ : _____

Student: _____ Soc. Sec. #: _____ Instructor: _____

What are you going to learn (objectives)	How are you going to learn it (resources and strategies)	Target date for completion	How are you going to know that you learned it (evidence)	How are you going to prove that you learned it (verification by judges)
B or A Level (so indicate)				

Source: Adapted from Knowles (1975).

teractive reading log or development of a theory log that summarizes what a learner believes are important theoretical constructs. In
a training workshop, a participant might select certain learning kits
within the company's resource center that will be studied over a
subsequent several-week period.

The target date for completion of each learning objective is
designed to help learners manage their own time. Rather than im-
pose some arbitrary time line, we indicate to participants that since
they are in a better position to judge the demands made on their
time, they should be responsible for determining when various assignments will be due. We, in turn provide feedback on their scheduling decisions to help them meet any institutionally imposed
deadlines, maintain an appropriate sequence, and complete activities in coordination with other learners.

The evidence that learners present to demonstrate accomplishment of each objective may take a number of different forms.
For the knowledge domain, learners might prepare a written report
or make an oral presentation. For the skill domain, they might
prepare a demonstration or complete some type of performance
exercise. For the attitude domain, learners might present a simulation game or offer a critical incident case and then ask for feedback
from participants and/or observers. A participant in a one-day
workshop might need to plan for subsequent on-the-job results as
a means of demonstrating how workshop activities meet any stated
objectives. We stress that there should be an appropriate linkage
between the types of learning objectives that participants are pur-
suing and the form of evidence that they select to demonstrate their
accomplishments.

The final task in developing a learning contract involves
determining the criteria and means for validating how the evidence
will be judged, as well as who will do the judging. For a learning
objective in the knowledge domain, appropriate criteria might include clarity, depth, precision, and/or comprehensiveness. For skill-
based objectives, appropriate criteria might include poise, speed,
flexibility, precision, and/or gracefulness. Attitudinal objectives
might require judgments or feedback from outside experts.

In addition to the instructor, validators could include fellow
learners, employment supervisors, faculty from other institutions,

or experts from the community at large. It is not at all unusual for someone other than the instructor or training session facilitator to be in a better position to validate the learning evidence. For example, a participant in a workshop on new computer graphic techniques may want to select an immediate supervisor or a work colleague to judge whether some new skill has been mastered. The important point for us, and we believe for learners, too, is that the contract can be used as a mechanism for careful planning and execution of learning activities all the way from an assessment of needs through verification that the needs have or have not been met.

Learners typically need some initial guidance from the instructor if they are to make good use of the contract as a learning resource. We introduce participants to the learning contract by means of four steps. In step one, as noted in Chapter Six, we provide learners with a number of handouts related to the learning experience or with similar materials compiled in a workbook or study guide. These materials typically consist of the syllabus, bibliography, guidelines for developing learning contracts, a needs assessment form, and related readings. We ask participants to familiarize themselves with these materials, and we try to answer any questions about them or clarify any confusing points. Learners are also asked to consider what competencies (knowledge, skills, attitudes, values) they wish to develop in concert with the course content.

In step two, participants develop a first draft of their learning contract. We encourage them to develop this draft as soon as possible so that we can provide feedback or answer additional questions that may arise. In a one-day training session, this frequently involves setting aside time toward the end of the day during which participants develop a personal contract for follow-up learning activities beyond that day. In a week-long workshop, learners frequently can complete contracts as early as the beginning of the second day. In a semester-long graduate course, we recommend that they wait until the general direction for the learning experience has been established (perhaps after ten to fifteen hours of time together) and specific topics for group as well as individual study have been determined. Thus, in a typical fifteen-week course, we ask learners to have an initial draft completed by the fourth to seventh session.

In the third step, learners typically share their preliminary contracts with a small group of colleagues (usually three to four) who serve as consultants. The purpose of this step is to provide participants with feedback on the clarity of each learning objective, the appropriateness of the learning strategies and resources selected, the relevance of the suggested evidence, and whether the criteria and means for validating the evidence are clear and convincing. Our own experience has been that this step is crucial in the development of a learning contract, as peers can be very helpful and can present insights different from those we suggest.

In the fourth and final step, participants turn in their learning contracts to us, typically updated after receiving feedback from peers. We look them over, seek clarification as needed, offer suggestions, negotiate alternatives if appropriate, and then return them for a final draft. Occasionally we will provide ideas on alternative or supplemental learning resources, ask learners to cut back on their planned activities, or ask them to take on additional tasks if we believe they need to do so. Once this has been completed, we ask each participant to keep a copy for personal reference and give us a copy for our own files.

Learning contracts are important tools in helping learners specify what they intend to learn; at the same time, they should be flexible enough to accommodate changes in plans or ideas. In fact, one of the central features of the learning contract is its inherent flexibility. Perhaps because of its legalistic feel or tone, we have found that learners often get the idea that they may not change their learning contract once it has been put in final form. In order to counter this view, we periodically remind participants that they may renegotiate their learning contract at any time up until the end of the learning experience if plans or ideas change. Thus, a learning contract should be specific enough to enable learners to accomplish their learning intentions, yet flexible enough so that new insights or revelations may be easily incorporated into the learning mix.

Some Related Issues

There are a number of other issues in using learning contracts that must be addressed, including alternative approaches to contracting, how to deal with learners involved in contracting for the first time, whether to link grading to learning contracts, and how to deal with institutional requirements.

Learning contracts are employed most often within institutions of higher education. They are used in a range of delivery modes, including correspondence courses and independent study, external degree programs, clinical placements, and continuing professional development programs, to name only a few. The learning contract is also being used more and more often in academic classroom courses.

However, learning contracts are increasingly being used in other agencies and institutions, including training programs in business and industry, staff development programs in governmental units, and continuing professional education programs in a variety of health-related organizations. Knowles (1986) reports that learning contracts are even being used in elementary and secondary schools, and he speculates that they are probably being used in some form in voluntary organizations as well. Thus, alternative ways of designing and thinking about contracts are increasing.

For example, in the case of a highly technical subject such as nuclear physics where learners are newcomers to the discipline, it is often necessary for the instructor to prepare the learning objectives for participants to follow. In addition, in such a situation, the types of learning activities might be planned by the instructor. But even in this kind of situation, learners could be given some opportunity to decide what resources and strategies to use in meeting the desired proficiency level.

Or take the case when the goal is to develop precise motor skills—for example, the skills needed to carry out a particular surgical procedure. Here, the instructor would retain considerable control over what is to be learned and how it will be learned, as well as how the learners are to demonstrate competence. However, even in this case, the instructor and learners might mutually agree on the pace and sequence of learning, as well as interaction activity among learners or between the instructor and learners.

A highly structured apprenticeship program where the instructor is required by government regulation to follow a prescribed curriculum provides another example. In this situation, the instructor would likely need to be quite directive, for example, in selecting the instructional topics and methods of evaluation. But even here, a good deal of negotiation between the instructor and learners could be instituted in terms of demonstrating mastery of content, the nature of the learning resources used, and the style of presentation.

Using a learning contract is not an all-or-nothing proposition. Learning contracts can be used successfully in nearly every instructional situation, provided that you have considered how much responsibility learners can assume in determining what they will accomplish. In some cases, an approach that provides for complete choice by learners may be warranted. In other cases, an approach calling for a more limited selection may be the best course of action. Whatever the situation, we recommend that every attempt be made to place at least some responsibility for learning squarely on the learners' shoulders so that the skills of self-directed learning can be encouraged.

Another problem you may encounter in using learning contracts is the anxiety and confusion some learners feel when first exposed to the process. We have found this to be a very normal reaction and have come to expect it. The chief reason for this uneasiness among learners is probably their prior educational experiences, where their role was that of passive receiver of the information transmitted and submissive executor of the instructor's directives.

One of the most effective techniques for dealing with initial learner hesitancy is simply to spend time discussing self-directed and contract learning. One of the hardest things in life is to give up something that has been reinforced many times over. This is especially true of adult learners when they are asked, often for the first time, to assume the role of a self-directing learner. We explain that, in this role, they share responsibility for determining what will be learned as well as showing how their learning will be evaluated. An important tool we use to promote this shared responsibility is, of course, the learning contract.

Another approach is to involve learners who have had some prior experience with learning contracts. We ask these individuals to share their experiences. Typically, they mention the anxiety and confusion they felt when first introduced to the idea, how they became more comfortable with the process, and how it has made their learning more relevant and meaningful. We have found this kind of peer testimony to be worth much more than what we could ever hope to attain through our own words.

Another helpful technique is to provide, in the workbook that learners use, an example of a completed learning contract using simulated information. Or, after removing each learner's name to maintain confidentiality, we distribute sample contracts during our first session so that participants can get an idea of what a learning contract looks like. We also mention that individual learners may borrow a copy or two for use as a model in developing their own contracts.

When introducing contracting, we also note that even though a suggested format is provided, learners may choose another style more to their liking. These can and have taken many forms, including outlines, narrative descriptions, concept maps, and audiotapes. We tend to accept almost any format as long as the submitted product communicates the intention clearly enough so we can provide feedback.

An additional technique that has worked very well is the scheduling of individual conferences with learners. We have found this helps us get to know individual learners better and to find out their particular interests in relation to the course. At this meeting, we try to provide both psychological support and information about resources, as well as clarification of the contracting process.

Although initial learner anxiety and confusion are typical with contract learning, we believe that this is a good thing. It often places the learner in a "zone of discomfort" that is necessary for critical learning to occur. Once learners have worked through their initial fears and concerns, our experience has shown that they often become quite excited about carrying out their own plans. Often, by the second or third course or workshop in which contracting has been used, learner excitement and creativity have become so contagious that the best we can do is stay out of the way. We feel this is the true essence of self-directed learning, and it is one of the main reasons why we enjoy working with adults.

In a formal credit-bearing setting, it is appropriate and helpful for learners to link the grades they will be given with their learning contracts. Linking grades to learning contracts may be a problem for some instructors, but it is something that we have done for many years now with consistent success. As noted earlier in the chapter, we assume that such learners will want to receive a grade of B or A if they are using contracts in a graduate course. Thus, rather than being kept in suspense, learners find it comforting to have some idea of what grade they are working toward.

We also note that achieving the grade learners contract for is tied to satisfactory completion of all their described assignments or a renegotiation of the assignments at some later date in the learning experience. We also mention to learners early in a learning experience that, as instructors, we retain the right to assign a grade that we feel reflects the quality of the work presented. We then spend some time talking about the issue of quality and responding to the questions of participants about this issue, the nature of our expectations, quantity of material expected, and even such minute details as the stylistic guidelines to be used in their writing efforts. If it seems appropriate, we talk about what a grade of A or a grade of B might mean in terms of the number of hours that they should invest in the learning experience.

Even given this candid discussion about expectations, there will be times when a lower grade than originally contracted for is warranted. Occasionally, it will make the most sense to simply give the learner an incomplete grade and ask for more or higher-quality work to be submitted before the incomplete can be removed. In addition, we realize that some instructors feel very strongly about retaining the right of issuing a grade based on evaluated performance rather than tying it to a contract.

A decision to use contracting should be based on a careful analysis of both your own philosophy and your institution's policies regarding evaluation or grading. Some educational agencies or institutions will have certain requirements, policies, or administrative constraints that inhibit the use of learning contracts. For example, some large corporations may require trainers to use a preplanned training package. In this kind of case, opportunities to use learning contracts may be severely limited. Even here, however, some discussion about the value of learner responsibility and possibilities for learner choices can be integrated into the instructional flow.

The philosophy of a particular institution or agency may make if difficult for you to use learning contracts. For example, in a vocational center, the prevailing instructional philosophy might be tied to behavioral objectives and the expected instructional style might be teacher directed. If you teach in this kind of setting and do not have the option to use learning contracts, you could nevertheless use a modified learning agreement between yourself and the learners as a substitute.

We have not encountered any difficulties in using learning contracts in our own institutions. However, a few colleagues have raised questions about what we were doing. Inevitably, these questions represented a reaction to learners who had a contracting experience with us and then, in turn, asked those instructors if they could also use a contract in their courses. Rather than seeing such questions as threats, we have viewed them as opportunities to respond to colleagues proactively. For example, we have met with colleagues over coffee or tea and discussed the use of learning contracts as a way of increasing self-directedness in our learners. Once we begin such dialogues, the conversational tone typically changes from anxiety about, to acceptance of, our approach—in some cases, even enthusiasm for it.

Constraints regarding contracting are often more self-imposed than otherwise. In view of this, we recommend that you conduct an "instructional audit" of your agency or institution to find out how firm the instructional policies and practices are. Our bet is that you will find considerable freedom and toleration for the approach that you believe is best, including contract learning.

Does Contracting Make a Difference?

It should come as no surprise that we believe contracting does make a difference. But we are not alone. Knowles (1986, p. 46), for example, believes that learning contracts have a number of practical benefits:

- It gets the learners more ego-involved in their own learning; it "turns them on" to learning. . . .
- It causes them to make use of a much wider variety

of resources for learning, such as peers, other people in the institution and community, field experiences, and [the] like, thus lessening the load carried by instructors who see themselves as the only resources available.

- It sharpens learners' skills of self-directed learning, thus giving them a tool that will enhance their ability to learn from their experience and their environment for the rest of their lives.
- It increases the accountability of the program by providing more functional and validated evidence of the learning outcomes.
- It provides a more functional way of structuring learning—a process structure in the place of the traditional content-transmission structure.
- It replaces the conventional teacher-imposed discipline with self-discipline in the learning process.
- It provides a way for the learner to obtain continual feedback about progress being made toward accomplishing learning goals.
- It is more cost effective than traditional teacher-directed learning, in that the learner is less dependent on exclusive use of the resources of instructors, and it takes some of the responsibility for directing the learning off their shoulders.

At the same time contract learning has some limitations. For example, in certain situations where the content is totally new to learners, an approach that provides more direction would probably be better, at least initially. Learning contracts can also cause problems for both instructors and learners who have "authoritarian" personalities. Finally, learning contracts appear to work best in agencies or institutions that support the idea of increasing learners' competence for self-directed learning.

Nevertheless, we are confident that contract learning affords the greatest flexibility for instructors and learners alike. This has been substantiated in our own experience as well as through the research of others. Yet the process of adaptation will probably vary according to an instructor's experience. In many ways, novice instructors may find our approach easier to apply than experienced instructors, in that the beginning teacher or trainer usually is eager to try various means to ensure success and is willing to experiment with new ideas or techniques, whereas the experienced instructor may be set in ways learned many years before. We of course hope that this book will provide the motivation and means for teachers and trainers of all levels of experience to try new ideas and approaches for helping learners achieve their highest potential.

9

Evaluating Learners,
the Learning Process,
and Yourself

As an instructional designer for a local community college, Mark Hayes knew that evaluation was one of the most important aspects of any program. After all, the information obtained from evaluations leads to various improvements in the program, instructional methods, and decision-making process. But Mark was concerned by a recent phone conversation that he had had with Miriam Rashad, an instructor in the psychology department, who argued that evaluation was a waste of time. Miriam believed that teaching evaluations amounted to little more than popularity contests. Worst yet, she felt that they did not provide any meaningful information about how to improve the instructional process or the learning experience.

Mark decided to investigate why Miriam had such negative views about evaluation by paying her a personal visit. He quickly learned that Miriam viewed evaluation very narrowly; she saw its purpose to be that of evaluating students, not instructors. In her mind, moreover, it was something that occurred at the end of a learning experience, so how could it be used to improve instruction. Mark showed Miriam how evaluation could be used as a tool for improving the learning experience—for example, by using a sentence-completion test midway through the course. He also discussed various evaluation techniques that could yield fair and objective information about teaching performance. Miriam thanked Mark for sharing some of his ideas and views about evaluation and promised to consider some of the techniques he had suggested.

As Mark pointed out, a key feature of any educational endeavor is the process of determining what is to be accomplished. Our society places great value on how well we are able to attain our goals and objectives. The skill that we exhibit as instructors in providing feedback to learners, guiding the teaching and learning transaction, and evaluating instruction is central to our overall success (Steele & Brack, 1973).

Learners, too, often need to develop skills for evaluating and validating their own learning experiences. The process that we use to assess teaching and learning outcomes is typically referred to as evaluation. This chapter discusses what evaluation is and how we can use it effectively in the context of individualizing instruction.

What Is Evaluation?

The concept of evaluation is not new. As early as 2,000 b.c., Chinese officials were conducting civil service examinations. The famed Greek teacher and philosopher, Socrates, reputedly used verbally mediated evaluations as part of the learning process. In the United States, the first reported user of program evaluation was Joseph Rice, who in 1897–1898 compared the spelling performance of 33,000 students in a large city school system. With the advent of IQ testing and other standardized achievement measures in the 1920s and 1930s, evaluation practices began to flourish in the United States. More recently, such evaluation measures as the Scholastic Aptitude Test (SAT) and the Graduate Record Examination (GRE) have come to be used very widely as measures of aptitude and ability (Worthen & Sanders, 1973).

Some typical forms that evaluation takes in institutional settings include course grades, scores on standardized measures such as an IQ test or the measures noted above, and performance feedback from a supervisor. So pervasive is the need for evaluation today that it can be found in nearly every type of organizational setting.

Most instructors would define evaluation as the process of judging the quality of an educational enterprise. Put another way, the term *evaluation* means appraising the value or worth of some educational undertaking such as a curriculum, a particular instructional procedure, or an individual performance in some area of learning (Popham, 1972). Generally, most evaluation efforts in education are undertaken with the aim of improving a given instructional situation. For example, evaluation can be used to answer such questions as how effective is the use of discussion with a group of experienced adults? Or, in a more personal way, how well am I communicating with the learners with whom I work?

The two main approaches to analyzing educational activities are summative and formative evaluation. There are many different types or models of evaluation. Some emphasize process, others product, while still others focus on learner outcomes. Despite these varying emphases, however, there are two main approaches to evaluation. The first of these is called summative evaluation. Summative evaluation is usually conducted for the purpose of assessing learner performance, justifying the worth of a program, or ensuring that a course has been effective. Such evaluation is usually undertaken after a learning experience has been completed. Some common examples used to assess how well participants performed include final examinations, term projects, oral presentations, and supervisor ratings. We ourselves use summative procedures to determine how well we did as instructors and how well the course or training session was received. These procedures include instructor evaluation forms, questionnaires used to obtain reactions to a particular session or technique, and course or workshop evaluation forms.

A second approach is called formative evaluation. Here, the instructional process is evaluated while it is being implemented with the aim of using any resulting information for ongoing improvements or changes. This evaluation approach seeks to assess how well the instructor and learners are doing so that any problems or shortcomings can be remedied. Examples of formative evaluation include an end-of-session evaluation slip; a sentence-completion form that asks, among other things, what is the most interesting and the least interesting of the learning experience; and informal interviews with selected learners.

One of our colleagues also has had success using evaluation teams made up of class members who provide periodic feedback on the course, instruction, and learning materials. We have found that all these formative evaluation techniques work well with adults since these techniques are highly responsive to their needs and are at the same time consistent with our goal of ensuring learner success.

Effective instruction results from evaluating both how well learners are performing and how well you are doing as an instructor. One of the key characteristics of good instructors is that they are constantly finding ways to improve their instructional skills. Even the best instructor realizes that there is always room for improvement. But exemplary instructors go even further. They realize that the true test of their instructional effectiveness is how well each learner performs. To some instructors, this view may seem threatening since it is customary to place the burden of learning entirely on the learners. However, in our view, instructors have a responsibility to organize and deliver their instruction in such a way that optimal learner performance is assured. One of the most effective ways to ensure that this occurs is by using both instructor and learner evaluations that follow the formative approach described above.

Instructor evaluation involves direct feedback from learners. As will be described in more detail later in the chapter, we ask learners to provide both formative and summative evaluations of our facilitation efforts. We also help learners design evaluation strategies through the learning contract and assist them in thinking about evaluation in terms of planning efforts. We also encourage them to become more adept at assessing their own learning activities.

We have found that some instructors carry out evaluations

only because they are required. At the same time, we have found many instructors to be extremely interested in receiving feedback about how they are doing as well as how they can further improve their instructional methods. There are many reasons for these varied views of evaluation but most relate to the instructor's evaluation philosophy and to the institutional constraints with which the instructor must deal.

Evaluation efforts should be designed in light of both the instructor's personal philosophy and the sponsoring institution's philosophy. In a number of chapters throughout this book, we have discussed the importance of understanding your own instructional philosophy and that of the sponsoring agency or institution in which you work. We have noted that there should be some consistency between your philosophy and your classroom practices (Cervero, 1988; Schön, 1987). As we have noted, too, our own philosophies of instruction have evolved from a point where we tried to control all aspects of the instructional process to our present position of sharing that responsibility with learners. Evaluation feedback from learners about our instructional skills and procedures has been instrumental in helping us make these changes. We hope that reading this book will prompt you to take a hard look at your own instructional practices and associated philosophy, and we urge you to use various evaluative strategies as you carry out such reflection.

Evaluation should be put in the context of learning goals and objectives. One of the most important aspects of the individualizing process is linking evaluation to what is to be learned or accomplished. This can be initiated by having the learners set forth their learning intentions in the form of objectives. Clearly stated objectives that emphasize such terms as *writing, solving,* and *listening,* which emphasize certain behaviors or goals, are desirable since they can be used to assess learners' progress in achieving minimal to optimal proficiencies (Knox, 1986). They also provide the basis for specifying the resources that will be used to accomplish the learning goals, the various activities that will be employed in the learning effort, the resulting products or evidence, and any assessment procedures.

Grading and Testing

Perhaps nothing is more sacred in educational settings than the assignment of grades. Nearly everyone has an opinion on the subject, although people often accept prevailing views uncritically. We have agonized over the appropriateness of grading and have concluded that it is acceptable as long as learners know what is expected of them and have some say in what grade they are working toward. Thus, as we noted in Chapter Eight, in our credit courses we ask participants to specify on the learning contract the grade that they are working toward. Our experience with this approach has consistently been that adults appreciate this grading practice once they become familiar with it.

At the same time, conflicts can arise between institutional expectations and those of the learners or the individual instructor. Certain educational agencies or institutions might view as scandalous the idea of granting learners some role in determining their grades. If this is the case, you will need to reckon with this philosophy and exercise some caution in allowing learners to choose the grades they are working toward. With careful planning and a solid rationale for why and how you are implementing your grading practice, however, few educational agencies or institutions will put too many roadblocks in your way.

The grade that a person earns should be based on criteria negotiated between the learner and the instructor. Although grades are something we all must live with, they often present a dilemma for instructors who use the individualizing approach. Thus, grades are actually normative measures designed to assess an individual's performance with respect to other individuals who have been measured similarly. For example, an instructor might use standardized midterm and final examinations to compare and grade learners (Popham, 1972).

The individualizing process advocates a different kind of evaluation procedure. Referred to as criterion-referenced evaluation, it is designed to help learners assess personal progress according to certain criteria or standards of performance. The performance criteria often are self-established and based on the needs and competence levels of each learner, who works individually at demonstrating mastery or accomplishment. In this form of evaluation, each learner indicates on the contract what is to be learned by listing learning objectives, the activities that will be used to achieve these objectives, and the criteria that will be used to demonstrate mastery of them. Thus, in such an evaluation effort the instructor's role becomes one of helping learners know when they have accomplished their learning objectives while at the same time helping them to become more competent at assessing their own learning.

Differences between an instructor and a learner in respect to grading and evaluation plans should be negotiated early in the instructional process. We have occasionally encountered differences between learner expectations and our own. For example, certain learners have felt that they deserved a higher grade than they ultimately received for a particular learning experience. The reason for this discrepancy can best be described in terms of the difference between summative and formative evaluation measures.

For example, we attempt to link grades with learning activities as early as possible in a course. We provide thorough explanations of each learning activity and what the criteria are for demonstrating mastery. We also grade on a pass/incomplete basis, issuing incompletes for those learners who do not provide evidence of mastery or competence as initially set forth in the contract. We then encourage learners to follow a formative evaluation approach by turning in materials on a regular basis as the learning experience unfolds. We are thus able to offer any necessary suggestions for improvement so that modifications can be made, critical thinking can be demonstrated, and ultimate mastery can be achieved. Although some learners do challenge our assessments, in general we are able to negotiate an acceptable compromise through individual conferences and discussions.

Unfortunately, what happens in a few cases is that learners fail to adhere to their contracted time lines and wait until the learning experience is over to turn in assignments. We remind learners when assignments are due through announcements in class or short memos. However, if someone falls far behind a reasonable schedule, we must move from a formative evaluation approach to a summative process. This necessitates evaluating the quality of the various written materials or other evidence of learning received. In many cases, learners who have procrastinated receive a lower grade than expected unless it is possible to work out with the learner and within institutional guidelines an incomplete grade that can be improved at a later date.

In order to cut down on these situations, we frequently discuss our evaluation practices during the first few hours together with learners, noting the differences between formative and summative evaluation and the consequences of waiting until the end to turn in learning activity materials. We also stress that individualizing their learning and subsequent evaluation activities require advance planning and careful time management. Despite such interventions, we still get an occasional learner who has a problem completing the learning activities on time.

Tests are, of course, another evaluation process that can be used, depending on the instructor's philosophy or the institution's requirement. We generally view testing as an appropriate tool for evaluating competence, but we tend not to use it in our own graduate classes or training workshops unless a particular learner requests it on the learning contract. In most cases, learners select other means for demonstrating mastery, such as simulation exercises, interactive reading and writing activities, or some sort of project.

We feel strongly that if you use testing, you should provide opportunities for follow-up discussion and debriefing. Tests should be developmental tools that give people the opportunity to learn from the mistakes they make. Too often, especially with summative forms of assessment and evaluation, learners simply take a test and then have no opportunity to know how they did other than their given grade or score.

Learner Assessment

There are any number of techniques that can be used to assess learner progress and competence, ranging from observations, to interviews, to written reactions to materials that are submitted. We encourage use of a mixture of assessment practices or tools organized around a set of suggested learning activities. We have successfully used these learning activities many times in our courses, and we present them as guides for thinking about possibilities or as presumptive devices for designing contracts or learning approaches. However, such activities are only suggestions, and alternative activities may be selected and completed through the learning contract.

We also encourage participants to select activities that reflect different levels of learning, ranging from basic knowledge or comprehension to higher-order synthesizing and analyzing. Such a selection process includes thinking creatively about how their learning activities will be assessed and evaluated. The evaluation process can also involve two or more learners working together on various learning activities, where they can carry out self-evaluations through synergistic exchanges.

Initially, learners tend to rely on familiar assessment measures such as tests or final exams, and, in some cases, expect us to tell them what assessment techniques to select. We spend considerable time discussing such alternatives as peer evaluations and professional assessments from experts in the community or their place of work. We also describe the specific assessment roles the instructor can play. Following this kind of discussion learners usually begin to think critically about the relationship between their intended learning objectives and how these objectives will be assessed. This typically leads to enhanced responsibility for and greater confidence in their learning.

We also use a number of less formal assessments in tracking learner progress. These often take the form of in-class discussions with the learners, personal observations, and informal interviews with learners during a break period. What we are typically looking for is whether learners are internalizing the course-related information and how this is affecting them as developing professionals. We are also constantly on the lookout for nonverbal cues such as puzzled facial expressions and angry gestures. These sources of information provide us with further data about how each learner is absorbing the material and the resonance they feel with it.

During breaks we try to make contact with as many learners as possible. We ask participants informally about any problems they may be encountering, how their learning activities are progressing, or what they feel is a high point thus far. Inevitably, various problems emerge with acquiring particular resources, or there may be misunderstandings about a learning assignment. With this information in hand, we are better able to help learners find acceptable solutions so that they can focus more of their energies on their various learning activities.

It is important to obtain formative and summative evaluation feedback on how you conducted your course or learning experience. We also make extensive use of course evaluations in our individualizing process. We typically use two procedures that are in keeping with the formative and summative evaluation approaches described earlier. The first is a midterm evaluation instrument that consists of five open-ended questions (Exhibit 3).

We can adapt this form to workshops, conferences, and even staff training settings. The midpoint evaluation effort allows us to gather information about the progress of the learning experience so that adjustments can be made to improve it. On many occasions, such evaluation efforts have turned up some important items that we had simply overlooked. For example, in one graduate course, participants asked for more lectures and less group discussion in response to the question "I wish we had . . ." In a training workshop, learners indicated that one particular instructional topic was so meaningful that they wanted additional group time spent on it. In both instances, the information provided by the midpoint activity resulted in corresponding changes in the remaining learning experiences.

A second approach that we have used with considerable success is an evaluation instrument administered at or near the end of the instructional experience (an example of this instrument is reproduced in the resources section). It consists of a variety of items designed to gauge the overall effectiveness of the learning experience. We ask participants not to include their names unless there is a particular reason for letting us know that they have raised certain points. We are interested in receiving anonymous feedback on the various techniques used to present information during the experience, whether it was a lecture, a group discussion, or a guest speaker. We also want feedback on the various topics explored during the learning experience as well as on the materials utilized, such as handouts and workbooks or study guides. Additionally, we ask for each learner's assessment of the textbooks, the learning activi-

Exhibit 3. Midterm Evaluation Form.

Please Complete Each of the Following Statements

This class has been . . .

The most interesting part of this class has been . . .

The least interesting part of this class has been . . .

I wish we had . . .

I learned . . .

ties, and the learning contract. This evaluation procedure follows the summative approach. We conduct an extensive analysis of the information provided by each participant and use this information to improve subsequent offerings.

We also recommend that you ask for an evaluation of yourself as a learning facilitator. In addition to receiving information about the conduct of a learning experience, we also believe that some appraisal of our performance as instructors is vitally important. For many instructors, this area may be a highly sensitive one. Yet, receiving feedback on your teaching is essential if you are to improve your performance.

Many instructors must also solicit some sort of evaluative information because their sponsoring agency or institution requires this of them. For example, as a requirement for tenure, junior faculty at most colleges and universities must demonstrate instructional effectiveness. In business and industry, trainers must show instructional competence if they are to keep their jobs. In adult basic education, literacy instructors are evaluated on how well they can teach, and their continued employment is often tied to this appraisal.

For our classes, we use an instructor evaluation form that consists of a number of items arranged on a scale of 1 to 5 with opportunities to provide open-ended comments. (A sample of this form is reproduced in the resources section.) It provides substantial information about how effective group time was in promoting learning, the instructor's interest in learners, and the instructor's mastery of the content. Additionally, the instrument helps assess whether the material was presented at an appropriate level, the instructor's control of the group and tolerance for dissenting opinions, and how effective the instructor was overall. We take this information very seriously and incorporate the findings into our instructional activities. In fact, such an evaluation procedure was very instrumental in helping us refine the individualizing process.

The importance of conducting both formative and summative evaluations cannot be overstated. Both types of evaluation provide information that can make the difference between success and failure as you employ the individualizing process.

PART THREE

ACHIEVING SUCCESS IN INDIVIDUALIZING INSTRUCTION

The individualizing process can work in various settings and with various types of audiences. Part Three presents some of our ideas on the adjustments that need to be made in different situations. We may not have touched on the particular audience or setting of relevance to you, but we think that our examples will help you make the appropriate adjustments.

Chapter Ten addresses the question of how individualizing instruction can be used in various nontraditional settings. The chapter begins with a discussion of the impact of technology on instruction and learning. A variety of design issues are raised, as well as some ideas on the future of nontraditional learning. Description of a nontraditional effort using on-line computer conferencing for distance education concludes the chapter.

Chapter Eleven focuses on answering the question of how the individualizing process can be used with various audiences. Two different audiences, those with special needs and older learners, are addressed as a means of describing some of the problems or concerns that you may face when you adapt the individualizing process to a particular audience. The chapter includes two tables that outline some of the special instructional requirements of the two groups. The last part of the chapter contains some questions that you may need to consider as you analyze the various audiences with which you come in contact.

Chapter Twelve provides some insights and recommendations on how to use the process successfully. It reviews the six-step model and provides a figure that raises some questions that you should ask during each step. A discussion is included on how to deal with those times when Murphy's Law affects your instructional efforts. The "instructor's first-aid kit" is offered as one means of preparing for the inevitable. The chapter concludes by discussing some of the benefits of individualizing your instruction, some of the problems associated with the process, various future implications, and some research needs.

10

Adapting the Process to Nontraditional and Informal Settings

Robert Givens was preparing for a well-deserved sab-batical leave from his university. He planned to investigate how academic courses could be delivered at a distance. Robert's plans involved a trip to England for a first-hand look at the British Open University, best known for its efforts in the field of distance learning. He also planned visits to several respected American universities to see how they used technology to deliver academic instruction off campus.

Part of Robert's motivation to study distance education came from his own experience. While stationed in West Germany as a military officer, he had been able to continue his own education through correspondence study. Later, he directed an overseas program for an American university that used a variety of instructional formats. More recently as an adult education professor, he had been teaching courses on weekends at various sites throughout his state.

Robert felt strongly about the importance of paying personal attention to individual learner needs regardless of that learner's location or proximity to instruction. He thought that this could be accomplished by using teleconferencing techniques, assigning faculty to receive telephone calls or electronic messages during certain hours, and using fax machines. Although he had some ideas about how learning could be maximized at a distance, he looked forward to finding new approaches that he could use in his instruction at home and off campus.

Although much of our discussion to date has focused on more formal settings, we have found that the individualizing process can be adapted to most instructional settings. In prior chapters we provided examples of changes that we make when using the process in short-term training sessions or intensive workshops. However, this chapter discusses the potential of individualizing instruction (1) in the growing number of nontraditional and distance learning forms that have resulted from technological developments and (2) in reaching learners in other than formal classrooms. In addition, the chapter will describe an innovative effort under way at Syracuse University to use computer technology for some nontraditional learning efforts similar to those in which Robert Givens was interested.

Technology's Impact on Learning

There are many forces at work that influence the ways in which people learn. Not the least of these are various technological developments. The greatly expanded use of computers for personal as well as institutional activities, satellite transmission of communications, and various workplace electronic innovations are some of the obvious changes that have taken place. The recent introduction (and expected rapid expansion) of material stored via images or in digitized formats (CD-ROMs, optical disks, interactive videos, and so on) also requires new thinking about the way we access information.

The number and type of resources available to learners and educators alike also are growing at an astounding rate, primarily because technological developments have speeded up the process of accumulating and disseminating information. Books, journal articles, conference proceedings, newsletters, monographs, films, video-tapes, slides, and numerous electronic resources are only some of these information sources. This ever expanding mountain of knowledge affects all of us as learners in many ways and has prompted the development of various means for the acquisition of new knowledge. The result has been a multitude of learning opportunities in formal, short-term, and nontraditional settings.

There has been a continuous increase in the number of learning opportunities in various nontraditional settings. There are several reasons for this increase:

- Many adults with full-time jobs or heavy family responsibilities want to participate in some form of education or training but are unable to study in a formal setting because of time or scheduling barriers.
- Adults in many parts of the world are living longer, are healthier, and have increasing levels of educational experience. Their subsequent desire for more education has put considerable pressure on traditional programs and has resulted in the development of various nontraditional programs to meet their needs.
- The growing number of adults with special needs who desire education (see Chapter Eleven) is increasing the pressure for nontraditional learning opportunities.

Gross (1979) interviewed a person who described why he prefers participating in a course delivered via a teleconferencing method in this way: "I can stay home and study at my own pace, at my own desk, in my pajamas with a good cup of coffee." When he is called away to work, he doesn't worry about missing any lessons: "I am able to tape entire programs, which is a great advantage because I can then replay them as many times as I want" (p. 5).

Teleconferencing, correspondence study, internships, apprenticeships, and a multitude of distance or open learning programs are only some of the nontraditional learning experiences in which adults throughout the world are engaged. In fact, the rapid advance of electronic communication technology suggests that an ever increasing number of adults will be involved with learning in nontraditional settings.

Administratively, nontraditional learning programs are open learning systems used to overcome spatial or distance barriers. In discussing nontraditional programs sponsored by institutions of higher education, Gross (1979) notes that open learning refers "to systems that reach out beyond the campus, often by using television and other mass media to bring instructors to learners wherever they are" (p. 3). We would add that a variety of learning resources and instructional modes should be made available if a truly individualized system is to be developed. As Gross notes, "If a system of open learning . . . is to be successful, it must link together a variety of instructional modes, allowing students to move from one form to another when circumstances require it" (p. 16).

Morrison (1989, p. 10) suggests that there are five features that best characterize an open-learning system: "the absence of a discriminatory entrance requirement, a results-driven concept of equality, a success-based concept of programme and service design, a multiple strategy and matching model approach to program delivery, and a developmental concept of quality." Morrison believes that not all nontraditional programs can now be evaluated against such features and urges that educators and administrators work toward satisfying such criteria, so that these programs will become more readily accepted.

Preserving the autonomy of the learner is an important feature of nontraditional programs. Chene's (1983) philosophical discussion of the concept of autonomy is germane here: "Autonomy refers to one's ability to choose what has value, that is to say, to make choices in harmony with self-realization" (p. 39). For many of us who have worked with self-directed learners, autonomy has come to be associated with such concepts as independence, self-responsibility, helping learners assume responsibility for their own learning, and self-determination based on some perception of needs or interests. Brookfield (1984a) suggests that care is needed when thinking about autonomous learning. Although autonomy carries with it a sense of learner control, it also implies "separateness from fellow learners, as well as from institutional recognition" (p. 27).

Nontraditional study typically involves some form of independent, individualized study on the part of learners, as well as the incorporation of various learning resources. It certainly has been our experience that individualizing the involvement of learners promotes increased self-direction and the assumption of personal responsibility for learning (Hiemstra, 1975; Leean & Sisco, 1981; Sisco, 1988). This carries over to learning in nontraditional settings. As Moore (1973) notes: "Because . . . [of being alone] the learner is compelled to accept a comparatively high degree of responsibility for the conduct of a learning programme" (p. 666).

Dressel and Thompson (1973) suggest that taking personal responsibility involves deemphasizing any of those practices, means, or resources that diminish autonomy and emphasizing those that increase it. The latter include learning contracts, study guides, lists of resources, involvement in networks, the educative use of institutions such as libraries, museums, and galleries (Hiemstra, 1981a), and various mediated instructional materials. Smith (1982) also discusses alternative ways of learning through various community or everyday experiences and mentions such resources or aids as study guides, diaries, journals, and mentoring experiences.

The enhancement of independent learning skills generally requires that instructors learn how to relinquish control over many learning decisions: "Properly used, individualization fosters self-discovery and the development of motivation for independent efforts, but as that independence develops, the obligations and privileges of adaptation must be transferred from the teacher to the student. Rather than the professor drawing on . . . [personal] expertise to formulate an individual project, the student gradually takes over responsibility for planning and carrying out . . . [personal] intents" (Dressel & Thompson, 1973, pp. 5-6).

Some Design Issues

A number of crucial design issues arise in implementing nontraditional learning opportunities. The participation of learners from a distance, flexibility in terms of normal institutional expectations, and success for those involved are some of the general expectations underlying any design effort. There also are more specific issues with which a design or content specialist needs to be concerned, including issues such as incentives, quality control, and availability of appropriate learning resources. The following list summarizes some of these issues (Gross, 1979):

- Specific, clearly defined, and well-researched needs of potential learners must be addressed.
- The learning process, itself, rather than the technology to be used for delivering or mediating an experience should be the focal point.
- Credit and degree incentives often are required to maintain learner involvement.
- High-quality learning materials should be a goal of the designer.
- The resource materials and educative process should be adaptable to local needs and learning expectations.
- A variety of means for obtaining learning resources and other necessary materials should be made available to learners if feasible.
- The best possible communication and support system should be made available.
- The availability, cost, and ease in use of any necessary hardware should be considered.
- Various levels of local support and learning resource possibilities should be studied.
- Good cooperative arrangements with any necessary broadcast outlets or resource providers should be sought.
- Ways to develop cooperation or to share resources related to production, distribution, expertise, promotion, and funding should be examined.
- Diverse sources of funding should be obtained.

Such design considerations highlight the need for careful planning, obtaining various cooperative agreements, and working to build high-quality learning opportunities. The fact that efforts such as open university courses require the work of large teams of design and content specialists over fairly long periods of time indicates how important issues such as planning, cooperation, and quality control are in enabling nontraditional programs to stand up to the scrutiny of more traditional educators and those officials who eventually must provide some sort of institutional or governmental approval.

Various learner-specific needs also must be considered in designing nontraditional programs. For example, as Niemi and Gooler (1987) point out, the learners must be trained to use any hardware required for participation in a learning experience: "If technology is to be effectively used for learning outside the classroom, careful thought must be given to how to prepare people to use such technologies . . . empowering people to understand and use information resources and technology is one of the major challenges confronting instructional designers and distance educators" (p. 107).

It is also important in nontraditional settings, as in more formal settings, that learners be involved in the needs assessment process. In addition to using individual or personalized needs assessment instruments, in many instances it will be possible to allow small groups of learners who live in close proximity to discuss each other's needs and subsequently provide guidance to a designer or facilitator responsible for building or prioritizing the contents of future learning activities. Group discussion via the mail, by phone conferencing, or even by computer conferencing can be used if learners are separated by long distances.

The type of assistance or resources provided to learners is another issue that should be examined. Cabell (1986) argues that learning contracts can be used in nontraditional settings to reduce ambiguities and confusions between the instructor and learner because they set forth specific goals, resources, and time lines. McKinley (1983) describes how important it is to provide adequate training for learners in using various resources. Loewenthal, Blackwelder, and Broomall (1980) encourage the development of well-designed study guides: "The study guide is the means by which you will give the student instructions on the mechanics of the course—how to submit assignments, make examination arrangements, and so forth—and, more importantly, guidance on mastery of the subject matter" (p. 37).

The Future of Nontraditional Learning

Predicting the future of any activity is always risky and certainly has the potential of being in error. However, some ideas about the future are possible just by extrapolating current developments, making some assumptions about the ability of world leaders to continually solve problems that often seem catastrophic in nature, and finding an acceptable path between various options: "It is believed we will continue to find a middle ground, although there certainly are various options still open to people throughout the world. Finding such a central path depends, perhaps optimistically, on rational uses of technological development, wise expenditures of available resources. . . ." (Hiemstra, 1987a, p. 4).

The continual advance of personal computers will have a major impact on both the hardware and software developed for nontraditional learning situations. Davis and Marlowe (1986) believe that computers and telecommunication networks have enabled learners in remote locations to feel that they are part of larger groups: "Computers, through teleconferencing and electronic mail, can readily serve groups of interested learners as well as they serve individuals in an office or at home. . . . The computer reduces isolation, enabling colleagues and learners to make contact and keep in touch with one another. Networking with computers promotes the development of special-interest groups and expands one's circle of professional contacts and friends" (p. 94).

Networking with computer and teleconferencing technology generally is referred to as computer conferencing. As Florini (1989) and Harasim (1988) note, it provides for interaction among learners who are geographically dispersed.

Davis and Marlowe (1986) also point out that computers can be used to access a variety of data bases, to customize various communication channels, and to participate in public bulletin boards. Sheckley (1986), too, describes how personal computers can be used by learners for networking, but he also believes that they have value as individualized teaching tools for drill and practice activities and as learning tools in such activities as word processing, computations, and decision-making simulations. Rachal (1984) values the privacy afforded by personal computers and their ability "to individualize instruction. This allows the student to work at . . . [an individual] pace and to focus the learning effort where it is most needed" (p. 93).

A variety of future roles for educators of adults are emerging because of the many technological changes now taking place. Hiemstra (1987a) suggests what some of these roles may be:

- Information counseling that helps adults obtain and use the information that is needed for their learning efforts. Such support will be possible at a distance and with learners from various cultural or geographical settings.
- Assistance for learners who require facilitation in organizing, prioritizing, evaluating, and using the multitude of information that will be available both electronically and through more traditional means.
- A corresponding need is to help instructors who have had experience only in more traditional settings learn how to facilitate individualizing learning in nontraditional settings.
- Providing expertise in the skilled use of technology with individualizing and adult learning principles in mind.
- Providing continuing education opportunities to learners in dealing with societal changes and various technological developments.
- Carrying out research related to technological change and its effect on adults as learners, including an examination of related administrative features such as costs, time requirements, and learning evaluation needs.
- Working as advocates for adult learners in developing countries who often will have little access to technological hardware or, at the very least, will have difficulties adjusting to technological change.

Nontraditional Learning in Action

Syracuse University has quite a few programs and resources for the education of adults. These include an active graduate program in adult education, a large university extension division, an active off-campus program in adult education and other educational disciplines sponsored through the School of Education, and an extensive collection of resources for educators of adults. In addition, the city of Syracuse has numerous adult education resources, including the national headquarters for Laubach Literacy International and the Literacy Volunteers of America, prompting one person to refer to it as "the Mecca of adult education" (Brightman, 1984, p. 2).

The Kellogg Project at Syracuse University builds on such resources using computer technology in finding ways to individualize how adult educators use information and knowledge. To explore how technology could be used in nontraditional and individualized ways to assist learners and adult educators in retrieving and using information, Syracuse University and the Kellogg Foundation of Battle Creek, Michigan, initiated in 1986 a partnership designed to create a system for disseminating knowledge about adult education through advanced computer technology. The result has been a multimillion-dollar project whose central purpose is to process and provide broad access to the university's outstanding collection of adult education materials. Greater access to this information and the various ancillary activities that have evolved as a result of Kellogg Project activities have created a center for scholars and practitioners devoted to enhancing the field of adult education.

Formally known as Syracuse University Resources for Educators of Adults (SUREA), the world's largest repository of English-language adult education materials is housed in the university's libraries. This collection was assembled during the past three decades under the leadership of various individuals. At the start of the project, the collection contained nearly 900 linear feet of manuscripts, including personal and organizational records of current and historical importance to the field of adult education. It also included a large collection of films, audiotapes, slides, and photographs. Currently, the collection is being expanded in various ways.

The project has two major features. One centers on the electronic transmission of information. This involves a process of optically scanning and storing printed materials so that the information is recorded either in image or ASCII (character codes for standard computer communication) form for later retrieval. A large computer, several optical workstations, laser printers, optical scanners, optical storage units, and connections for various electronic exchange media make up the main hardware configuration. Another set of equipment provides capabilities for future optical work with the collection's color slides, photographs, and audiotaped material.

In addition, project personnel can communicate readily with each other via an internal LAN (Local Area Network) that links all the project's personal computers together electronically. Project staff also hope to create ways for people in other cities and countries to access the data from the collection while sitting at a personal computer or a mainframe computer terminal. The project's initial computer-mediated network (referred to as AEDNET—Adult EDucator's NETwork) is used for the communication effort. AEDNET operates on BITNET, an international computer network that currently links universities and a few other institutions in North America, Europe, and several other locations. It features electronic messaging, electronic conferencing, cooperative publishing, and an electronic journal entitled *New Horizons in Adult Education.*

The second feature centers on a number of educational components. To begin with, research on the historically rich adult education collection at Syracuse University by faculty, students, and visiting scholars from throughout the world is strengthening the field's self-knowledge and identity. It also is helping to ground future practice in adult education. In addition, the project holds periodic meetings or conferences designed to stimulate new ideas, sponsors several visiting scholars at Syracuse University each year, and disseminates a variety of annual publications. Project personnel also are developing and delivering credit courses via the computer conferencing system that will be described in the next section.

Although the project has considerable computer technology as a base, personnel are concerned that the individual learner does not become mesmerized by the glamor and interesting uses of hardware that surround the effort. Internal discussions among staff, advice from members of both internal and external advisory councils, recommendations from various outside consultants, and interdisciplinary conversations with people from across the Syracuse University campus are helping to keep the individual learner or user of the project's electronic system as a central focus of the total effort. The long-term result should be some major inputs to the adult education field and a better understanding of how to individualize learning efforts.

On-line computer conferencing uses mainframe computers, personal computers and modems or computer terminals, a sophisticated electronic communication tool, study materials, and the guidance of a facilitator to individualize instruction on any given subject. The Syracuse University Kellogg Project also makes a special effort to individualize instruction through the delivery of graduate credit courses in adult education for learners in nontraditional settings. After several alternatives had been examined, a decision was made to use on-line computer conferencing as the primary distance education medium. With on-line conferencing, learners can participate in small- or large-group discussions, submit assignments, interact with other learners and with faculty, and exchange information via computer mediated electronic communication. The medium permits flexible scheduling for learners, rapid responses from instructors and fellow students, and access to various resources.

The courses are facilitated via an on-line computer conferencing software program entitled Participate (Parti is the nickname used to refer to it) that resides on the university's VAX mainframe computer. Learners currently access courses in three ways: (1) by utilizing on-campus terminals; (2) by connecting personal computers to the mainframe with modems, telecommunication software, and telephone lines; or (3) by connecting personal computers via internet, a high-speed fiber optic network that links an ever increasing number of higher education and governmental institutions.

The general design of courses taught via Parti includes the following:

1. Development of an extensive course study guide. The guide provides introductory information, a summary of the course activities, various supplemental resource materials, and descriptions of course components. For each component, it describes introductory information, relevant resources, learning activities, expected computer conferencing activities, learning requirements, and any necessary supplemental material. Textbook readings, supplemental reading and media materials that learners access, and descriptions of information that learners are to secure by themselves are normally included.

2. Training learners to use the software. Various training options are made available to learners. These include such activities as face-to-face meetings with individual faculty for tutorials on using the software, an initial large-group orientation to the course

and relevant software, a manual on using the software, and ongoing electronic communication with faculty members.

3. Electronic communication. The course is built around electronic networking among learners and the instructor. A series of topics designed to elicit ideas, reactions, and comments are posted within the course environment by an instructor. Learners can write messages or make responses to the topics to members of a small group, to each other as private communications, or to the instructor. Larger course-related writings also can be transmitted to the instructor or other learners for evaluation and feedback. A typical course will have a student-centered topic for informal conversations, a bulletin board for the instructor's comments, several small-group discussion topics, some large-group topics, and supplemental read-only topics.

4. Various learning options. A course will use various learning options to stimulate learner participation and interaction. These options involve using computer conferencing for small-group discussion of individual needs, debates, polling activities, dyadic learning partnership exchanges, one-on-one message exchanges, and small-group coordination in developing learning activity materials for distribution to other class members or to the instructor. The system allows larger papers or statements to be sent to and from personal computers so that word-processing capabilities can be used and permanent paper copies of any materials obtained.

5. Use of learning contracts. Participants in the on-line conferencing courses, like learners in more formal settings, use learning contracts so that individualized plans can be developed in conjunction with the instructor. After completing a form to assess individual needs, participants use computer conferencing to discuss and clarify needs via small-group interactions. They complete a first draft of a contract that matches their needs with available resources, as well as with suggestions for learning activities that the instructor has presented in the study guide and learners' own ideas for ways their needs can be met. Another advantage of the system is that learners then have an opportunity to receive electronic feedback from colleagues on their plans and activities, if desired, prior to discussing their individual plans with the instructor.

6. Varied evaluation opportunities. Because some learners participate in the on-line conferencing courses without ever coming to the campus, a variety of evaluation options are made available. Face-to-face or electronic conversations with the instructor, electronic communication with colleagues, telephone, mail, or fax exchanges, and the use of outside resource specialists if appropriate are among the possibilities. In addition, learners are asked to evaluate the instructor and the course via electronic, face-to-face, mail, or telephone communications.

Although still in its infancy as a distance education medium and with various problems still to be solved, on-line computer conferencing shows considerable promise. It has potential as a means for individualizing instruction, providing education to learners in various locations, and even providing learning opportunities to people who ordinarily would have difficulty participating in educational programs. As Roberts (1988) notes, "The computer is active. Unlike television which can only present to the student, the computer can only work with the student. It is individualized, interactive, and diagnostic. And through networking and conferencing the computer is out reaching" (p. 38).

There also are some issues directly related to individualizing instruction that need to be better understood. For example, the ability to retrieve considerable information at a workstation and to access a wide variety of data has many connections to individualizing approaches and the use of learning resources. In the very near future it will be possible for an individual to have access to more information than can ever be processed or understood by a single human mind. An important question that must be answered is, How do adult educators help such an individual understand the learning requirements associated with processing and using needed information?

There also is now a very chaotic proliferation of information and information resources. Various commercial groups offering networks or data bases are springing up quite steadily. Each may well have a slightly different protocol than the other, with the result that a person has to learn slightly different ways of even getting access to the information that is available. Adult educators thus need to communicate such concerns to system developers, software programmers, and hardware manufacturers. Perhaps educators also should insist on more standardization in regard to information dissemination and resources.

Individualizing instruction in nontraditional settings has tremendous potential for meeting the needs of many learners, especially if the facilitator can find ways of empowering the learner to take personal responsibility for much of the learning that occurs. It has been our experience that such empowerment is possible, but it takes patience and perseverance on the part of both learners and facilitators. Fortunately, the payoff for learners is the realization that they can make decisions that result in real personal benefits.

11

Responding to the Needs
of Special Audiences

Janice Freeman had used a wheelchair for the past fifteen years as a result of an automobile accident that had injured her brain stem and left her paralyzed from the waist down and with some speech problems. She had overcome many of her disabilities and was able to work as a computer operator for a financial institution.

Now forty-five years old, she was looking for a way to enhance her career. Her supervisor told her about a new certificate program in computer programming offered by a nearby university that could lead to job advancement. Janice decided to look into the program to see if it would fit her needs.

After work, Janice called the university to inquire about the certificate program. She was told that it was designed for working people who wished to obtain new skills or upgrade their current skills in computer programming. All classes were offered late in the afternoon or evening, and financial aid was available. Janice explained that financial aid was unnecessary since her employer would cover the tuition costs, but she wondered if the instructors could work with adults who had disabilities. She was assured that they could and that, in fact, each instructor was required to take a workshop in special education before he or she could teach in the program. This delighted Janice, who then mentioned that she was confined to a wheelchair and had some speech difficulties. The university representative emphasized once again how ready and willing everyone would be to help her and encouraged her to stop by soon for more information. She said that she would do so the next day.

George Hammond was very spry for a man of seventy-eight. He walked to just about every place in the city that he needed to go. Widowed for three years now, he found that his church and senior citizen center activities did not sufficiently occupy his time. He finally visited the Volunteer Center, where the director, Jane Paige, asked if he would be willing to volunteer in the Red Cross Center three afternoons a week. He enthusiastically agreed, and Jane signed him up for the orientation workshop that was to begin the following Monday.

      The workshop coordinator, Ralph Jameson, began with an introduction activity that George enjoyed. By the time that first hour was over, George knew the names of and something about the other six senior citizen volunteers in the group. He also felt at ease with Ralph's instructional process. Ralph took special care to involve each of the seven people in the learning activities and helped them establish personal learning goals. He employed a pace appropriate for people in their sixties and seventies. George was especially pleased that Ralph made sure that he could hear and see all that was going on, as George's eyesight and hearing were not what they used to be. By the end of the two-day workshop, George was confident that he would be a useful volunteer at the center.

Most instructors or trainers of adults will work with learners who have varying abilities, backgrounds, past experiences, and expectations, including learners such as Janice and George. The individualizing process, we believe, works very well with elderly learners, adults who have disabilities or special needs, adult literacy groups, institutionalized people, vocational rehabilitation participants, and people from foreign countries who need special language or cultural training.

This chapter examines how the individualizing process can be used with different audiences. We focus on only two groups—adults with special needs or disabilities and the elderly—to describe some of the different problems or concerns that can affect the individualizing process. Some of the instructional adjustments that we recommend for working with these two groups will be valuable as you adapt the individualizing process to special audiences with which you work. In addition, the resources section contains material related to instructing adult students in graduate courses, as well as individuals involved in apprenticeship training. Finally, the last portion of this chapter contains some questions that instructors should consider in analyzing the various audiences with which they may come in contact.

Adults with Special Needs

Instructors need to master considerable knowledge specific to adults with special needs or learning disabilities if they work with such groups. In many ways, individuals who have physical, emotional, developmental, or psychological disabilities can be treated as typical learners. However, it is important to understand how such disabilities may affect instruction. Public Law 94-142 pertains to education for the disabled, and corresponding research and development during the past several years has produced new ideas on ways instruction can be adapted to their needs. The teaching experiences we and others have had with special groups of adults have also made us aware of ways in which the individualizing process can be modified for adults with special requirements or disabilities.

"The term *learning disabilities* came into use in the early 1960s, replacing such terms as brain damaged, minimal brain dysfunction, word blindness, and perceptual handicaps. . . . manifested by significant difficulties in the acquisition and use of listening, speaking, reading, writing, reasoning, or mathematical abilities" (Hebert, 1988, p. 7). Polloway, Smith, and Patton (1984) earlier noted that, "somewhat surprisingly, learning disabilities in adulthood received limited attention until the last decade. This is especially perplexing since some of the most important early work in the field was conducted with brain-damaged adults. . . . However, the degree of attention paid to LD [learning disabled] adults has increased dramatically in recent years" (p. 179).

This attention has resulted in several efforts to build categories or frameworks for understanding the concept of learning disabled in relation to instruction and learning needs. Brown (1982) describes four kinds of functional discrepancies: (1) dyscalculia, inabilities related to performing mathematical operations; (2) dysgraphia, inabilities related to writing skills; (3) dyslexia, inabilities related to reading and comprehending; and (4) cognitive and perceptual problems or inabilities related to taking in or processing information via any of the senses. Jordan (1977, 1988) includes dyslexia within a framework of disabilities that are all tied in some way to faulty processing by the central nervous system: "Minimal Brain Dysfunction (MBD), Primary Dyslexia, Attention Deficit Disorder Syndrome, residual type" (1988, p. 3).

Lean (1983) talks about types of learning disabilities in terms of the problems that an affected adult faces:

1. Visual perceptual problems—difficulties in obtaining information via the sense of sight.
2. Auditory perceptual problems—difficulties in obtaining information via the sense of hearing.
3. Intersensory problems—difficulties in using two or more senses at the same time.
4. Motor problems—difficulties in using the body efficiently in performing some task.
5. Directional problems—difficulties in distinguishing physical directions or in telling left from right.

Regardless of the framework used, any such functional discrepancies can affect a person's ability to perform in an educational setting.

Polloway, Smith, and Patton (1984) describe some of the problems that learning-disabled adults can have that educators should take into account: affective deficits, emotional instability, social imperception, communication difficulties, low social skills, and low self-esteem. Problems associated with learning disability have even had an impact on training in the workplace, although Lean (1983) points to the difficulties that most trainers have in identifying the learning-disabled, many of whom become quite skilled at disguising personal problems. She outlines several behaviors that provide clues for trainers or teachers of adults with some type of learning disability (p. 60):

- Demonstrates marked difficulties in reading, writing, spelling and/or using numerical concepts, in contrast with average to superior skills in other areas.
- Has trouble listening to a lecture and taking notes at the same time.
- Is easily distracted by background noises or visual stimulations; may appear to be hurried and anxious in one-to-one meetings.
- Has trouble understanding or following directions; is easily overwhelmed by a multiplicity of directions.
- Confuses similar letters or numbers, such as 'b' and 'd' or '6' and '9'; confuses the order of letters in a word or numbers in a sequence; may misspell the same word several different ways in the same paragraph.
- Omits or adds words, particularly when reading aloud.
- Appears clumsy or poorly coordinated.
- Seems disorganized in space; confuses up and down, right and left; is disoriented when a familiar environment is rearranged.
- Seems disoriented in time; is unusually early for appointments; is unable to finish assignments in the standard time period.

- Exhibits low self-image; has a low frustration threshold.
- Misinterprets the subtleties in language, tone of voice, or social situations.

A similar checklist is provided by Jordan (1988), who adapted it from a George Washington University document, although he adds poor handwriting and difficulties in sticking to simple schedules as other problem signs. Mays and Imel (1984) add vision problems, production of extraneous vocal sounds, inability to match sounds or symbols, and physical conditions resulting from metabolism problems.

Increasing attention is being given to some of the instructional needs associated with adults who have special needs, problems, or disabilities. Many different kinds of instructional resources are becoming available. The U.S. Department of Education's Division of Adult Education has developed a Clearinghouse on Adult Education under the leadership of William Langner. This clearinghouse has funded projects, coordinated national conferences, and produced various documents of value both to persons with disabilities and to instructors of the learning disabled. In 1987 Langner coordinated the compilation of a directory of resources for adults with disabilities. Rees (1988) has produced another directory on the resources available at various governmental levels.

These directories provide someone interested in the individualizing process with good descriptions of various federal and nonfederal organizations that work with learning-disabled adults, mobility-impaired adults, deaf and hearing-impaired adults, blind and visually impaired adults, mentally retarded adults, and mentally ill adults. The directories also provide descriptions of media services and other resources of value to instructors of persons with disabilities. You may come across additional directories, clearinghouses, or resource guides as you seek assistance in adapting aspects of the individualizing process to your particular audiences.

Various individuals have also provided ideas and suggestions regarding the disabled and the instructional process. Daily (1982) believes that instruction for disabled adults requires considerable innovation, creativity, and new thinking about the teaching process.

Fettgather (1989) is concerned about the patronizing, condescending language that some use when speaking to persons with disabilities. He suggests that, in the case of special audience adults, we should become sensitized to the use of childlike labels for retarded adults, such as certain "nicknames (e.g., Little Ron) or collective terms (e.g., gang, kids) [that] may clearly characterize the adult student as a child. In some instances, informal versions of first names with 'y' or 'ie' endings may subtly infantilize the adult student as well" (Fettgather, 1989, p. 4). This also can include using unusually high-pitched voices, speaking in baby talk, providing unnecessary assistance to slow responses, affectionate touching or patting, threats, or even criticisms. The North Carolina Council on Developmental Disabilities (n.d., p. 2) urges that words be chosen with care and that the reference be to the person rather than to the disability:

- Avoid: afflicted with blindness
  Use: person who is blind
- Avoid: afflicted with deafness
  Use: hearing impaired
- Avoid: crippled
  Use: physically disabled
- Avoid: dumb
  Use: unable to speak, nonverbal
- Avoid: epileptic
  Use: person with epilepsy, person with a seizure disorder
- Avoid: mentally defective, retarded
  Use: person with mental retardation, person who is mentally handicapped
- Avoid: palsied
  Use: person with cerebral palsy
- Avoid: stricken with . . .
  Use: person who has . . .
- Avoid: mongoloid
  Use: person with Down's syndrome

Any audience with which you work may find various terms, labels, or gender-specific pronouns to be demeaning or derogatory, so you should endeavor to learn what they are and avoid their use.

The Council on Exceptional Children (Imel, 1986) has proposed four basic principles to be used in developing educational programs for adults with disabilities. Although they are specific to a certain audience, the principles have applications for many groups of learners (pp. 1-2):

1. Individuals with disabilities should be respected as adults, and their rights to make decisions about their education should be respected. Belief in the autonomy of the individual is an underlying principle of adult education and should be applied to all adults.

2. Handicapped individuals should have available to them the wide range of programmatic options available to nonhandicapped individuals. Adult education programs will need to ensure that there are no barriers to participation for handicapped individuals in the programs offered to the community.

3. Handicapped individuals should be provided with educational programs on the same economic and administrative terms as are applied to non-handicapped individuals. Any adjustments in these terms should be made on the basis of an individual's ability to pay, not on the basis of handicap and condition.

4. Handicapped individuals should have the same benefits as the nonhandicapped when they participate in adult education. If necessary, facility and program adaptation should be made to achieve this result.

Table 3 provides further suggestions for instructors of the disabled, several of which fit well with the various individualizing concepts presented in earlier chapters. We would add to such suggestions the ideas that we presented earlier about the value of involving learners in assessing needs, using learning contracts, and utilizing a variety of learning resources.

Table 3. Techniques and Strategies for Teaching Learning Disabled Adults.

Technique or Strategy	Instructional Implications
Break learning tasks into small increments.	Present material in a paced or sequential manner. Make shorter and more varied assignments. Break directions into steps that can be presented one at a time. Deemphasize timed tests and provide additional time for task completion.
Sequence learning tasks.	Build on acquired skills or knowledge only after ascertaining what levels have been achieved. Teach new concepts as concretely as possible. Relate new materials to life experiences whenever possible.
Provide frequent feedback.	Let learners know periodically how they are doing in terms of quality and appropriateness of their learning. Provide activities that allow learners to experience small successes. Review and preview major points. Use nontraditional grading and reinforce with comments.
Use many sensory modalities (sight, sound, touch, and so on).	Outline materials in more than one way (for example, written on a board or flip chart, presented orally, outlined in a handout, and so on). Use a variety of devices to present material. Help learners use their strongest sensory channels to obtain information. Teach to students' learning strengths (visual or auditory, for example) whenever possible. Provide opportunities for handling and touching materials when possible. Use color and color coding whenever possible.
Use direct approaches in presenting information.	Review new vocabulary, use a directed-reading approach, and establish purposes for all readings. Make announcements in both oral and written forms. Speak at an even speed, emphasizing and enumerating important points.
Manipulate the physical environment.	Encourage learners to sit where they can hear and see well. Ensure that physical comfort is as high as possible. Ensure that the learning environment is as free from sensory distractions as possible.
Enhance self-concept.	Encourage learners who are self-conscious about talking in front of groups to provide short answers. Provide opportunities for learners to repeat verbally what has been learned as a check for accuracy.

Source: Adapted from Fluke (1988).

Finally, as in the case of other audiences, technological advances are making the task of instructing learning-disabled adults easier: "Several computer enhancements that permit wide access to educational resources have been developed for learners with disabilities. For example, voice recognition systems help students who cannot type but can vocalize sounds. . . . For people with visual impairments, there is access technology, which endows the computer with synthetic speech, enables the output to be produced in large print on the screen and from the printer, and produces output in braille. . . . For students with impaired learning, modems can be used to communicate with others, with or without learning impairments, over the phone. . . . Word-processing programs, with their capacity to identify misspelled words, mistakes in punctuation, and grammar errors, should reduce the impact of these disabilities on the production of documents" (Carrier, 1987, p. 58).

The Older Adult as Learner

The growth of the elderly population in the United States (as well as in many other countries) has been accelerating rapidly over the past two decades. By the year 2000, it is estimated that at least 13 percent of the U.S. population will be sixty-five years of age or older and that that figure will climb to as high as 22 percent by 2030 (Fowles, 1984). Most older people are reasonably healthy, have active minds, and want to be involved in various activities. Some, like George Hammond, enjoy volunteer work, including participating in the training required to be a successful volunteer (Hiemstra, 1987b). Some find great satisfaction in participating in activities at senior citizen centers, traveling, or working in part-time jobs. Others spend considerable time taking courses, carrying out independent study activities, or participating in specially developed learning experiences such as the elderhostel (Kinney, 1989; Knowlton, 1977).

An increasing number of educators are now working with the elderly in some type of instructional capacity. In addition, an increasing number of institutions of higher education are discovering the potential of the older adult as a learner and consumer of education. In fact, educational opportunities for the older learner have increased significantly in the past two decades (Fisher, 1986; Knowlton, 1977; Peterson, 1983; Sheppard, 1979).

Coinciding with this growth in the number of elderly persons participating in learning activities has been an explosion of research on older adults as learners or participants in various educational programs. This research has often focused on the physiological problems that adults face as they age, such as visual or hearing losses. But the research has ranged over a number of other areas, including how information is processed, the nature of short- and long-term memory, intelligence measures, and life stages. Other areas of interest have included the importance of understanding cognitive or learning styles, the learning needs and activities of older learners, and how satisfaction with life can affect involvement in learning.

It is clear that individual differences among older people do exist. The elderly cannot be treated or viewed as a single group; rather, they should be viewed as heterogeneous, multidimensional in their characteristics, and quite varied in terms of their needs and abilities. Although some still lump them all together as one group (Hauwiller & Jennings, 1981; Hiemstra, Goodman, Middlemiss, Vosko, & Ziegler, 1983; Kasworm, 1978), Arenberg and Robertson-Tchabo (1977) believe that some seventy-year-old adults can match—or even surpass—younger people as learners if they are able to overcome certain obstacles.

What are these obstacles? Although there will be some problems specific to a location or economic group, some of the more common obstacles include lack of transportation, lack of time, prohibitive costs, lack of confidence, negative stereotypes regarding education, and lack of knowledge about specific educational opportunities. A variety of health-related factors also can affect the learning abilities of older adults. These include fatigue, personal perceptions about declining health as a barrier, along with declining hearing or visual abilities (Hiemstra, 1975). The resources section later in this book contains material that outlines some research findings and related instructional applications for guiding older learners.

Research on older adults and their learning abilities has resulted in some specific findings about their instructional needs. The increased attention to providing educational opportunities for older learners has corresponding instructional implications. For example, Table 4 describes some of the instructional requirements associated with visual and auditory changes that occur with age. We incorporate many of these instructional requirements into the individualizing process when we work with older learners, but we are quick to point out that most of our experiences have been with healthy older adults who have been quite capable of, and generally very interested in, learning. If you work as an instructor of frail,

Table 4. Visual and Auditory Changes with Age:
Implications for Instruction.

Visual or Auditory Condition	Normal Change Patterns	Instructional Requirements
Color intensity: Strength or sharpness of a color	Losses begin to occur from about age 45 on.	Don't depend on color coding and use sharply contrasting colors.
Depth perception: Ability to judge distances	Declines begin as early as the late 30s.	Be alert for adults who need to sit near the front of the class.
Presbyopia: Regression of eye's ability to focus on near objects	Declines can begin as early as the 40s.	Make sure that learners can focus on and see all visual aids.
Sclerosis: Yellowing of lens	Slow decline after age 50; causes light to become scattered.	Ensure proper illumination, don't rely on color coding, and reduce glare.
Visual acuity: Visual ability and distinctness	Sharp decline probably beginning in the 50s.	Be sensitive to visual needs, especially to whether a learner needs to be closer to learning materials.
Presbycusis: Impairment in sensori-neural hearing for both volume and high pitch	Losses can become noticeable in the 40–55 age range.	Be alert to hearing problems and to learners who need to be nearer the instructor; need may exist for sound enhancement or slower pace of speech.

institutionalized, or home-bound older learners, you will need to make some adjustments beyond what we describe in this chapter.

Fortunately, because a fair amount of attention has been given to teaching older adult learners (Hiemstra, 1980c), information and resources are available to assist you in making adjustments to your teaching approaches. Siebles (1988), for example, presents a directory of resources for older learners. Peterson (1983) wrote an award-winning book that provides considerable information on facilitating the learning of older adults.

On the one hand, Brockett (1985b) suggests that adult educators who work with the older learner can promote self-directed learning opportunities as a strategy for increasing their independence and life satisfaction. Hiemstra (1975, 1976b) also has determined that older adult learners prefer to take personal responsibility for their learning whenever possible.

On the other hand, not all learners are able to be self-directed at all times. For example, self-concept and self-confidence can decline when a person begins to experience visual, auditory, or psychomotor skill losses. Arenberg and Robertson-Tchabo (1977), Carpenter (1967), and Kuhlen (1970) all have found that a lack of self-confidence is a problem. In many instances, women have been found to be more anxious or to have lower self-concepts than men (*Symposium on Adult Learning Psychology*, 1973). Jones (1979) noted that a learner's attitudes and self-perceptions may have as much effect as age on learning abilities. Other researchers who have examined the self-concept of the elderly include Brockett (1984), Bolton (1978), and Goulet (1970).

Thus, it is important for facilitators to find ways of enhancing self-concept, self-confidence, and the ability to become self-directed. As Ripple and Jaquish (1981) note, "Self-esteem appears to be a key variable in implementing educational interventions with older adults, and success of such interventions depends on supporting it, capitalizing on it, and building on it" (p. 9). Such advice may apply to many of the learners with whom you work.

Lack of self-confidence may also result in hesitancy, cautiousness, and a reluctance to risk making errors among some older learners. Okun (1977) and Okun and DiVesta (1976) suggest that tendencies toward caution in older adults can be motivation inhibitors. Lack of risk taking and a concern for accuracy also are thought to be learning obstacles (Botwinick, 1973; Canestrari, 1963, 1968). Obviously, the facilitator interested in the individualizing process needs to use various methods or approaches that minimize the possibility of making errors or of entering high-risk situations.

Slowness of recall and corresponding fears about making errors also can affect the instructional process. Several steps can be taken in regard to recall problems. For example, instructors can make the time allowed for assessment instruments or for responses to queries flexible, and they can pay close attention to how various learning activities are paced (Arenberg & Robertson-Tchabo, 1977; Labouvie-Vief, 1976). We also believe that facilitating self-paced learning whenever possible is important.

The facilitator's role is important, too—the pace for presenting information and the expectations about learners' response speeds clearly affect learners' reactions (Witte & Freund, 1976). Thus, if a facilitator allows for adequate response time, older learners normally will perform about as well as younger people (Eisdorfer, 1965).

Several researchers have cautioned against the use of traditional testing procedures for older learners (Guttman, 1984). For example, complicated experimental instructions may result in misconceptions that create problems (Arenberg & Robertson-Tchabo, 1977). Similarly, complicated assignments, unclear task instructions from the teacher, and test anxiety (Kooken & Hayslip, 1984) may also create problems in the classroom. The ways in which information is presented also appear related to cognitive performance (Arenberg, 1976).

Recognition rather than recall techniques, frequent feedback on learner progress, and self- or peer-evaluation techniques have been recommended as evaluation procedures (Eysenck, 1975; Knowles, 1980; Mullan & Gorman, 1972; Witte & Freund, 1976). Hulicka and Grossman (1967) suggest using review strategies as a regular part of a learning activity.

Techniques that employ concrete stimuli but that reduce stimulus discriminability and avoid competition or too much complexity also have been recommended (Arenberg & Robertson-Tchabo, 1977). Research by Witte and Freund (1976), as well as a

discussion in Winn, Elias, and Marshall (1976), suggests the usefulness of concrete learning stimuli and techniques that facilitate
matching or associating related ideas and concepts.

The speed with which previously learned information is recognized appears to correlate with its meaningfulness for the learner
(Eysenck, 1975). Gonda, Quayhagen, and Schaie (1981) found an
association between cognitive performance of older learners and
their perception of how meaningful the material being learned was.
(See also Alpaugh, Renner, and Birren, 1976; Calhoun and Gounard 1979; Hultsch, 1971; Norman, 1973; and Taub, 1977.)

Many experts argue that a variety of advanced organizing or
cuing techniques are essential for efficient learning. Reviewing or
visual analogies, instructor assistance in helping learners integrate
new information with old, and various practice techniques are
among the important organizing means. The use of outlines, abstracts, summaries, prequestioning techniques, instructional objectives, and pictures or other visual aids is also recommended.
Hiemstra (1980c) provides two examples:

"One day some colleagues and I were discussing a way of
remembering the names and order of five components in a model
for learning they had been working on: differentiating, structuring,
integrating, abstracting, and generalizing. I pushed the pencil
around for awhile and came up with a sentence using the first letter
from each word in order. Dear Sir, I Am Good! It took, it works,
and now my colleagues and I refer to the dear-sir-I-am-good model
in our normal conversation" (p. 33).

"A colleague works as a volunteer in a senior citizens center.
She uses a trick for helping a person or group to remember some
name that is on the tip of the tongue but not quite out yet. She has
the person or the group go through the alphabet, letter by letter.
Very frequently it results in the remembered name, usually to the
delight and amazement of all" (p. 33).

Remember, too, to consider the best ways of having learners
interact with one another. For example, White and Hansen (1976)
suggest that five to twenty people is the optimal size for small-group
work, with seven to ten the best number for good interaction and
communication. They also recommend the use of discussion groups
for optimal interaction. Finally, it is important to limit the factors

that may interfere with the ability of older learners to undertake effective learning, such as any number of physical, bureaucratic, or social distractions that may cause debilitating anxiety (Schaie & Strother, 1968).

Applications for Various Audiences

Obviously, it is up to you to determine the special limitations and strengths of your learners. This may require specific assessments on your part, or you may want to turn to various organizations, resource guides, and clearinghouses for help and information. Once you have a better understanding of the people whom you will be instructing, you can begin to alter or adapt the individualizing process to suit their needs. Following are several questions that may help you to do this. You will probably want to add more questions as you work on adapting the individualizing process to your instructional requirements.

- Are there special physical, emotional, developmental, social, or psychological conditions regarding your learners that need to be considered?
- Are there certain anxieties characteristic of your audience, such as math anxiety?
- Are there any listening, speaking, reading, or reasoning limitations?
- Are there any visual, auditory, sensory, motor, or directional problems?
- Are there any problems associated with verbalizing anxiousness and communication skills, on the one hand, or with anxiety, self-esteem, or low frustration thresholds, on the other?
- Can your learners follow directions?
- Are there potential problems because English is a second language for your learners?
- Is any of the language used in the learning setting condescending, derogatory, or belittling?
- Do your learners want more or less autonomy in the classroom than is normally provided?

- Do you have a thorough understanding of the physical environment and its effect on various audiences?
- Are there any new technologies that could be used to improve your instructional efforts?
- Do any of your learners have special health problems?
- Do your learners have the ability to be self-directed?
- Are there any problems related to memory or speed of recall among your learners?

We believe that the individualizing process can be used successfully with most audiences. However, it will require some adjustments based on your specific knowledge of the learners and your own philosophy of instruction. Remember, too, that we urged you in earlier chapters to try each part of the process at least three times to discover which aspects work, which need to be changed, and which should be discarded or replaced.

12

Realizing the Potential of a Personalized Approach

Marge Winter had just returned from her first evening class of the semester, Contemporary American Fiction, and she was excited because it really sounded interesting. The instructor was enthusiastic about the subject, and there were many older learners such as herself in attendance. One thing stood out for Marge: the instructor had started the class in a most unusual way. He had members of the class first introduce themselves to their partners and then to the group as a whole. He then talked about his own background as an instructor, and, finally, he discussed the purposes of the course and his own instructional philosophy.

Marge thought about how helpful this approach was since it enabled her to know something about the other learners, the instructor, and the course material. She thought to herself, "I think I'm really going to enjoy this course. I like the technique he used to help us identify what we wanted from the course. All the learners seem so interesting, and I especially appreciate being treated like an adult. What a refreshing feeling it is to have an instructor who seems to understand something about teaching adults. Yes, I think I'm going to like this course."

As we have demonstrated throughout this book, successful instruction such as that Marge Winter experienced does not happen accidentally; it requires an instructor to have a good knowledge of the subject matter, an understanding of the clientele, a willingness to plan carefully, a good deal of patience and flexibility, and a commitment to helping learners reach their potential. Perceptive instructors of adults realize all this and measure their success accordingly. For them, instruction is never a routine matter to be taken lightly.

In this book we have presented a six-step model to help you become more successful as an adult instructor. Yet, you may feel like the person in a recent airline commercial who kept answering the telephone and saying, "Yes, I can do that," "Yes, I can do that," "Yes, I can do that," and finally realizing, "How am I going to do all of that?" This is understandable since we have presented you with a great deal of material about adults and adulthood, and we have discussed at length how such knowledge suggests a particular way of organizing instruction. Many times during the initial development of the individualizing process, we felt overwhelmed by its numerous details and subtleties. We wondered if it would be possible to incorporate our principles into a workable system for instructing adults. But with a commitment to the idea that adults have the right to expect instruction consistent with their roles, responsibilities, maturity, and expertise, we were able to put our theories into practice. We think that you will be able to adapt the process to your own situation and experience the same kind of success that we have enjoyed.

In this concluding chapter, we synthesize the various elements that comprise the individualizing process. We offer a checklist related to the six-step model for you to use in examining and organizing your instructional efforts. Additionally, we provide some ideas for successfully employing the process, along with our views on possible implications for future changes affecting instruction and the kind of research into the individualizing approach that is still needed.

Individualizing Process Model

The individualizing model is designed for optimum use with adult learners and consists of six specific steps. Each step involves continuous planning, analyzing, and decision making on the part of the instructor. The model should be used flexibly as a framework for organizing instruction. If certain elements do not seem applicable to your particular context, then simply modify or remove them; that is one of the strengths of the process.

As you can see from Figure 3, the model requires a number of preplanning activities prior to the first session of the class. These include developing a rationale statement that describes why learners should be interested in the learning experience, how and why it will enable them to develop additional competencies, and what the instructional experience will be like. Other preplanning activities include identifying suggested learning competencies and requirements, locating support materials such as books, articles, and media-supported items, and securing human resources such as community experts and other specialists. Other preplanning activities include the preparation of a study guide or workbook in which materials such as syllabi, bibliographies, and suggested readings can be collected and organized.

In step two, the emphasis is on creating a good learning environment. Here, you will want to assess the physical environ-

Figure 3. Individualizing Instructional Process Model.

ment, noting how it can be made most conducive for learning to occur. This may involve rearranging the room, adding color to the space, and making provision for refreshments and food. In addition, you will want to think about how to best introduce the contents of the learning experience, how to help participants become acquainted with one another, and how you will get to know the participants.

The third step stresses development of the instructional plan. How you create this plan is crucial in operationalizing the individualizing process. We think that the best approach is a needs assessment process in which learners first individually complete a checklist of potential study topics. Once this has been done, small groups are formed for sharing ideas and building a consensus. The instructor then takes the information thus obtained and develops a learning plan that describes the topics to be studied, in what sequence, and through what kinds of instructional techniques.

The fourth step of the model consists of identifying the various activities that learners will undertake in preparation for and implementation of their learning contracts. Here, learners identify what it is they will learn, how they will learn it, and how they will evaluate their learning. Typically, learning activities take many forms, are dependent on the needs of each learner, and are negotiated between the learner and the instructor.

In the fifth step of the individualizing process, the learning plan is put into action, and learner progress is monitored. The instructor decides what instructional techniques will be used—minilectures, case studies, field visits, and so on—and implements these accordingly. In addition, as the learning unfolds, the instructor monitors learner progress through formative evaluations that enable modifications to be made as needed.

The sixth and last step of the individualizing model consists of evaluating individual learner outcomes. Using learning contracts, learners identify and complete various learning outcomes on the basis of their individual needs and competency levels. The instructor assesses the evidence or products presented by each learner and assigns the appropriate grade or achievement measure.

As we have noted throughout this book, the underlying intent of the individualizing process is to promote effective educational practice through the recognition of individual differences, experiences, and learning needs. By capitalizing on the expertise so typical of older, more mature learners, you are creating the conditions for good learning to occur. As a means of helping you organize your instructional efforts and assess the degree to which the various instructional elements have been incorporated, we have developed a checklist of items to be considered (Table 5).

Murphy's Law and the Individualizing Process

Most of us are familiar with Murphy's Law, which says, "if anything can go wrong it will." We suspect that nearly every instructor remembers some occasion when Murphy paid an unwelcome visit and disaster struck. In fact, many instructors may believe that Murphy lives on their shoulders! While we believe such disasters are unfortunate indeed, we always try to remember that life remains unpredictable no matter what you do. As a means of giving you the courage to press on and try the individualizing process, let us recount a few times when we encountered the unexpected and what we did to control the damage.

Take, for example, the time that one of us showed up for a class in an off-campus building only to find the room occupied by another group. In checking to see what had gone wrong, someone mentioned that a person by the name of Murphy had called to reserve the room. A sympathetic custodian was finally found and the problem resolved, but not without the loss of some valuable time.

Or take another occasion when one of us was conducting a two-hour training session for fifty community college teachers. The teachers were all sitting in a large circle around the room. We had just finished introductions and a quick informal needs assessment activity. The main points worked out by several smaller groups were organized on poster paper, and about eighty minutes remained for presenting the content. A large number of transparencies for this presentation were located on a table next to the projector with a cup of coffee situated close by. All of a sudden, one of the table legs gave way, and the table crashed forward with the transparencies spewing

Table 5. Individualizing Process Checklist.

Step 1: Preplanning Activities

_____ Learning rationale described?
_____ Potential learners understood?
_____ Instructional options considered?
_____ Learning competencies determined?
_____ Necessary support materials and resources considered?
_____ Workbook or study guide materials collected and prepared?
_____ Organizational constraints discussed and approvals negotiated?

Step 2: Creating a Positive Learning Environment

_____ Physical environment examined?
_____ Icebreaker activities considered?
_____ Opening activities decided?
_____ How to make learners feel at ease decided?
_____ Personal comforts of learners considered?
_____ How will learning materials, contracting examples, learning resources, and so on be introduced?

Step 3: Developing the Instructional Plan

_____ Suggested learning activities determined?
_____ Appropriate needs assessment tools created and used?
_____ Responded to related questions and concerns about the learning experience?
_____ The role of experience emphasized?
_____ How learners will be helped to feel comfortable with the process determined?
_____ Learning plan laid out and matched with resources?

Step 4: Learning Activity Identification

_____ Self-directed learning concepts emphasized?
_____ Learning contract process understood?
_____ Learning objectives identified?
_____ Necessary time lines established?
_____ Needed learning resources and strategies discussed and located?
_____ Needed evidence to show achievement of learning objectives discussed?
_____ Necessary validation and evaluation strategies identified?

Step 5: Putting Learning in Action and Monitoring Progress

_____ Optimal instructional techniques decided?
_____ Variety of instructional techniques used?
_____ Conducting formative evaluations understood?
_____ Frequent feedback to the learners provided?
_____ Feedback from learners encouraged and received?
_____ Feedback from learners used to make ongoing adjustments in the instructional process?

Table 5. Individualizing Process Checklist, Cont'd.

Step 6: Evaluating Individual Learner Outcomes

____ Appropriate summative techniques selected?
____ Competency and the transfer of learning to skills emphasized?
____ Various linkages from the learning activities and materials made to practice?
____ Ensured that mastery of learning took place?
____ Assessed that quality learning and critical thinking took place?
____ Prepared for the next instructional situation?

out in a fan across the floor, the coffee spilling across most of them, and the bulb burning out as the overhead projector hit the floor. Fortunately, the session was saved by some humorous sharing of ways to deal with this near disaster, while someone found another overhead and a couple of people helped dry off the transparencies.

Or there was the time when both of us were making a presentation before a regional chapter of the American Society for Training and Development. Our topic was the linkage of self-directed learning and training. Both of us had spent a good deal of time preparing for the session, and we had developed a number of overhead transparencies. The morning of the session, one of us (the one who was to bring the transparencies) had an emergency at home that required personal attention. Well, as you might imagine, the time needed to solve the emergency put everything behind schedule, so much so that the individual responsible for the transparencies dashed off with what he thought to be the correct set. Arriving just as the session was scheduled to begin, we pulled out the transparencies only to find that they were the wrong ones. We were able to save the day, however, by talking about Murphy's Law and drawing up new transparencies (admittedly briefer ones) by hand.

On another occasion, one of us was initiating a week-long, intensive summer workshop. Unfortunately, one of the participants just happened to have a nervous breakdown that first day. He proved to be quite disruptive and made it almost impossible for the rest of the participants to carry on with their work. We were able to salvage part of the first day by helping him focus on some specific tasks. We also made some quick phone calls to a university counselor and then to family members of the participant with the result that he was under medical care by the evening of that same day. Since he did not attend the remainder of the workshop, the learning situation returned somewhat to normal. The group spent the first two hours of the second day discussing what had happened and talking about the implications for teaching, learning, and just plain caring for others. At the end of the workshop, many participants noted that the entire experience, including the first day and the way it was handled, was one of the most meaningful they had ever had.

Coping with the Unexpected

As described above, instructors can learn to control, and even diminish, the effects of Murphy's Law. The first and perhaps most important step is planning, planning, and more planning. Failures in programs almost inevitably occur because of some breakdown in the planning process. To control for potential breakdowns, we recommend that you err on the side of overplanning. We also suggest you build in redundancy measures—backup systems that will work if the primary system fails. By following this approach, you will diminish the probability of a breakdown in the instructional process.

However when some disaster does strike, it is imperative that you handle the situation gracefully and professionally. We have found that being open and honest is a policy that learners appreciate, and discussion of any particularly disruptive situation often proves very instructive for everyone. The ability to laugh at yourself and the situation is another way of defusing the situation, since humor tends to have a cleansing effect.

Another way of countering Murphy's Law is to carry out a dress rehearsal, particularly if the learning experience or audiovisual support device is new to you. The old adage that practice makes perfect certainly applies here and usually is a sure way of reducing the effects of Murphy's Law. In addition, your confidence will be heightened to a point where any unplanned interruption is little more than a mild annoyance.

Perhaps the most important thing you can do is carry an "Instructor's first-aid kit." We have carried one for years and recommend that you do so as well. The kit contains essential items that often mean the difference in dealing successfully with the unexpected. Recommended items include: a grounding adapter for two-way electric cords and outlets, extension cords of various lengths, magic markers that work, poster paper, masking tape, extra blank overhead transparencies and frames, extra bulbs for audiovisual equipment, pencils and pens, extra paper, spare food or snacks, note cards, rubber bands, paper clips, stapler, glass cleaner and paper towels for cleaning overhead projector glass, chalk, telephone numbers of important people, extra institutional forms such as registration cards, maps, resource guides, throat lozenges, aspirin, tissues, Swiss army knife, magnet, thumbtacks, scissors, post-it stick-on papers, folders, envelopes, and the like. By assembling such a kit, you are lowering the chances that an unforeseen problem will affect the instructional situation, while at the same time increasing the odds for success.

Benefits of Individualizing Your Instruction

Perhaps the greatest benefit from individualizing your instruction with adults is the joy that you will derive from teaching and the joy that they will derive from learning. But there are other advantages. One is that you will find your teaching duties much easier to carry out in the long run. Because the individualizing process stresses flexibility, adaptability, utilization of various human and material resources, cooperative learning, and personal responsibility for learning, it reduces the kinds of anxieties common to conventional pedagogy (anxiety about taking tests, competing, or keeping up, for example). You will find that learners thrive on the individualizing process, that they become highly motivated to engage in learning, and that they work actively to fulfill their potential.

A second benefit comes from the satisfaction that you and the learners will experience in learning together. This may seem mundane, even unimportant, but our experience suggests that satisfied learners are motivated learners. The old adage of leading a horse to water may be appropriate here: your role isn't to make the horse drink, rather it is to make the horse thirsty. And so it is with satisfied learners; they are ever thirsty for more.

A third benefit comes from the satisfaction that you will feel in knowing that learners are responding to a learning approach tailored to their abilities and needs. Yes, many will balk when first exposed to the individualizing process, and this may dampen your enthusiasm for it, too. But soon, as the learners come to understand the process and begin experiencing the freedom of choice that it permits, they will respond to it in an infectious way. Their enthusiasm will increase to the point where you will know the harmony of teaching and learning.

Problems with the Individualizing Process

As effective as the individualizing process is, we realize there are certain problems in using it. For example, if you work in an agency that frowns on giving learners a voice in their learning, you may have difficulty in employing the process. You will probably need to be cautious initially in using individualizing techniques, but we have found that once co-workers and supervisors see the kind of results that are sure to occur, they generally become at least tolerant of this approach. Some may even ask for assistance in emulating what you are doing.

Some learners with very rigid learning styles may have difficulty with the individualizing process. We recommend that you not penalize such learners but rather encourage their learning efforts and point out options that they may want to consider. One of the strengths of the individualizing process is that it allows you to work with each learner individually. Thus, with certain learners you may need to be more directive than you would with others.

Some instructors who have fairly rigid teaching styles may have difficulty in adopting or adapting the process that we have described. We recommend that such instructors give the individualizing process at least three honest tries. We are confident that once they become comfortable with the process, so will their learners. However, there still may be some instructors who are more comfortable with a socratic or directive approach. If so, we still hope that they will find some useful tips in this book.

Future Implications

We think that, in the future, the individualizing process will become commonplace and that aspects of it will become available to learners of all ages. We say this because there is a clear need for an instructional system that capitalizes on the intrinsic capacities of learners, helps them to be more critically aware of their own needs; and links personal choice with responsibility.

In order for us to realize this vision, several changes will need to be made in the way that instructors are trained. Currently, most instructors who receive any formal training to teach do so in colleges of education, where the emphasis is on teaching children and adolescents. While this practice may have been acceptable in the past, it will be less acceptable in the future. As the number of adults requiring continued learning increases, the need for instructor training based on knowledge of adulthood will also increase. This means that colleges and universities that provide the bulk of instructor training must revise and expand current curricula so that principles of adult learning are incorporated into them. More important, those college instructors who will provide the training of future adult instructors must themselves be trained in adult learning principles so that they use the individualizing approach in their own teaching.

Significant changes also must be made in the way physical environments are designed and created if we are to serve adult learners well. Currently, most learning environments are designed for young people. With increasing numbers of adult learners demanding educational services, there will be a greater need for physical spaces that are consistent with the requirements of adult learners. Already, much has been written about the subject, and we suspect more will come in the future. Educational leaders, when thinking about and planning physical environments, must do so with an eye for serving learners of all ages, including adults.

Lastly, agencies and institutions must become more supportive and understanding of self-directed learners and their learning needs. The days when education was reserved almost exclusively for youth, and schools were places where the bulk of learning occurred, are over. Frankly, we wonder if they ever existed. We know, for example, that most adult learning is of a self-directed kind and occurs in the home or work setting. We also know that the prime motivations for such learning are the anticipated benefits. If adult learners see little or no benefit in continuing their learning in institutional contexts such as colleges or universities, they will not do so. One way of ensuring that educational settings will be desirable places for adults to attend is to organize them on the basis of what we know about adulthood and to provide services and instruction that are in keeping with this knowledge. The individualizing process is one proven way of organizing and providing the kind of instruction most adults want.

Research Needs

The individualizing process has its sources in research in self-directed learning, knowledge of how adults grow and develop, material pertaining to andragogy, and our own teaching and learning experiences. We are confident that you will find the individualizing process an effective way of organizing and delivering instruction, particularly with adults. At the same time, we realize that more research needs to be done to demonstrate the value of the process with various groups of adults, in various educational settings, and in various types of agencies or institutions. This is the proper function of research, and we welcome any comments readers have as to their experiences and outcomes.

A Final Word

The joy of watching adults grow and develop is something so special that we wanted others to benefit from our experience. That is why we wrote this book. We believe that the individualizing instructional process will enable both you and your learners to experience success. Yet this success will not be won without some trials and tribulations. For in the words of John Ruskin, "Education does not mean teaching people what they do not know. . . . It is painful, continual, and difficult work to be done by kindness, by watching, by precept, and by praise, but above all—by example."

RESOURCES FOR INDIVIDUALIZING INSTRUCTION

The resources section provides you with a variety of materials from which you can pick and choose according to your interests and needs. The section is divided into two parts. The first part, which contains nine units, is entitled "A Guide to Practical Applications." It includes various materials and examples that can be used with learners. The second part, "Research and Theory," contains five units of information derived from current research on adult teaching and learning.

"A Guide to Practical Applications" discusses some common concerns about the individualizing process. It describes alternative introduction techniques and several needs assessment techniques, it provides a sample course evaluation form and a sample instructor evaluation form, and it discusses several learning activity resources. This first part concludes with a discussion of how the individualizing process is used to train apprentice instructors and to develop graduate courses. It also provides some specific information on guiding the instruction of older learners.

"Research and Theory" provides in-depth information on several topics. It begins with a summary of the current thinking about two areas fundamental to the individualizing process—andragogy and self-directed learning. Literature and research on learning style differences and on needs assessment are included. The resource concludes with a summary of the latest information on the physical learning environment.

 A

A Guide to
Practical Applications

COMMON CONCERNS ABOUT THE INDIVIDUALIZING PROCESS

There are a variety of questions you may have about the individualizing process as you begin to adapt it to your own instructional situation. In our various classes and workshops for adult educators, for example, most of the following concerns are invariably raised in some manner.

New Instructional Skills Required

"Will new instructional skills be required to use the individualizing process and to be successful with it?" An answer to that question really depends, of course, on what skills you already possess. Individualizing your instructional process will require you to have those qualities necessary for any kind of human interaction: the ability to communicate, a willingness and desire to help, honesty, openness, and true enjoyment in being with other adults.

However, the process may also require the development of some new abilities. These include the ability to utilize the input of learners, to organize a variety of resources to meet their needs, and to inspire them to assume ownership of their learning endeavors. It also will require your willingness to give up a certain amount of control and transfer that control to learners.

Time Needed to Individualize Instruction

"The individualizing process seems too easy—it is the lazy instructor's method!" It is true that some will misuse, abuse, or not completely understand the process that we have described. But we have found that fostering and utilizing learner input typically promote an exciting, positive, and rewarding educational climate. Indeed, we believe that really good instructors have known and employed aspects of the individualizing process for centuries. This process is not a means of letting learners do the teaching but one of finding ways in which the many skills of an instructor can best be used to meet the needs of learners and take advantage of their experiences and skills.

Involving the learner is by no means an easy way to handle an instructional assignment. The instructor is often required to spend considerable time outside of class in organizing resources, uncovering new resources, meeting with learners to help them organize and implement their own learning activities, and staying on top of the relevant content areas. The instructor may also have to spend extra time tailoring and guiding special programs or learning activities and providing supplements to an individualizing environment, such as evaluating the wide variety of products that learners will submit. Indeed, as noted in Chapter Nine, the evaluation activities required of the instructor often exceed what would be found in a standard testing or grading situation.

In terms of organizational acceptability, many of your colleagues simply will not understand or will refuse to understand what you are doing when you encourage individualizing activities. Further, you may experience bureaucratic problems in respect to your evaluation or grading policy, your attendance policy, your stance on textbooks, and so on. You may need to demonstrate equivalent competency achievement in your learners or trainees or explain to others just how your instructional process works.

Instructor as Expert

"My learners expect me to teach them; they expect me to be an expert!" In addressing that often-repeated statement, we usually ask whether it is the learner who expects the instructor to lead the class or whether it is the instructor who insists on playing that role. There is no question but that many learners come to a classroom or workshop thinking that the instructor will share expertise with them. Much of this expectation stems from years of conditioning and role model expectations. Perhaps even more critical is that many instructors themselves believe that the instructor's role is to hand down the truth and show followers the way.

We have found, however, that most adult learners adapt quite quickly to whatever environment is being fostered. The evaluation reports that we have received over the years invariably have commented on the pleasure and excitement experienced by learners on realizing that they could become experts on some topic and could share that expertise with their colleagues as they grew and learned together. The real value, in our estimation, comes when learners realize that they are expected to take responsibility for their own learning.

Lack of Knowledge of Subject Matter

"My learners really don't know enough about the subject matter to play a large role in determining what should be taught!" We frequently hear this statement when first meeting with other instructors in a workshop. Such feelings are tied to the belief that an instructor has spent years preparing to become an expert on some subject and that the expertise acquired at such cost must somehow be poured into the ready but empty reservoirs called learner minds.

We have absolutely no quarrel with the notion of maintaining expertise in one's chosen subject matter; after all, that is the *sine qua non* of intellectual growth and capability. But, if the learner is bored, if the learner spends more time trying to figure out how to please the instructor than in really learning the subject matter, or if the instructor is not in fact very skilled in sharing expertise with others, then what is the use of all the knowledge the instructor might possess?

Building Learner Confidence and Trust

"How do you build the confidence of learners so that they will take responsibility for their own learning and be willing to participate in individual and group activities?" It is true that some learners who enter a learning situation in which involvement is the norm may feel threatened and may even resist the whole process. We have seen this happen frequently at the start of our classes and workshops. Our solution? We simply talk openly and honestly to participants about our expectations of them, about the process of involving them that we will use, and about some of the problems that they will encounter initially. This approach seems to help, and we can then move ahead with the process knowing that almost every learner will soon become involved at a level that feels comfortable.

From time to time throughout a learning experience, however, participants will revert to prior expectations about learning and the role of the instructor. This is where patience becomes very important. Learners in a course or workshop with us for the first time frequently ask What would you like on this activity? or May I do it this way? We attempt to maintain consistency and answer with some such statement as It is what you want or feel comfortable with that is important or Is this something that will meet some of the needs you uncovered earlier or are experiencing now? We view this as responsible permissiveness: we want to help learners realize that their own input is important, but we also try to provide guidance when necessary. We have also found that by the time of the second experience with the individualizing process, a learner has usually developed self-directive attitudes and approaches to learning. Thus, we often attempt to pair up experienced learners with new learners in the initial stages of the process.

Applicability to Various Content Areas

"This process simply won't work in my subject matter area!" Another set of concerns about the individualizing process centers on doubts that a certain content area can be taught other than in a fairly traditional, instructor-directed manner. As a matter of fact, there are certain subjects—for example, an introductory course on physics or chemistry—where the instructor must wear the hat of the expert or specialist purely for safety reasons. (A chemistry experiment could blow up if the instructor is not providing appropriate control or guidance.) There are also situations in which an instructor or trainer by contract must assure that each learner achieves a certain level of proficiency. But the instructor can still involve the learners in a variety of ways and foster in them a sense of responsibility for their own progress and mastery by helping them lay out learning goals and evaluation plans.

Adaptability of Process to Nonformal Settings

"This process might work in a regular classroom but not in a workshop, a noncredit class, a training session, or a short meeting!" This final objection is one that we often hear. Actually, instructors will need to adapt the process or use only certain aspects of it as they move from one instructional setting to another.

For example, in a one-day workshop less time will be used in getting acquainted and assessing needs than in a semester-long course; however, to ignore completely such activities may result in a bored or even disillusioned audience if the content has no real relevance to their needs and expectations. In a one-hour training presentation, the instructor can raise needs-related questions at the very beginning or have participants raise questions among themselves in small groups. Such information then becomes the basis for discussion and presentations by either the trainer or someone from within the learning group who may happen to be an expert on a particular topic that is uncovered.

ALTERNATIVE INTRODUCTION TECHNIQUES

In Chapter Six we prepresented some introduction techniques that we typically use with the individualizing process. However, there are other such techniques that can also be used:

1. Learners can introduce themselves progressively around the circle by telling the others something about their personal or professional lives, what they would like to accomplish during the course, and so on.

2. A slight variation on this is to add the stipulation that each person must also work "backwards," so to speak, and give the names of all the people who have already spoken. However, each person should have the right to pass on this portion of the introductions or to use a crib sheet.

3. A technique that can be used in very large groups (that is forty-five to fifty or more) is to ask people to form themselves into groups of three or four (whatever is convenient in terms of seating arrangements and proximity). They can then spend about twenty minutes becoming acquainted with each other.

NEEDS ASSESSMENT TECHNIQUES

Games or Group Interaction Devices

A number of techniques fall under the rubric of what adult education literature refers to as gaming and simulation devices. Today, however, *games* is a more descriptive term. Many of the techniques are especially useful for stimulating interactions among group members.

Brainstorming. Group members (usually in a small group) spontaneously generate various ideas or descriptions of needs, with a facilitator providing support (Clark, 1980).

Uses

1. Where quick responses are desired or needed.
2. When initial ideas or lists of needs are required.

Limitations

1. Spontaneous responses may not always be accurate.
2. Some people may not want or be able to participate.

Games and Simulation Devices. Role-playing is facilitated by some sort of board game or other device that allows for self-observation (Horn & Cleaves, 1980).

Uses

1. To determine a participant's knowledge about certain topics.
2. To facilitate interest in or practice with some topic.

Limitations

1. Viable games or devices that will maintain participant interest are difficult to find or create.
2. Some people have difficulty with role-playing.

Nominal Group Involvement. Group decision-making in which all suggestions related to a topic are recorded and ranked (Delbecq, 1975).

Uses

1. When contributions need to be encouraged.
2. When synergistic results from group involvement or commitment are desired.

Limitations

1. Not all people will participate fully in the ranking process.
2. The process can be quite time consuming.

Outside Consultants or Groups

Advisory Council Input. An outside group is asked to serve in an advisory capacity (Hiemstra, 1985a).

Uses

1. To obtain advice, insight, or factual information from a group of people knowledgeable about an area or organization.
2. To evaluate ongoing or completed educational activities for the purpose of determining new needs.

Limitations

1. Advisory council members may not truly represent all the areas of interest of the people for whom they are providing input.
2. It may be difficult to compare advice obtained from outside groups with information obtained by other techniques.

Consultants or Outside Experts. A professional helper's advice is used in assessing needs or evaluating performance (Long, 1972).

Uses

1. When participant observations are appropriate.
2. When outside advice can be combined with information obtained from the participants.

Limitations

1. Relying solely on an outside expert for advice on needs may reveal only that person's view.

2. Participants' real needs may differ considerably from those suggested by outside experts.

Paper-and-Pencil Devices

Diagnostic Form. Respondents individually or in groups check on a form and/or prioritize answers, interests, or perceptions of need from a list of statements (Knowles, 1980).

Uses

1. For groups of people in a class or meeting.
2. When forms can or must be completed at a later date.
3. To collect evidence of progress made as a means of assessing future learning needs.
4. To obtain an individual's perception of needs or interests.

Limitations

1. It may be difficult to interpret the results.
2. It may be difficult to compare one person's perceptions of competencies with those of another person.

Interest or Attitude Inventory. A device used to determine what participants or potential participants are interested in or their attitudes toward some area of concern (Knowles, 1980).

Uses

1. To study personal interests relative to potential areas of study.
2. To assess attitudes toward learning.
3. To assess attitudes toward a particular subject.

Limitations

1. Interests and attitudes can change over relatively short periods of time.
2. It may be difficult to isolate specific areas of study for a group when individuals' needs vary greatly.

Questionnaire. A survey form, usually mailed, used to obtain a broad analysis of needs, interests, or opinions (Sudman & Bradburn, 1982).

Uses

1. For reaching a wide distribution of potential learners.
2. For reaching a relatively homogeneous, fairly well-educated group of people.
3. To determine factual material.

Limitations

1. Reliability of the results can be quite low at times or difficult to determine.
2. The rate of return frequently is quite low, and increasing this rate is costly.
3. Any open-ended responses or added comments may be difficult to interpret.

Systematic or Structured Devices

Content Analysis. The objective, systematic, and quantitative description or analysis of the contents of written materials to determine any trends or weaknesses indicative of educational needs (Holsti, 1968).

Uses

1. For the analysis of materials representative of a group of people.
2. For the development of particular need statements that can later be placed in some type of diagnostic form.

Limitations

1. The analysis process can be quite time consuming.
2. It may be difficult to access appropriate materials.

Critical Incidents Assessment or Task Analysis. An interview with a supervisor, judge, or someone knowledgeable about an individual to determine specific behavior patterns considered critical to a skill or behavioral area (Rigors, 1971).

Uses

1. In studies of leadership ability or potential.
2. For determining qualifications of individuals for certain levels of instruction.
3. In studies of individual behavior or on-the-job behavior.
4. To examine training needs in relation to job performance.

Limitations

1. It may be difficult to obtain the cooperation of busy supervisors or persons in authority.
2. This approach can be quite time consuming.

Peer Evaluation. The evaluation of behavior by an individual's peers to provide feedback on perceived training needs (American Medical Association, 1971).

Uses

1. To assess certain aspects of human behavior.
2. To obtain another assessment of a person's job performance (usually used with supervisory ratings).

Limitations

1. The technique requires trained observers with considerable skill and sensitivity if it is to produce reliable results.
2. Peers may not always perceive or report information accurately.

Supervisory Rating or Performance Appraisal. Ratings of an individual made by someone in a supervisory role (Mager & Piper, 1970; Nadler, 1982).

Uses

1. To analyze individual behavior, performance, or training needs.
2. To determine where performance gaps can be interpreted as educational needs.

Limitations

1. It may be difficult to obtain the cooperation of the appropriate supervisor.
2. A supervisor presents only one view, and that view may be influenced by particular organizational requirements.

Systematic Study of Available Records. An analysis of any available records related to a particular individual, subject area, or need area (Hiemstra, 1985a, Nadler, 1982).

Uses

1. When an interview or questionnaire procedure is impossible.
2. When past information can suggest current needs.
3. When a case-study technique is desired.

Limitations

1. Historical information may not portray current needs or situations very accurately.
2. It may be difficult or impossible to gain access to certain records.

Test or Pretest. Completion by an individual of a device designed to test or measure some aspect of behavior or knowledge (Hopkins & Stanley, 1981).

Uses

1. To determine needs by assessing deficiencies in knowledge.
2. To measure performance or status on some task, attribute, or attitude.

Limitations

1. There are potential problems with validity, standardization, and measurement.
2. This technique will often need to be combined with other techniques.

Verbal Devices

Informal Interview. An unstructured and unstandardized method of obtaining answers to various questions and gaining information on various topics (Tough, 1979).

Uses

1.   To begin discussion of a topic.
2.   To initiate small-group discussion.
3.   For gathering qualitative information about needs.
4.   For obtaining new insight into a particular problem or need.

Limitations

1.   This technique requires excellent interviewing and interpretive skills.
2.   Data analysis can be complicated and time consuming.

Personal Interview. Gathering information through direct verbal interaction between individuals in face-to-face or telephone conversations (Hyman, 1970).

Uses

1.   To obtain specific facts, opinions, and specific information about needs.
2.   To measure specific attitudes and interests.
3.   To obtain an understanding of current needs or learning situations.
4.   When a high degree of participation is needed or desired.

Limitations

1.   It requires a standardized approach and interviewing schedule to obtain comparable data.
2.   It is time consuming and can be expensive.

SAMPLE COURSE EVALUATION FORM

ATE 604 – Community and the Adult Educator
Course Evaluation – Spring Term

Instructions: The following form includes several statements designed to evaluate the course and to help me and other faculty members improve future courses taught via Parti, our distance education computer conferencing system. Each statement or item requires a response. In addition, if you wish to add any evaluative remarks, personal comments, recommendations, and so on, please use the backs of these sheets. Please do not sign your name unless you have a particular reason for wanting me to know it.

I. Following are several of the techniques used to present information or to promote learning during the semester. Please circle the number on the 3-point scale that represents your opinion as to how frequently each technique should be used. In other words, in another course where Parti was used as the primary delivery mechanism, would you hope that each technique was used less often, more often, or the same?

		less	*same*	*more*
A.	Study guide information on the course (basic information and learning activities)	1	2	3
B.	Discussion of study guide materials	1	2	3
C.	Materials distributed by participants via Parti	1	2	3
D.	Large-group discussion via Parti	1	2	3
E.	Small-group discussion via Parti	1	2	3
F.	Learning partner discussion and activity via Parti	1	2	3
G.	Debate activity and discussion via Parti	1	2	3
H.	Polling via Parti	1	2	3
I.	Initial face-to-face orientation to Parti	1	2	3
J.	Suggested reading—textbook/study guide	1	2	3

K.	Suggested reading—other than above	1	2	3
L.	Availability of video and other materials on media reserve at Bird Library	1	2	3
M.	Availability of library reserve readings	1	2	3
N.	Learning activity requirements	1	2	3
O.	Feedback on progress from instructor	1	2	3
P.	The role of the instructor as a facilitator of the learning process	1	2	3
Q.	Use of learning contracts			

II. The following are the content areas on which some time was spent during the course. Please circle the number on the three-point scale that represents your opinion as to the time that should have been spent on the topic during the semester.

		less	*same*	*more*
A.	Getting started—becoming acquainted with Parti and related technology	1	2	3
B.	Assessing needs and completing learning contracts	1	2	3
C.	Developing a definition of community	1	2	3
D.	Building a community or agency planning model	1	2	3
E.	Activating the educative community	1	2	3
F.	Power structure analysis	1	2	3
G.	Community study techniques and information	1	2	3
H.	Assessing community needs	1	2	3
I.	Community coordination and cooperation	1	2	3
J.	Change agents and community intervention strategies	1	2	3

III. The following centers on the various materials in the study guide. Please evaluate them in an open-ended fashion. In other words, did you find them informational and educational, should such materials be discussed in greater detail, should other types of information be contained in a study guide for a course taught via Parti, and so on (continue your comments on the back side of this page if you need more space).

_____

_____

_____

_____

IV. In an open-ended fashion, please evaluate the text:

_____

_____

_____

_____

_____

V. Please evaluate the use of the textbook, the supplemental readings provided in the study guide, and suggested other readings or resources as aids for stimulating thinking and electronic discussion.

_____

_____

_____

_____

_____

_____

_____

VI. The learning contract is intended to help you individualize your learning in a course. Did it serve that purpose for you? Feel free to add any other thoughts that you may have regarding learning contracts.

_____

_____

_____

_____

_____

_____

VII. Computer conferencing obviously has strengths and weaknesses. Please list some that come to your mind after having participated in a semester-long course via Parti.

_____

_____

_____

_____

_____

VIII. Please suggest ways in which you would change the course if it were to be taught again via computer conferencing.

_____

_____

_____

_____

_____

IX. Facilitating a course via computer conferencing requires some different roles for instructors. Having participated in the course, how would you recommend that I do things differently the next time?

_____

_____

_____

_____

_____

X. There were certain combinations of individuals in some groups that triggered either a great deal of discussion or very little. We even talked about this during the course. Please provide any thoughts that you have on ways to trigger discussion, the importance of discussion, the role of the instructor in promoting discussion, and so on.

_____

_____

_____

_____

_____

_____

_____

_____

XI. The general purpose of this course was described in the study guide as follows: The purpose of the course is to provide an opportunity for Adult Education students, community workers, and any other interested people to develop skills in dealing with the community and its educational problems.

Was this accomplished for you? _____ Yes _____ Partially _____ No
Please add any appropriate explanation in the space provided.
Explanation: _____

_____

_____

_____

_____

_____

_____

XII. As we discussed at the beginning of the course, the use of such techniques as learning contracts, reading logs, and discussion activities is fundamental to individualizing the instructional process. Individualizing also is based on student initiative, self-directed learning assumptions, and the use of the instructor as resource and facilitator. Please evaluate the effectiveness of this class in establishing these conditions. In other words, did you have the freedom you wanted, yet some guidance from the instructor? Were you stimulated and challenged to learn, grow, and change? Did you have a satisfactory learning experience? Were you able to think critically about what it means to be an effective community adult educator? Did you learn new ways of studying and understanding communities? Were you able to individualize your own learning in a manner satisfactory to your needs and expectations? Please explain on the next page.

Explanation: _____

_____

_____

_____

_____

_____

_____

This concludes the structured portion of your evaluation. If you have additional comments and suggestions, please make them on the back of this page. These could include an evaluation of the instructor, the value of the bulletin board and the student center topics we established on Parti, the value of posting various topics, and so on.

THANK YOU!

SAMPLE INSTRUCTOR EVALUATION FORM

Indicate by means of a check anywhere on the 5-point scale how you rate your instructor on each quality. Any related comments (or any other comments) may be placed on the lines provided or on the back of any page. Please do not sign your name unless you have a particular reason for wanting me to know it.

Instructor's Name: _____

Course No.: _____ Date: _____

1. Was the time we were together as a class used to effectively promote learning?

      Ineffectively   Effectively

         1   2   3   4   5

_____

_____

_____

2. Evaluate the instructor's interest in the students, including his/her availability for questions and consultation.

      Low   High

        1   2   3   4   5

_____

_____

_____

3. Evaluate the fairness of the instructor's grading policies and practices:

      Very Unfair   Very Fair

        1   2   3   4   5

_____

_____

_____

4. The instructor's knowledge and command of the subject matter covered in the course was:

Poor				Excellent
1	2	3	4	5

_____

_____

_____

5. The preparation and organization of materials used in individual class sessions were:

Poor				Excellent
1	2	3	4	5

_____

_____

_____

6. Was the material in this course presented at an appropriate intellectual level?

Too Simple				Too Complicated
1	2	3	4	5

_____

_____

_____

7. The instructor's control of the class was:

Too Loose				Too Tight
1	2	3	4	5

_____

_____

_____

8. What effect did the instructor have on your interest in the subject matter that was covered?

	Decreased It				Increased It
1	2	3	4	5

_____

_____

_____

9. How tolerant was the instructor of student opinion, input, and involvement in the course's operation?

Intolerant   Encourages Varied
                                                        Student Expression
    1   2   3   4   5

_____

_____

_____

10. How would you rate the clarity of suggested individual, group, and course learning activities?

Unclear   Clear
    1   2   3   4   5

_____

_____

_____

11. Which of the following comes closest to your opinion of the instructor's overall effectiveness?

Low   High
    1   2   3   4   5

_____

_____

_____

LEARNING ACTIVITY RESOURCES AND IDEAS

There are a number of learning activity resources, ideas, and approaches that can be brought to the attention of learners as they begin the process of developing a learning contract. This section describes the kinds of contracts that we have found to be both popular with learners and helpful in promoting critical thinking and reflection.

Interactive Reflection and Information Collection Tools

In our experience, most adult learners prefer information of a practical nature. Thus, the facilitator must ensure that learners spend some time reflecting on a subject, becoming aware of available resources, and thinking through how new information or knowledge might influence them as educators.

We accommodate this instructional need by encouraging learners to select one of the four tools that we have developed or adapted for use in collecting information. Each tool provides opportunities for learners to reflect on what they are learning. And, in keeping with the foundational premise of individualizing the instructional process, the reflection is interactive in that learners must simulate dialogues either with themselves or with the author of the material being read.

Most learners will be willing to try out at least one of these tools after their intended purposes have been described. Moreover, in short-term training sessions, participants seem to appreciate receiving information on the various tools because they see them as devices that they can utilize for follow-up work once the session or workshop is completed.

Interactive Reading Log. When using this technique, the participant first reads certain materials and then uses writing as a means for growth in knowledge, ability to think, and skill to express oneself. For example, in a beginning level graduate course, we would counsel a learner to take a broad or general approach in reading and writing about an initial exploration of available information. However, in an advanced course, where a learner may already have considerable knowledge on which to build or is quite experienced with reading logs, or in a short-term workshop where participants might want quite specialized follow-up activities, we encourage the design of a reading and writing experience that will provide in-depth knowledge of a specific area.

The interactive reading activity places more stress on reading and interaction with the author and less stress on intensive or structured writing on a limited topic. The log is not an outline and, except in certain circumstances, not a summary.

Knowles (1975) writes about an exercise in reading a book proactively. That entails looking for signposts an author might have provided, such as a table of contents, dust cover statement, or index. It also entails writing out some guiding questions the reader might want answered, and then reading those parts of the book that seem to answer the questions. Elbow (1973; 1981) describes a concept that he calls *cooking*, in which the interaction of contrasting and conflicting material in a document becomes central to getting at the heart of that document's idea or message.

These types of techniques are described, and the learners are then encouraged to find a reading approach that will match their particular levels of self-directedness. The following is a list of recommendations we make to learners as they seek advice on how to begin or proceed on their logs.

- The interactive log is essentially a series of reactions to those elements of the reading material that are particularly meaningful or provocative to the learner.
- The written materials that a learner selects may include books, professional journal articles, government reports, unpublished manuscripts, conference papers, and in-house organizational documents.
- We suggest that readers skip those sections that do not appear of interest, skim others, read still others at a "once over" normal rate, and read some passages much more carefully and in depth.
- We give no particular instructions to learners on how the reading is to be undertaken. We simply suggest that they adapt a style of reading with which they feel comfortable, and we make ourselves available for oral or written feedback.
- The actual spacing and number of interactions that a person has

with the material read usually depend on the scope of the reading and the reader's purposes.

- Writing the log during the reading experience might involve the selection of sentences or longer passages that are striking for their clarity, insight, stimulation, or usefulness. It might also include items that the reader considers ambiguous, exaggerated, poorly reasoned, insufficiently supported, understated, or questionable. The reader may also decide to record information that might be useful in a later period of study.
- We emphasize that a reader should also try to explain why an item, concept, or section is stimulating, provoking, exaggerated, useful, and so on.
- We suggest that the reader ask questions like the following: If this fact, point, or idea is true, then what does it mean for other facts, for practice, for my personal beliefs? An advanced learner might ask, can this idea be verified or refuted by research?

The approaches to recording interactive comments can be quite varied. Some people prefer to summarize certain passages and then perhaps make one or two observations before moving on to interact with the next part of the text. Some learners will record mainly personal observations as they read a document. Others not only will record personal reflections and comments but also will use the reading experience as a source of future reading or research ideas. In fact, for certain readers, we encourage digression, reading several documents at the same time, and branching off into entirely unexpected areas to gather new or advanced ideas about the field of adult education. Some learners will have the self-confidence and expertise to engage in simulated debates with the author in which ideas are challenged and counterarguments presented.

The length and scope of the log will vary with the type of reading materials selected and the intensity of the treatment given to each item by the reader. In one case the log might consist of widely spaced reactions to a variety of selections. In another case the log might include a number of longer reactions to fewer selections—selections that have been carefully chosen for in-depth reading. We also encourage learners to think through whether or not they will want some type of feedback from the instructor.

The format of the product to be turned in for examination and feedback will again vary from person to person and should be based primarily on the plans noted in the learning contract. For example, one person might choose to provide a brief introduction that explains why she selected particular reading materials. The interactive log of comments would follow, and there might also be a summary section at the end. Another learner might choose to submit a stack of index cards on which thoughts had been recorded during the reading process. Still another person might employ a coding scheme that uses color, printing font, or some off-setting technique to divide the reader's comments from the author's words. This latter format can be especially helpful when the reader has set up the interactive experience as a debate or dialogue with the author.

The facilitator's role is to provide a description of the technique and to encourage learners as they think through a personal approach to interactive reading. During the initial steps, we encourage learners to accept responsibility for decisions about resources, approaches, and writing style. During the reading and writing stage, we make ourselves available to those who request time for discussion and feedback about their efforts. Learners may have to renegotiate personal plans or learning contract goals if they encounter a stumbling block, want to change focus, or decide to shift from a broad to an in-depth approach.

The final role for the facilitator is to provide feedback, if desired or contracted for by the learner, on the completed log. We read through the log and write our observations, comments, and suggestions for follow-up reading or reflection in the margins. Occasionally, however, learners will prefer a face-to-face discussion. We also comment on the choice of reading materials and summarize our perceptions of the value of the experience for the learner.

Media Log. This media-supported activity has both advantages and disadvantages. On the positive side, a voice or visual presentation provides opportunities for a variety of stimulations typically impossible in printed material. A lecturer on an audiotape can use voice inflection, word emphasis, and specialized sound effects to make or stress certain points. A video or film on some subject can use actors, interviews with experts, or varied visual effects to enhance a topic.

On the negative side, it is difficult, as well as expensive, to create high-quality audio or visual materials. In addition, access to media may be limited due to costs or lack of needed equipment. It is also frequently difficult to hold a viewer's or listener's attention beyond a certain length of time. As a consequence, it may not be possible to provide much in-depth coverage of a topic through audio or visual materials.

Nevertheless, there are many films, audiotapes, slide-tape learning kits, and so on available for the self-directed learners, who can find videotapes on an expanding number of topics, and on-line conferencing systems and knowledge bases that provide new ways to gain access to information. Supplemental learning resources can generally be placed on media reserve in the university library.

Over the past several years we have collected a large number of our own audiovisual materials. These include videotapes that we have produced on our own or through special grants and audiotaped conversations with adult educators. Thus, we are frequently able to provide learners an opportunity to complete media logs. We suggest that they adapt the interactive reading log guidelines described above to the media log experience. Some people even use a type of mediated means for recording their thoughts, interactive comments, and reflections. We provide feedback to learners, if desired, in the same way as we provide it to those who use reading logs.

Theory Log. We typically use theory logs in advanced courses where learners have a fairly good grasp of the subject matter. Not everyone finds theory logs easy to use, but they can be valuable in promoting an advanced understanding of a topic and corresponding research needs. The facilitator has a quite important role to play here. It is in using the theory log that many learners first attempt to extract concepts from the literature and synthesize information. Thus, they usually need feedback on the accuracy and completeness of their thinking. We try to provide written comments on the log or theory statements, and we also make ourselves available for discussion of their work. We provide the following outline of a theory log to each reader:

I.   Preparation
   A.   The assumption underlying this assignment is that learners taking an adult education course will need and desire to increase their personal understanding of the field. In keeping with this, the instructor will facilitate appropriate learnings related to the course and representative of the group's needs.
   B.   On your own, discover what is meant by the term *theory*.
II. Activity and Presentation
   A.   Throughout the course, for both your work outside class and information presented in class, make notes on what you perceive to be theoretical concepts, salient points, truths, bridges to known theory, ideas to be tested, gaps in knowledge, and so on. The instructor will attempt to point out theories or important constructs throughout the course.
   B.   During and/or toward the end of the course, attempt to organize your notes and thoughts into some cohesive format. This can be in the form of a log, a statement, an outline, or whatever else is appropriate for you in expressing the grasp you have of the theory or theoretical constructs that are the foundation for course content— or the absence of theory, theory gaps, and so on. This does not need to be a long statement. Its purpose is to allow you to work through and refine your understanding of adult education theory and knowledge.
   C.   Turn in your report, log, or paper by the end of the course. Keep a carbon copy for yourself.
III. Educational Goals for the Activity
   A.   One goal is that you gain experience in analyzing and deriving the theory underlying a content area, that is, a body of basic knowledge.
   B.   Another is that you gain experience in stating the theory, in making contributions to the theory, and in determin-

ing where an understanding or determination of theory
is still needed.

IV. Miscellaneous

    A. This is not intended as an assignment to please the in-
structor; the hope is that it will contribute to your own
growth and understanding. Therefore, do not make the
assignment a burden; it is intended to be a facilitating
activity that promotes learning.

    B. A pass/incomplete grade will be given to assess your
fulfillment of course requirements.

    C. The following statements about theory may be helpful:

    –A theory is a generalization or series of generalizations
that attempt to explain some phenomenon in as systematic a manner as possible.

    –A theory is a set of assumptions from which can be
derived a set of empirical laws or principles.

    –A theory can be used as a guide to action, a guide to data
collections, a guide to new knowledge, or a means of
explanation.

    You do not prove a theory—you build a theory by em-
pirically testing a variety of related assumptions (expand, clarify, build).

Personalized Journal or Diary. The use of a diary or journal
to enhance learning is not a new phenomenon. However, until the
past couple of decades, it was used primarily in conjunction with
professional writing, for religious, psychological, or meditative reasons, or for personal pleasure. Beginning in 1965, Ira Progoff, a
psychologist and therapist, and his colleagues began to emphasize
the value of journals in enhancing personal growth and learning.
Progoff has written several books about personal growth, but the
one most directly related to the journal-writing activity is *At a Journal Workshop* (1975). Christensen (1981), Gross (1977), and Rainer
(1978) have also discussed the diary as a learning tool for adults.

    Journal or diary writing usually involves the recording of
personal feelings and reflections on a topic. Typically there are no
set rules for writing a journal, and the content, structure, and style
are left up to the writer. We encourage learners to look on the

personal journal as a resource that facilitates the growth of self-awareness and self-reliance. Within the solitude of the blank page, writers "can reflect on their life experience, contemplate future directions, and come to trust more deeply their own answers" (Christensen, 1981, p. 4).

We suggest to learners that they use Progoff's book as a guide if they decide to work on a personalized journal. His method involves more than just recording thoughts about a subject or a set of readings. It calls for active dialogue and feedback by the journal writer reflecting on what is currently being written, compared with what was written earlier.

We have found the role of the facilitator to be most important in the early stage of diary or journal writing. It is then that the learner may need someone to act as a sounding board or to provide encouragement. In later stages a journal may become more personal, and the learner frequently becomes less desirous or in need of outside feedback. We regard this as a sign of personal growth, but we always try to be available if feedback is wanted.

Small-Group Activities

We have found it valuable to involve learners in small groups whenever it seems feasible. Three techniques that seem to be effective in promoting learning are study groups, debates among learners, and teaching teams.

Study Groups. We are firm believers in synergism, the notion that one plus one can often equal more than two in terms of the energy, excitement, and products that result when people work together on some study-group activity. A study group consists of two or more people (we have found four to seven to be the optimum number) who join together to explore a topic. If used to meet some of the requirements in a graduate-level course, for example, the study group typically focuses on a topic related to the overall subject of the course and one that is mutually agreed upon by the group members and approved by the facilitator. We also have used the study-group technique in a training workshop to help participants design a procedure whereby they could carry out further study on a topic after the training experience concluded.

Once the group has formed, its members should meet together to explore a probable topic, to determine workable meeting times, and to select a group coordinator (and group recorder if deemed necessary). This initial discussion period is quite important, because it allows members to begin to take ownership of the topic selected. Some may even decide to back out if they do not find the topic interesting. In a graduate class, we typically provide some time during the first few sessions for groups to form and to begin work on a topic. In a short-term workshop, we encourage the group to meet during a lunch break or immediately following the initial training session.

After the topic is selected, we suggest that group members work out a focal point for their study efforts. This might include establishing specific goals, coming up with one or more specific questions that they would like to explore, and deciding on readings, learning objectives, and end results.

Next, group members begin to read the materials they have selected. We stress that the reading responsibilities be divided among all group members. This typically permits a wide range of materials to be covered. It is not unusual for members to use other ways of obtaining information, such as through interviews or other data collection efforts.

Group members are encouraged to prepare abstracts, summaries, or reading logs of the materials they read for later sharing with other members. Throughout all these efforts the group coordinator serves to keep things moving forward on target, to schedule meetings as needed, and to serve as a liaison with the course facilitator. We encourage members of the study group to meet periodically and discuss their various materials, as a way of promoting learning, and building some sort of group consensus.

In a graduate course we ask study groups to produce a final report (a typed, double-spaced report ranging in length from ten to thirty pages) that summarizes the general focus of the study effort, the materials read and discussed, the conclusions drawn, and the nature of the involvement by various group members. This report usually is submitted to the facilitator for evaluation, comments, and feedback. If time permits, it can be very educational and worthwhile for an oral summary of the study effort to be presented to other members of the class. In a training workshop we make ourselves available for later feedback if a study group elects to send us its final report. It is possible to conduct study groups via electronic mail or electronic conferencing, but more time usually is required.

Debates. We have found that most learners appreciate an opportunity to provide some in-depth information to each other during a course, even if they do not have the opportunity to participate in a study group. Thus, setting up a debate with one group for and one group against some topic can be a worthwhile and enjoyable learning experience. This activity, too, can be carried out electronically if the course is on-line or if learners have access to each other through some electronic mail procedure.

Teaching Teams. It also can be a valuable experience for learners to teach each other about some aspect of the course. In such cases, we prefer that a group or team of three to five people work together by studying the material for a while and then deciding on an instructional method, choosing one or more teaching techniques, and adding whatever supporting media or other devices they will need. We have found that a teaching period of between sixty and ninety minutes is about right. The team should also seek coaching help from the instructor because this kind of session may not be well received by fellow learners unless it is carefully designed and delivered.

Learning Resources in the Community

A large number of learning resources and valuable educational experiences exist in any community. The purpose of this section is to describe three techniques involving experiences within the community that we have found beneficial as learning activities.

Agency Visits. The literature provides several conceptual frameworks that aid the reader in understanding different types of agencies. In our courses we provide learners with information about various schema (Hiemstra, 1976a; Schroeder, 1980) and discuss the inherent value of learning firsthand about an adult education agency or program. We also provide three or four handouts that describe various guidelines to use when conducting research on an agency. These include topical study outlines, structured interview schedules, and suggestions for studying only specific aspects of an agency.

This learning experience may be most beneficial to a person not very familiar with or new to the field of adult education (or whatever field of interest is pertinent to your content area), but we also encourage more experienced learners to consider the activity as a means of validating or clarifying their current understanding of adult education or to learn something about an unfamiliar agency. Some learners will purposely choose to visit more than one agency in a semester-long course just so they can quickly broaden their view of the field.

Evaluation typically is in the form of written feedback (or oral if so desired) from the instructor. However, we encourage learners to consider the best means for validating what they have learned as a result of visiting an agency. For example, an agency administrator or the people interviewed may be much better able to evaluate the final report than the course instructor. In addition to written summaries, which we encourage, we also urge people to make oral reports to the whole group if time permits.

Mini-Internships. A short-term internship in a community organization or agency has many of the same values as an agency visitation. A typical internship for a three-credit, semester-long course would require the learner to work with an adult education practitioner for some forty to fifty hours. The intern might simply follow the practitioner around for a week and observe the various activities involved in carrying out the job. Or the intern might participate in a special program on which the agency is working— serving, for example, as a member of a planning committee for a conference or training workshop. This might require the intern to work with the agency for a few hours each week during the entire semester. We also have suggested internships to noncredit workshop participants as a learning technique that could be employed after the workshop has been completed.

The instructor's role is to serve as a liaison with the agency as needed, to discuss periodically with one learner what progress is being made, and to help evaluate the experience. We typically ask people undertaking this kind of internship to keep some sort of log or make a report of their experience. The report should include a self-evaluation and some overall statement about what was learned. We will then provide written (or oral if preferred) feedback to the learner. We usually call workers at the agency to ask if any problems developed during the internship and to obtain their overall assessment of the value of the experience for both the agency and the learner.

Community Studies. We recommend such study efforts primarily to those interested in community education programs or to those advanced learners who wish to become more skilled in understanding the educative potential of the community. There are several dimensions of a community that can be studied, such as its social, educational, or economic characteristics, historical background, the nature of the citizenry, and its power structure (Hiemstra, 1985a). We tell learners that collecting information through a community study is only the beginning of the learning process. The information gathered will need to be processed, analyzed, and interpreted.

We encourage people who undertake this kind of study to develop a report that will include information on a variety of categories, including such topics as the history of the community, its leadership structure, the makeup of its formal and informal groups, and what the future may hold for it. Written or oral feedback from the instructor and/or community members provide some evaluation information for the learner.

Learning Activity Sheets

When teachers or trainers encourage learners to assume responsibility for learning, then they must also provide clear information about the various course requirements. In a typical course we provide a learning activity descriptor sheet for each suggested learning activity. Even if a learner contracts for some alternative activity, the guidelines will be useful either for preparing materials or for deciding on the alternative experience.

We use a similar format for describing most learning activities (see the outline list for a theory log presented earlier in the chapter). The learning objectives we provide in any write-up are based on our assessment of what information, knowledge, or skills a person should get out of the experience in relation to the overall goals of the course or training session in question. They also are intended to suggest what the person may use as a personal goal statement in the learning contract.

We also use the term project to provide learners with an opportunity to integrate what they have learned in a course. In most of our graduate courses we tell learners as they are developing their learning contracts that completing the various learning activities or their equivalent is necessary to achieve the grade of B. Thus, the term project normally is used by the learner to achieve the grade of A. It represents an effort on the part of the learner to obtain as much as possible from a course.

We provide learners with a descriptive sheet that lists several options. These usually include some sort of examination or testing procedure, a study-group option, an extensive reading and writing assignment, a term-paper option, and one or more additional ideas depending on the nature of the subject matter (for example, a program-planning course might include suggestions for a term project that allowed learners to plan or evaluate a program of some sort). In addition, learners always have the option of designing an activity of their own choosing.

TRAINING APPRENTICE INSTRUCTORS

One of us participates in an annual summer institute for journeyman and apprentice instructors. These typically are workers who have been designated to teach what they do as a trade. They represent a variety of trades, such as carpentry, electrical work, drafting, boiler making, and plumbing. Although most participants have never had any teacher training, they are usually very enthusiastic and highly motivated.

The institute involves an intensive week-long seminar designed to help participants become better teachers. Four topics are covered: adult learning processes, communications, testing and evaluation, and using media.

The individualizing process is used for the first topic mentioned above. Rooted in adult learning principles, this class consists of five sessions that last ninety minutes per day. The sessions are: (1) setting a climate; (2) helping adults learn; (3) Howard McClusky's power-load-margin theory (Baum, 1978; Hiemstra, 1980a, 1981b; James, 1986; McClusky, 1963, 1967, 1970; Main, 1979); (4) learning styles (Smith, 1982); and (5) motivation and teaching in a motivated way. This curriculum has been preset by earlier arrangements with the sponsoring organizations. Thus, needs assessment activities and learning contracts are not feasible. However, other aspects of the individualizing process are employed, and the use of needs assessment activities and learning contracts is discussed throughout the week.

On the first day, for example, we begin with some activities designed to set a climate for mutual learning. This initial session emphasizes the three relationships described in earlier chapters. These are introductions and icebreakers, and participants are given the opportunity to exchange stories on the trials and tribulations of teaching adults. The instructor also has an opportunity to share personal stories about his initial teaching efforts and how much he had to learn in order to become a better teacher.

The second day of the institute is devoted to the topic of helping adults learn. Participants are asked to take the Educational Orientation Questionnaire (Hadley, 1975), which is then scored and processed during the group session. This activity always creates a great deal of discussion since it allows participants—usually for the first time—to see where they fall on some sort of teaching continuum. Participants discuss the differences between pedagogical and andragogical assumptions. Usually the instructor also talks about the problems inherent in a fairly structured program such as that at the institute, where principles and concepts of adult learning such as andragogy, self-directed learning, and individualizing instruction are discussed but where the structured setting makes applying such principles difficult. The importance of listening, of treating learners like adults, and of using humor is discussed, along with such topics as what it means to be a facilitator.

The rest of the week is devoted to a discussion of learning styles, power-load-margin in adult life, and how to motivate learners. A variety of techniques are used, including minilectures, small- and large-group discussion, simulations, role playing, and learning exercises. The instructor supplies a great deal of feedback and also seeks feedback from participants. An important key to the continuing success of the institute is the inherent flexibility and adaptability that is central to the individualizing process.

DEVELOPING A GRADUATE COURSE

If you are using the individualizing process and want to develop a new course, you may have to depart somewhat from more traditional curricular development processes. The reference base we are using in this description is an adult education graduate program.

One of our first steps is to develop a course statement of rationale for the course. In a rationale statement, we do more than simply develop a course description, although some descriptive information is included. We provide a statement that describes why learners should be interested in the course, how it will help them as professionals, and how we will implement the individualizing process.

When we are developing a new course, we also identify colleagues at other universities who are offering similar courses and request copies of their syllabi for review. We read as much as possible about the subject to be taught, talk to colleagues at our university about it, and do some personal brainstorming on it. For example, we wanted to develop a course entitled, Controversies in Adult Education. As initial preparation, we read *Examining Controversies in Adult Education* (Kreitlow & Associates, 1981), we browsed through many copies of four adult education journals looking for controversial topics, and we talked with several colleagues about what a learner should obtain from such a course. We also use this searching process to identify one or more textbooks for use in a course.

We also begin to look for some unusual types of materials that learners could not easily obtain on their own. For example, in the Controversies course described above, we phoned several of the chapter authors for the Kreitlow book and asked them to record on an audiotape their current views on the topics they had written about, so that we could make the tapes available to learners. For a course on Professional Writing and Publishing, we provide examples of virtually every type of article that can be written, copies of stylistic guidelines from several journals, and various tips for writing and publishing in professional journals. For a research seminar, we make available a large collection of research proposals, along with several sets of data from past studies. Our view is that even if only one person uses a resource during a course, it was worth the effort to make the material available.

The next step is to develop a workbook or study guide that contains a basic description of the course and resource materials. The statement of rationale, textbooks, and supplemental resource materials thus serve as a foundation for developing the workbook or study guide. We then begin the process of drafting some preliminary goals, detailing various learning activity ideas, and describing the resource material that we have located. We also include items such as bibliographies, samples of learning contracts, and copies of papers or reports pertaining to the subject matter that have not been published in any other source. We think it much better to distribute all this material at once rather than hand it out in a piecemeal fashion. We typically make arrangements with a local copy center to duplicate and bind all materials in an attractive cover. The workbook is sold to learners as a normal text requirement for the course.

For our university courses, we accumulate special reading or mediated materials and place them on library and media reserve. An activity common to almost all types of instructional and training approaches is the development of reading lists or bibliographies. This requires an instructor first of all to do considerable reading in the given subject matter. Our approach is to develop both an extensive bibliography that can be updated periodically and a list of selected materials that are then placed on library reserve. The selected reading materials will provide a basic understanding of the subject, while the larger bibliography facilitates additional or specialized study.

If a university course is held off campus, especially at a location distant from the university library, it becomes even more crucial that some sort of extra reading capability be provided. In our off-campus courses, we usually make arrangements with our own library, a public library, or another university's library for materials that can be loaned to learners or placed on reserve. For the weekend scholar program in adult education at Syracuse University, a number of books have been purchased for each off-campus site. We also bring along materials from our personal libraries and loan these to participants. When carrying out a training workshop, we often bring along material to loan out or ask the organization to provide access to various items for trainees.

Finally, we look for resource people in the community who

will be willing to make a presentation in a formal setting or work with learners in some other setting. One of the most pleasing aspects of seeking out experts in the community is the very positive response that they usually give. Most people seem to love sharing what they know about a subject and are eager to work with learners. We also ask learners to evaluate all resource people at the end of a course so that we can obtain a good sense of how each performed and whom we might ask to participate again.

It may also be necessary to obtain other kinds of resources and make a variety of other arrangements. Films, panels of experts on specific topics, internship assignments, attendance at conferences, and telephone interviews are some of these. Advance planning and communication often are required when using these kinds of resources.

GUIDING OLDER ADULT LEARNERS

The literature on older adults as learners is quite extensive. The following material has been adapted from Hiemstra (1980c) and updated with more current information.

Attention to the Pace of Learning

- Allow for long periods of time between stimuli, for responding to questions, and for group discussion.
- Allow more time for all aspects of the learning experience.
- Avoid sudden surprises or changes.
- Be sensitive to perceptions about life satisfaction and locus of control.
- Keep sessions short (perhaps fifty to sixty minutes), keep the discussion time on any single topic short, and present only small amounts of information at any one time.
- Keep time pressures at a minimum.
- Permit and promote self-pacing by learners.
- Promote certainty, confidence, and success by moving from easy material to difficult (build on earlier successes).
- Provide for frequent refreshment and restroom breaks.

For further application suggestions, see Freund and Witte (1976); Gounard and Hulicka (1977); Henry (1989); Jones (1980); Knox (1977, 1986); Lersten (1974); Long (1983); Mullan and Gorman (1972); Okun (1977); Peterson (1983); *Symposium on Adult Learning Psychology* (1973).

Evaluation and Assessment

- Be sensitive to issues of quality and life satisfaction in relation to educational participation.
- Encourage the use of outside validators who are knowledgeable about a topic area.
- Minimize the chance of failure and the impact of making errors.
- Provide regular feedback on progress.
    Use peer review and feedback.
    Use positive feedback techniques.
    Use review strategies.

- Reduce or eliminate required homework and graded testing procedures.
- Use interview techniques if feasible to help learners talk about what they have learned, their problems, and their aspirations.
- Use multiple-choice testing when testing is required.
- Use recognition techniques as opposed to more traditional recall methods.

For further application suggestions, see George (1986); Gordon, (1974); Gounard and Hulicka (1977); Hixson (1968); Hulicka and Grossman (1967); Jones (1980); Mullan and Gorman (1972); Okun and Siegler (1977); Rodgers and Herzog (1987).

Involving the Learner in the Instructional Process

- Facilitate the learner's active involvement in all aspects of the individualizing process.
- Facilitate self-directed learning.
    Encourage self-directed determination of learning goals, approaches, and resource needs.
    Help learners develop a positive self-concept.
    Reduce learner dependency on the instructor and increase self-responsibility.
- Promote self-motivation and learning efficiency.

For further application suggestions, see Brockett (1984); Gordon (1974); Hiemstra (1975, 1976b, 1985b); Knox (1977); Mullan and Gorman (1972); Peterson (1983); Tough (1979); Wass and West (1977).

Organization and Meaningfulness in Learning Activities

- Be well organized.
    Suggest instructional goals or objectives and help learners develop their own.
    Use outlines, study guides, and other advanced organizing techniques.
- Help learners gain confidence in their learning abilities.

- Help learners process the information that they receive.
- Help learners increase their reading proficiency.
- Help learners organize and reorganize their learning activities.
  Facilitate the use of learning contracts.
  Encourage practicing techniques.
  Show learners how to take notes or to make outlines.
  Encourage learners to use verbal coding.
  Explain the use of specific encoding procedures.
  Make organizing the material part of the learning process.
  Stress the tying together of concepts, the relevancy of information, and connections to learners' experience base rather than memorization.
- Utilize materials and information that will have real meaning to the learner.
  Use a stimulating approach that will appeal to several senses.
  Use concrete examples and base them on past experiences of the learner when possible.
  Be sensitive to cognitive or learning style differences among learners.
- Utilize various cuing devices.
  Encourage the learner to develop various mediators or mnemonic devices (visual images, rhymes, acronyms, and self-designed coding schemes).
  Seek cues that are familiar to learners or that can be tied to past knowledge.
  Use headings, summaries, and review aids.

For further application suggestions, see Camp (1986); Camp, Markley, and Kramer (1983); Cavanaugh and Murphy (1986); Craik (1977); Davis and Miller (1983); Franz (1983); Galbraith and James (1984); Glynn and Muth (1979); Gonda, Quayhagen, and Schaie (1981); Gordon (1974); Gounard and Hulicka (1977); Heisel (1985); Hultsch (1975, 1977); Jones (1980); Knowles (1984); Knox (1977); Lersten (1974); Mergler and Zandi (1983); Peterson and Eden (1981); Shadden and Raiford (1984).

Personal Approach of the Facilitator

- Be positive, supportive, and helpful.
- Help older learners compensate for both intellectual and non-cognitive changes.
- Help to promote learning confidence, self-discipline, and self-respect.
- Maintain an informal, friendly environment.
- Work to make learners feel welcome and at ease in a new learning setting.

For further application suggestions, see Brockett (1985b); Fisher (1986); Gounard and Hulicka (1977); Hiemstra (1982a); Hixson (1968); Jones (1980); Knox (1977); Mullan and Gorman (1972); Peterson (1983); Ralston (1981); Wass and West (1977).

Needs and Experiences of Learners

- Base learning activities and instructional approaches on the needs and interests of the learners.
- Be flexible in terms of the differing needs, interests, and abilities that learners may have.
- Be sensitive to life stages and the impact of life changes on needs.
- Be sensitive to the value of social interactions among learners.
    Use small-group discussion to help learners analyze personal and group needs.
    Encourage people to work together in groups when feasible.
- Help learners relate new knowledge to past experiences.
- Help learners understand the advantages and disadvantages of being an older person and the corresponding impact on needs.
- If text material is utilized, help learners tie the information to their current knowledge base.
- Try to understand the cognitive styles of learners and develop instructional approaches for different styles.

For further application suggestions, see Blanchard-Fields (1986); Fisher (1986); Glynn and Muth (1979); Goodrow (1975); Gordon (1974); Gounard and Hulicka (1977); Havighurst (1976); Hiemstra (1975, 1976b, 1977-78, 1979, 1985b); Labouvie-Vief (1977); Leclerc (1985); Lersten (1974); Levinson (1978); Marcus (1978); Merriam and Lumsden (1985); Peterson (1983); Peterson and Eden (1981); Ralston (1981); Sheehy (1976); *Symposium on Adult Learning Psychology* (1973).

Sensitivity to Barriers, Obstacles, and Physiological Needs

- Be sensitive to declining hearing and related problems for some older learners.
    Be prepared to help learners move closer to sound sources.
    Use voice and media amplification.
- Be sensitive to declining vision and related problems for some older learners.
    Allow adequate time for adjustment when going from light to dark areas or vice versa.
    Ensure that ample light is available.
    Reduce glare or direct sunlight.
    Use high contrast on visuals and handouts.
    Use methods and techniques that emphasize visual as well as interactive and aural approaches; deemphasize haptic, kinesthetic, or olfactory approaches.
- Be sensitive to memory losses and the corresponding impact on assimilating new information.
- Be sensitive to the manner of the presentation.
    Read material aloud when feasible.
    Use combined auditory and visual presentation modes.
- Carry out diagnostic evaluations of learners' needs, abilities, and limitations.
- Minimize distractions at the time of the learning, including background noise, room conditions, and personal anxiety.
- Pay attention to various obstacles that can interfere with learning.
- Pay attention to the physical environment.
    Analyze the environment (see Chapter Six). Ensure that heating and ventilation are adequate.
    Reduce distractions.

Take appropriate breaks.
- Provide for those with limited mobility and help learners compensate for declining energy levels or occasional depression.

For further application suggestions, see Arenberg (1976, 1977); Bennett and Eklund (1983a, 1983b); Brockett (1984, 1985b); Charles (1983); Cross (1981); Estrin (1986); Galbraith and James (1984); Gordon (1974); Graney and Hays (1976); Gounard and Hulicka (1977); Haase, Robinson, and Beach (1979); Hayslip and Kennelly (1985); Henry (1989); Hiemstra (1985b); Hulicka (1967); Jones (1980); Knox (1977); Lersten (1974); Merriam (1977); Ogle (1986); Ostwald and Williams (1985); Peterson (1983); Plopper (1981); *Symposium on Adult Learning Psychology* (1973); Tager (1981); Vosko and Hiemstra (1988); Wass and Olejnik (1983).

B

Research
and Theory

MOVING FROM PEDAGOGY TO ANDRAGOGY

There is little doubt that the dominant form of instruction in Europe and the United States is pedagogy. But a competing approach to instructing adult learners has gathered momentum within the past two decades—this approach is generally referred to as andragogy. The purpose here is to provide the reader with some background information on both instructional forms.

The pedagogical model of instruction was originally developed in the monastic schools of Europe in the Middle Ages. Young boys were received into the monasteries and taught by monks according to a system of instruction that required these children to be obedient, faithful, and efficient servants of the church (Knowles, 1984). This tradition of pedagogy, which later spread to the secular schools of Europe and America, became and remains the dominant form of instruction.

Pedagogy is derived from the Greek words *paid* (child), and *agogos* (leading). Thus, pedagogy has been defined as the art and science of teaching children. In the pedagogical model, the teacher has full responsibility for making decisions about what will be learned, how it will be learned, when it will be learned, and whether or not the material has been learned. Pedagogy, or teacher-directed instruction as it is commonly known, places students in a submissive role and requires them to obey the teacher's instructions. It is based on the assumption that learners need to know only what the teacher teaches them. The result is a teaching and learning situation that actively promotes dependency on the instructor (Knowles, 1984).

Until very recently, the pedagogical model has been applied to the teaching of both children and adults. But this involved an obvious inconsistency. As adults mature, they become increasingly independent and responsible for their own actions. They are often motivated to learn by the need to solve immediate problems in their lives. Additionally, they have an increasing need to be self-directing. In many ways the pedagogical model does not account for such developmental changes in adults, and thus produces tension, resentment, and resistance in them (Knowles, 1984).

The growth and development of andragogy as an alternative model of instruction has helped to remedy this situation and to improve the teaching of adults. But this change did not occur over-

231

night. Rather, it began some twenty years ago when Malcolm Knowles popularized the term *andragogy* and referred to it as a system of ideas, concepts, and approaches to adult learning. His contributions to this area have been many (Knowles, 1975, 1980, 1984, 1989; Knowles & Associates, 1984) and have influenced the thinking of countless educators not only in North America but in other parts of the world. For example, Griffin (1983), Jarvis (1984, 1985), and Tennant (1986) are only a few of the adult educators in Great Britain who have discussed the andragogical concepts. Knowles's dialogues, debates, and subsequent writings on andragogy have been a healthy stimulant to the growth of the adult education field during the past twenty years.

The first time that andragogy caught the widespread attention of adult educators was in 1968 when Knowles, then a professor of adult education at Boston University, introduced the term (then spelled "androgogy") in a journal article. In a 1970 book (a second edition was published in 1980), he defined the term as the art and science of helping adults learn. His thinking had changed to the point that in the 1980 edition he suggested the following: "Andragogy is simply another model of assumptions about adult learners to be used alongside the pedagogical model of assumptions, thereby providing two alternative models for testing out the assumptions as to their 'fit' with particular situations. Furthermore, the models are probably most useful when seen not as dichotomous but rather as two ends of a spectrum, with a realistic assumption (about learners) in a given situation falling in between the two ends" (p. 43).

The andragogical model as conceived by Knowles (1980) is predicated on four basic assumptions about learners, all of which are related to a learner's ability, need, and desire to take responsibility for learning (pp. 44–45):

1. Their self-concept moves from dependency to independency or self-directedness.
2. They accumulate a reservoir of experiences that can be used as a basis on which to build learning.
3. Their readiness to learn becomes increasingly associated with the developmental tasks of social roles.
4. They begin to count on immediate rather than postponed ap-

plication of knowledge and shift from subject-centered to performance-centered learning.

Andragogy as a concept and set of assumptions about adults existed before Knowles popularized the term. Anderson and Lindeman (1927) were the first to use the word in the United States in a published piece, although Stewart (1986a, 1986b) notes that Lindeman apparently used the term as early as 1926. Brookfield (1984b) suggests that Anderson and Lindeman drew upon the work of a German author of the 1920s, Eugene Rosenstock. However, Davenport and Davenport (1985) assert that the word was first coined in 1833 by Kapp, a German teacher.

Writers in several European countries, such as Hungary, Poland, and Yugoslavia, also had used the term prior to 1968. Hungarian educators, for example, place teaching and learning within an overall system called *anthropogogy* (Savicevic, 1981). This system is subdivided into pedagogy (dealing with youth education) and andragogy (concerned with adult education). There is some variety, too, in the application of related terms. Some countries use the term *adult pedagogy,* one (the Soviet Union) uses the term *autodidactic* to refer to adult education activities, and a few countries use the term *andragology* to refer to andragogical science (Knoll, 1981, p. 92).

Outside of North America there actually are two dominant viewpoints: "one by which the theoretical framework of adult education is found in pedagogy or its branch, adult pedagogy . . . and the other by which the theoretical framework of adult education is found in andragogy . . . as a relatively independent science that includes a whole system of andragogic disciplines" (Savicevic, 1981, p. 88).

In setting forth his particular version of andragogy, Knowles associated it with a variety of instructional suggestions and he also described the facilitating roles of instructors in detail and talked about ways of helping learners develop their learning abilities. His early work with andragogy and his subsequent interpretation of the learning projects research by Tough (1978) and others led to a 1975 publication on self-directed learning in which he provides a variety of inquiry projects and learning resources on the topic.

Knowles (1975) has offered some reasons for his decision to pursue research in the area of self-directed learning. One immediate reason was the increasing evidence that people who take initiative in educational activities seem to learn more and learn things better than do passive individuals. Second, self-directed learning appears "more in tune with our natural process of psychological development" (1975, p. 14). Knowles observed that an essential aspect of the maturation process is the development of an ability to take increasing responsibility for life. In addition, Knowles had observed that the many evolving educational innovations (nontraditional programs, Open University, weekend colleges, and so on) throughout the world require that learners assume a heavy responsibility and initiative for their own learning.

Knowles also suggested a longer-term reason for the study and promotion of self-directed learning, one that involves our individual and collective survival: "It is tragic that we have not learned how to learn without being taught, and it is probably more important than all of the immediate reasons put together. Alvin Toffler calls this reason 'future shock.' The simple truth is that we are entering into a strange new world in which rapid change will be the only stable characteristic" (Knowles, 1975, p. 15).

SELF-DIRECTED LEARNING

Interest in and knowledge about self-directed learning has been accelerating in the past decade:

- Many dissertations on self-directed learning, some federally funded projects, several monographs, and numerous books and articles have been written during this time.
- A self-directed learning task force has been created within the North American Commission of Professors of Adult Education (CPAE), and it conducts annual miniconferences on the subject.
- A multitude of related papers are read each year in North America at the Adult Education Research Conference, the CPAE conference, the National Adult Education Conference, the Lifelong Learning Research Conference, and many other national and regional conferences. The number of related papers read at conferences outside of North America also is increasing.
- Several recent grants sponsored by the Kellogg Foundation at various universities have given special attention to developing literature and knowledge about self-directed learning (Long & Associates, 1988).
- The topic receives an increasing amount of support and criticism in the literature, both of which reflect its impact on the knowledge base related to instructing adults.

Much of this information about self-directed learning has grown out of two different but related areas of attention. Both areas were developed in North America during the 1960s, but their impact has come to be worldwide.

The concept of andragogy has perhaps played the most important role in stimulating theories about, approaches to working with, and literature related to instructing adults. But parallel to many of the andragogical assumptions has been the thinking on self-directed learning that stemmed from learning projects research.

The concept of self-directedness in learning was first discussed in educational literature as early as 1926 (Brookfield, 1984b). From these writings, a preliminary description of self-directed learning emerged. In Lindeman's (1926) words: "Adults are motivated to learn as they experience needs and interests that learning will satisfy . . . adults have a deep need to be self-directing; therefore the role of the teacher is to emerge in a process of mutual inquiry" (p. 16).

Actually, self-directed learning has a long and rich history. Kulich (1970) noted that prior to the evolution of formal schools, self-education was the primary means individuals had of dealing with the changes going on about them. Self-education, for example, has been an important tool in the lives of scholars throughout the history of Western civilization—Socrates and Aristotle, for example (Tough, 1967).

Long (1976) noted that a spirit of self-directedness was prevalent in the learning of colonial American adults, and cited many self-improvement societies, the instructional content in newspapers, and an expanding subscription library system as supporting examples. Long (1983) also points to such people as Benjamin Franklin, Cotton Mather, Abigail Adams, Colden Cadwallader, and Eliza Pinckney as quintessential adult learners.

Fundamental to contemporary studies of self-directed learning was the pioneering work of Houle (1961). Houle used an interview technique with several adult learners to develop a motivational typology of learning styles. He discovered that people generally were either goal oriented (some specific goal or objective serves as the learning stimulus), activity oriented (being with others in the pursuit of learning is the primary motivation), or learning oriented (enjoyment of learning for its own sake is the stimulator). More recent research that involved both formal and informal learning prompted one of us to add to the typology a fourth category identified as "the self-reliant, autonomous, and independent learner" (Hiemstra, 1976a, p. 35).

The chain of research following Houle's work began with a study conducted for the National Opinion Research Center (Johnstone & Rivera, 1965). The researchers used interview techniques rather than the more commonly used polling procedures to estimate the amount of self-directed learning that had taken place during the year preceding the interview. They determined that at least nine million adults in the United States carried out one or more self-instruction projects during a year.

Tough then undertook some related research in 1966 as a doctoral student at the University of Chicago, where Houle was a professor. He based his work on the notion that people accomplish considerable learning without assistance by teachers (Tough, 1967). This research culminated in 1971 with his seminal work on adults' learning projects (Tough, 1979). Using a probing interview technique, Tough determined that most adults spend as much as 700 hours each year in deliberate learning projects. Nearly two-thirds of his original sample reported that these projects were self-planned. A number of subsequent studies have substantiated these original findings. Caffarella and O'Donnell (1988), Penland (1978, 1979), and Tough (1978) provide summary information about research on learning projects.

Cross (1977) also summarized this body of research by looking at several studies conducted prior to 1977. She drew the following conclusions about the learning efforts of adults: Almost every adult undertakes some sort of learning or receives some sort of training each year, with the number of activities falling between three and thirteen. She also noted that there are clear differences in the time spent in learning by different populations and that the majority of such learning is self-planned.

A different approach to examining the self-directed phenomenon was initiated by Gibbons and others (1980). Utilizing the biographies of twenty high achievers, the researchers determined that self-directed characteristics such as creativity and self-confidence were common among the subjects. Another approach to measuring self-directedness is found in Guglielmino (1977). She developed a scale to measure characteristics related to self-directed learning styles and readiness to undertake self-directed learning. Although the instrument has received some criticism (Brockett, 1985a; Brockett & Hiemstra, forthcoming; Field, 1989; Landers, 1989), it has been widely used during the past decade (Guglielmino & Guglielmino, 1988). Oddi's (1985, 1986) more recent instrument is another effort to provide an instrument to measure personality characteristics related to the self-directed learning phenomenon. Only very limited use of the instrument has been made thus far, and it, too, has received some criticism by other researchers (Landers, 1989; Six, 1987; Six & Hiemstra, 1987).

There has thus been a steady progression in our understanding of self-directed learning and, as a result, there have been numerous changes made in educational and training practices with adult learners. Some of this information has been developed into instructional suggestions (Hiemstra, 1980a, 1988a; Sisco, 1988), some into policy recommendations (Caffarella & O'Donnell, 1988; Hiemstra, 1980b), some into implications for future research (Hiemstra, 1982b, 1985c), and some into efforts to create new theories related to instructing adults (Brookfield, 1985). Most of this increased understanding centers on the view that the individual learner is capable of assuming considerable responsibility for and control of learning activities when such opportunities are provided. As such, the research serves as another foundational progenitor of the individualizing process.

LEARNING STYLE DIFFERENCES

For many years, perceptive educators have known that people differ in how they go about learning, thinking, and problem solving. Some people like to form pictures in their minds, while others are more comfortable if they are able to touch or feel an object. Some people prefer reading about something first and then trying it out, while others like to try something out and then read about it later. Some people find that working alone in a quiet environment helps them learn better. Others prefer working in a group with some noise in the background. In short, people have very different learning styles.

Learning styles refer to characteristic ways of processing information and behaving in learning situations (Keefe, 1979; Price, 1983). They are hypothetical constructs that provide clues as to how a person learns and adapts to the environment.

Numerous writers have addressed the concept of learning styles and the various ways in which they are measured (Canfield & Lafferty, 1974; Dunn, Dunn, & Price, 1981; Gregorc, 1979; Hruska & Grasha, 1982; Kolb, 1984; Reichmann & Grasha, 1974). Although much of their work has focused on children and adolescents, the usefulness of learning style assessment and analysis for older learners has also been clearly demonstrated (Smith, 1983; Marton, Hounsell, & Entwistle, 1984; Maxfield & Smith, 1987). In the literature of adult education, there is increasing emphasis on learning styles and their implications for educators of adults (Conti & Welborn, 1987; Dorsey & Pierson, 1984; Fox, 1984; Holtzclaw, 1985; James & Galbraith, 1985; Knox, 1986; Korhonen & McCall, 1986; Loesch & Foley, 1988). Knowledge and awareness of personal learning styles help individuals identify their strengths and weaknesses. They also assist the instructor in making better decisions about curriculum development and instruction as well as in counseling individual learners. Most important, learning style assessment and analysis are crucial to identifying individual differences and integrating these within the learning environment.

Following is an example of how knowledge about learning styles can help you be a more effective facilitator of learning:

As an instructor of English at a local community college, you are aware of the differences in learning styles among your adult learners. You know that some of your learners learn best through listening, others prefer to see the material, while still others are more comfortable relating information to a practical problem. By organizing your learning activities in a manner that involves telling, showing, and doing, you can ensure that each learner will be operating, at least part of the time, in a preferred or dominant style of learning. The result should be more effective learning for everyone involved.

How can you determine the learning styles of your adult learners? Learning style diagnosis is carried out in a variety of ways, ranging from informal analysis to formal testing. Informally, you can ask learners about their preferred ways of learning and what learning environments they like best. You can also watch learners in action, noting those who prefer concrete examples and those who are more comfortable dealing with theoretical explanations. Perhaps the most informative approach is to administer various instruments. There are many such instruments available to the adult instructor. Examples include the Canfield Learning Styles Inventory (Canfield & Lafferty, 1974), Kolb's Learning Style Inventory (Kolb, 1976), and Gregorc's Type Indicator (Gregorc, 1979). Learning style instruments are best used as tools to create an awareness that learners differ and as starting points for individual learners' continued investigation of themselves as learners.

A thorough examination of various learning style instruments is beyond this book's scope. However, Smith (1982) provides a review of more than fifteen such instruments that are appropriate for use with adults. Price (1983) reviews eight learning style instruments, what they measure, the approximate time needed to administer each instrument, and where they can be obtained.

In addition to learning styles, there are two related concepts that deserve some attention: cognitive styles and thinking styles. So closely related are these three terms that they are often used interchangeably, with some resulting confusion (Bonham, 1988a, 1988b; Keinholz, 1984). This is unfortunate since the terms point to distinct realities and should be used with greater precision. Learning style is the most inclusive and overarching term in that it refers to cognitive, affective, and physiological traits that indicate how learners perceive, interact with, and relate to the learning environment (Keefe, 1979). In short, learning styles include cognitive and thinking styles in addition to other dimensions such as personality and environmental traits.

Messick and Associates (1976) think of cognitive styles as information-processing habits—a learner's most common mode of thinking, remembering, or problem solving. These means of dealing with knowledge determine how people encode and decode information through such operations as selective combination and selective comparison (Sternberg, 1986).

Thinking styles are those modes of functioning that govern our perceptions and intellectual activities in a highly consistent and pervasive way. They describe systemized ways of apprehending that include a variety of perceptions and cognitions (Harrison & Bramson, 1982).

Messick and Associates (1976) describe more than twenty cognitive style dimensions derived from experimental research. These various styles are conceptually independent of each other. One dimension involves an analytical, impersonal approach to problem solving versus a more global, social orientation. A second dimension provides categories for measuring a person's tolerance for errors. A third dimension analyzes how well developed an individual's short-term memory is. A fourth dimension tests whether an individual is impulsive (selects the first answer that comes to mind even if it is incorrect) versus reflective (chooses among several alternatives before deciding which is correct). A fifth dimension measures the degree of cognitive complexity and simplicity.

Research into cognitive styles has made available knowledge about how various adult learners are likely to perform such tasks as remembering, selecting, comparing, focusing, reflecting, and analyzing (Sisco, 1987). Knowledge of these and other cognitive style dimensions can also help an instructor and learners make more informed decisions about which learning activities will be useful and productive.

An additional source of information about adult learners can be gleaned from the thinking styles research of Harrison and Bramson (1982). They have developed an instrument called the Inquiry Mode Questionnaire (InQ) that measures the characteristic thinking style of individuals and then classifies them as synthesists, idealists, analysts, realists, and pragmatists.

Briefly, the synthesist focuses on change, abstract conceptual ideas, and underlying assumptions. Idealists tend to be future oriented and to value process relationships, and they are also interested in social issues. Analysts focus on problem solving in a careful, logical, methodological way, paying great attention to details. Realists tend to be practical and concrete, focus on the here and now, and like to deal with facts. The pragmatist focuses on what is useful or utilitarian, values step-by-step thinking, strives for immediate payoffs, and emphasizes tactics.

Knowledge of your learners' thinking styles can help you be a more effective facilitator. You can provide examples that range from theoretical analysis to practical applications. You can provide a mixture of telling, showing, doing, and applying in each of your instructional units. By addressing each style, you can help learners employ their preferred style of thinking. To the extent that you do this in a systematic and attentive way, you will greatly enhance the likelihood of learner success.

NEEDS ASSESSMENT RESEARCH

Needs assessment has received considerable attention from adult education scholars for many years. Brackhaus (1984), Long (1983), McMahon (1970), Monette (1977), and Pennington (1980) provide useful overviews of needs assessment. Reading such sources in chronological order also provides an interesting summary of the changes in thinking about needs assessment during the past three decades. Some researchers have even demonstrated the value of involving learners in assessing needs in terms of corresponding positive effects on achievement or attitudes (Cole & Glass, 1977; McLaughlin, 1971; and Pine, 1980).

Much of the early attention to needs centered on Tyler's (1949) model for curriculum development. This model in turn focused attention on the importance of understanding a person's perceived or "felt" needs as a starting point for adult learning activities (Atwood, 1967; Hiemstra & Long, 1974; Knowles, 1980; Knox, 1968; McMahon, 1970). The Tyler model, the importance of felt needs, and the subsequent use of behavioral objectives (Mager, 1962) based on such needs served educators of adults in their instructional planning for many years.

Although behavioral, competency-based, and performance objectives are still discussed in the literature and are still used by many instructors as learning guides, their popularity has declined somewhat during the past ten years. Monette (1979) suggests one reason why use of the Tylerian approach has waned: "Tyler does not explicate a particular philosophy. Exactly what one's guiding philosophy is for stating objectives is extremely crucial. Stating objectives consistently with a philosophy can be as much a virtue as a sin depending, of course, upon what that philosophy is. Tyler's rationale offers neither the necessary criteria for prioritizing need statements nor a governing philosophy" (pp. 85–86).

Monette goes on to suggest that the writings of Paulo Freire (1970) provide a distinctive philosophical orientation and a means for taking personal values into account in designing instructional activities or educational programs. Apps (1979) also discusses the value of understanding Freire's work for interpreting needs information. Brookfield (1986) urges the determination of those critical incidents (often involving pressure or discomfort) in a person's life that may serve as a basis for subsequent educational programs.

243

Understanding a person's values or critical incidents is crucial to the individualizing process, where the personal values and experiences of a learner are examined in order to determine learning needs, plans, and approaches. Cheren (1983) refers to the roles of the instructor and of the learner in assessing needs as being codiagnostic in nature. Whatever it is called, devoting time to the diagnosis of needs is important. Knox (1977) suggests that up to one-fourth of the available instruction time can be devoted to initial activities such as assessing needs and translating needs into plans. Our experiences support this view.

The assessment of needs should take place throughout a learning experience, although many learners or instructors do not realize or take into account the normal changes that occur as a learner gains new knowledge. As demonstrated in earlier chapters, the individualizing process accommodates such changing needs in various ways.

PHYSICAL LEARNING ENVIRONMENT

One situation that every instructor faces is how to establish an environment in which adult learners can thrive. Because adults who enter a training setting, formal classroom, or self-directed learning activity have a variety of needs and expectations, the learning environment must be able to accommodate such variety. This section discusses some aspects of the physical environment, including such areas as anthropometry, ergonomics, proxemics, and synaesthetics, and suggests how an instructor can create an optimal setting for adult learning.

We recognize that an environment includes social, cultural, and psychological elements as well as physical features, but we want to concentrate on the latter in this section because such features are frequently overlooked, misunderstood, or taken for granted. James (1986) suggests that many learners believe that neither they nor their instructors have much control over their physical surroundings. It has been our experience, though, that it is almost always possible to shape the physical learning environment to some degree.

The concept of a physical environment has varied meanings. For example, Tagiuri (1968) discusses a similar concept in describing what he calls the organizational climate. Sommer (1970) calls this area "the ecology of study areas." James (1986) simply uses the term *environment* when referring to aspects of the physical setting. Knowles (1980) refers to some elements of the physical environment in discussing physical comfort, climate setting, and classroom arrangements. Knox (1986) talks about arranging facilities, equipment, and materials for adult instructional purposes. We place all these meanings under the physical environment label.

What We Know About the Physical Environment

A major goal of most instructors in facilitating learning is to use effective organizational arrangements and interaction processes. This goal, coupled with our growing knowledge about adults' interest in self-directed learning and the importance of increasing learner inputs, suggests the need to establish a learning

Note: The material in this section is adapted, in part, from Vosko and Hiemstra (1988).

climate that enhances learner commitment. Such environmental features as flexibility, attractiveness, and comfort, are very important in optimizing the learning that takes place.

White (1972) notes that "general estimates indicate that while about 75 percent of learning is accounted for by motivation, meaningfulness, and memory, the remaining 25 percent . . . is dependent upon the effects of the physical environment. In general, therefore, the success of adult education is dependent to a considerable extent upon the facilities and environment provided for the learner" (p. 1). Even if the impact is less than 25 percent, it still is worth understanding the physical environment and how to affect it in positive ways.

Unfortunately, questions about the physical environment for adult learning are often ignored by institutions and instructors and are passed over in the literature. For example: (1) adult learning activities often take place in spaces designed for other activities and age groups; (2) many adult learners and instructors are often not even aware that there are serious problems with the physical environment; (3) budgets for adult learning activities seldom include improvements for the physical environment; (4) many administrators and instructors do not feel it is their responsibility to ensure that learning environments are prepared adequately; (5) those who do feel responsible may not think themselves competent to prepare the settings properly; and (6) those who wish to do something about the environment do not know where to begin (Vosko & Hiemstra, 1988).

In fact, we have to look back three or more decades to find a time when adult educators were willing to give this area much attention. For example, in 1956, a commission on architecture in the United States published a document (Adult Education Association, 1956) that contained photographs and floor plans depicting several buildings constructed to accommodate adult learning (Adult Education Association of the U.S.A., 1956). Another commission document reported on a national conference on architecture for adult education (Hunsaker & Pierce, 1958), and a summary of a national survey on physical facilities was produced (Clark, 1958). About the same time, the New York State Education Department (1958) produced a report on the facilities and environmental needs of adults for use by educational planners and architects. In 1960, the same education department produced another report describing various educational programs for adults and several corresponding needs for school plants. Community education specialists have long urged that community school facilities be equipped with special rooms and furnishings that will be acceptable for adult as well as nonadult uses (Educational Facilities Laboratories, 1979; Hiemstra, 1985a).

Another study examined the inadequacy of adult learning in the United States: "To a very large degree adult education procedures in America are still carried on in hand-me-down or makeshift surroundings, an environment so primitive and meager that the creative imagination of the user is almost completely inhibited" (Becker, 1960, p. 156). Fulton (1988b) describes a few other efforts since 1960 that in some way take the physical environment into account. The expansion of community education, community colleges, and organizational training efforts in the past thirty years has helped to improve facilities in many settings, but numerous improvements still need to be made.

Knowles's publication of *The Modern Practice of Adult Education* in 1970 (revised in 1980) perhaps did more than any other work to focus attention on the actual setting in which adults learn and to help instructors and administrators begin thinking about needed improvements. At about the same time, White (1972) also began to call attention to the deficiencies of adult learning spaces: "Adults are often physically uncomfortable in child-size furniture, and they are psychologically uncomfortable in traditional classroom settings which emphasize the distance and inequality between teacher and student" (p. 3).

Kidd (1973) also made some suggestions about the environment for adult learning: "Luxury is not required, but comfort, excellent illumination without glare, absence from disturbing sounds or movements, provide a setting in which the chances for effective learning are increased" (p. 233). A few years later, the Council of Educational Facility Planners International (1976) published a guide for adapting educational facilities to adults: "With extended use of the school and the growth of the community/school programs, the age of the school users has expanded. The necessity for

accommodating persons of many ages has suggested that perhaps
the lighting standards recommended for learning environments
based on needs of children and younger adults should be reexam-
ined in light of an older group of users" (p. I-6).

As Fulton (1988a) notes, perhaps one of the most widely researched environmental issues is that of seating arrangements.
Becker, Sommer, Bee, and Oxley (1973), Koneya (1976), Sommer
(1967), and Stires (1980) are among those who have carried out such
research. However, this area and many other learning environment
features need far more attention than they have received in the educational literature to date. We need to understand much more
about such topics as access and egress from buildings and rooms
and the effects of color, light, acoustics, and temperature. Such
"hidden dimensions" (Hall, 1966) of instructional settings are frequently overlooked.

To facilitate research into the physical environment, we will
present some information about the four areas mentioned earlier:
(1) anthropometry, (2) ergonomics, (3) proxemics, and (4) synaesthetics. Much of the information actually comes from outside educational circles, but we have either applied the concepts in our
own instruction or discussed their potential implications with
colleagues.

Anthropometry

Adults have various learning needs and expectations. Adults
also come in different shapes and sizes. All these facts are relevant
for determining what kinds of spaces and furnishings are required
to meet their learning needs. We turn first to a discussion of anthropometry, which addresses the various human dimensions important
in the design of furnishings and equipment (McCormick, 1976).

For example, the comfort, size, and arrangement of chairs or
other seats are of considerable importance in the learning environment. Some adults have lower back problems that necessitate certain
kinds of seating support if discomfort is to be reduced. Some people
cannot sit for long periods of time in a chair without padding or
in one that prevents the frequent crossing of legs to relieve pressure
on knees or other joints. During a long lecture, any disturbing

features of a seat may reduce the listener's comprehension or involvement (Branton, 1969).

Croney (1981) notes that "sitting can be a tiring and painful business on a poorly designed seat. A good seat should allow for movement or a change in the sitting posture; there must be space for easement to maintain the best sitting posture for a lengthy period, but there should be enough control from the seating surfaces to effect the relief of body weight and give a sense of security" (p. 116).

Seat size and shape are problems in many learning sites. Adults often are required to sit in seats originally designed for much younger people. Even in training settings where only adults participate, esthetic criteria may have been the primary ones used to select seats. Damon, Stoudt, and McFarland (1966) believe that many chairs or other seats are simply too high. Generally, tall people can accommodate to low seats more easily than short people to high seats. They also believe that most seats should be flat rather than shaped because of the varied conformation of the human buttocks and perineal regions and because it is difficult to change positions or even cross one's legs in a shaped seat.

Huchingson (1981) has also studied the benefits of various types of seats. He believes that "seat pans, whether upholstered or solid material, should be slightly contoured at front without seam or ridge" (p. 273); otherwise, they might have pressure points that will create problems over time for some people. Branton (1969) has looked at similar problems in chairs and recommends that cushioning be used to relieve pressure points, spread the sitter's load over wide areas of the seat pan, and provide enough support so that the sitter does not slide into a slumped posture. Cushioning and fabric covering also help to absorb perspiration in warm rooms or humid climates.

Murrell notes it "is the requirement of good seating that the person sitting in a seat should be able to maintain a good posture which will not cause overstrain of any particular group of muscles . . . [and] cause fatigue" (1965, p. 143). Bennett (1977) believes it possible to provide seats satisfactory for all adults by making them (1) large enough to accommodate most people, (2) adjustable, or (3) in several sizes so that a proper one can be selected by a given person.

Certain kinds of furniture can even serve as hazards for people (Scheflen & Ashcraft, 1976). This includes furniture that is too heavy to be easily moved, furniture that may collapse if a person accidently leans on it the wrong way, or furniture with sharp edges on which a person can bump a leg or snag a piece of clothing.

A barrier-free environment, that is, one that provides easy access to any space to be used for learning, is a "must" for adult learners. However, many existing building interiors and furnishings inhibit mobility and accessibility for handicapped and elderly learners. The Council of Educational Facility Planners International (1976) offers criteria for the selection of furniture and equipment for "average" people (p. J-3) and "disabled individuals" (p. J-9).

Huchingson (1981) talks about writing arrangements and suggests that tables are better than chairs with the desk attached, even though the former take up more space. He notes that in small classes, slightly "oblique" tables "improve eye contact between students seated at one side" and that "round tables are optimal from this standpoint" (pp. 259-260). The best kinds of desks or chairs are those than can be arranged into circles (or squares) for large- or small-group discussions and that provide adequate space for writing or holding personal resource material. Knirk (1979) adds another piece of advice: "Don't forget the left-handed students" (p. 102).

Ergonomics

The term *ergonomics* refers to human factor engineering and to the design of spaces and objects (Burgess, 1981). The comfort of those who occupy a space or use a particular piece of equipment is what is involved here. Various kinds of research have led to designs based on what will be perceived by people to be pleasing. Sometimes research or design work must find solutions for complex situations. Fortunately, adults have considerable flexibility and can survive in many possible environmental conditions (Bennett, 1977).

Canter (1975, 1977), Heimsath (1977), and Krasner (1980) have also discussed design needs.

Most instructors will have to work with groups of various sizes, and many will want to use a variety of learning activities in their work with adults. Thus, employing ergonomic principles can be helpful in many ways. The size of the initial space for learning provides one example. How often have you found yourself assigned a space too small or too large for the participants with whom you must work? Farbstein and Kantrowitz (1978) describe the dilemma this way: "A space can be too small, cramping and hindering our performance. But a space can also be too large, leaving us feeling lost and insignificant or too far away to see and hear well. The best size spaces are those which are comfortable for the activities we perform in them" (p. 36).

What can you do about such a situation? By being more aware of concepts such as ergonomics, you can ensure that you are assigned a room of appropriate size or attempt to obtain a different room if the initial one does not meet the learners' needs or causes them discomfort. Huchingson (1981) also notes that room size and specifications should be determined by program activities. On the one hand, for example, there will be times when you want to foster a friendly or very informal setting. This may require a small, cozy room. You also may want to have additional rooms that can be used for discussion groups. On the other hand, "lack of a large enough meeting room to get a whole group together will [also] deter the development of a sense of community in that group" (Steele, 1973, p. 115). Here, too, in addition to providing seats and possibly tables that are designed for adult learners, you need to make sure that they can be easily moved for small- or large-group discussion activities.

The actual shape of a learning environment can also become an important factor as you work to create certain kinds of learning conditions or to promote certain kinds of relationships among learners. Narrow rooms or auditoriums with lecterns on a raised platform will work for some learning sites but not for others: "Sheer size and vertical relationships are not the only factors dominant in establishing a relationship between speaker and audience. Think of the plain shapes of auditori[ums]. If your purpose is simply to lecture to sponges, then adopt the narrow wedge or the straight row of seats. If, however, you seek discussion and interchange between members of your audience, then think of the semicircle or even the two-sided British House of Parliament, where your listeners are related to each other as well as to the speaker" (Will, 1958, p. 66).

Proxemics

One of the most significant contributions to the design and use of space has been in the area referred to as *proxemics,* a word that Hall (1966) associates with the "interrelated observations and theories of [people's] use of space as a specialized elaboration of culture" (p. 1). Hall (1974) urges us to think of an environment as more than just a physical setting. He describes several important proxemic features, including posture, body orientation, gestures, eye behavior, olfaction, thermal code, and seeking or avoiding touch.

Hall (1974) thinks that there are three aspects of space on which we should concentrate: fixed-feature, semifixed-feature, and informal. Fixed-feature space, such as a room full of seats attached to the floor, is a standard and often-used way to organize individuals and groups. Semifixed space, which may include movable desks, tables, and chairs, can be rearranged to suit the needs of an instructor or a group of users. These space features can encourage or discourage participation, depending on how well designed they are in terms of learning objectives.

Informal space is determined by what Hall calls the "distinct bounds" (1974, p. 112) that people create for themselves. Steele (1973) suggests that there is still another category, namely, pseudo-fixed-feature space. Space of this kind has components that can be easily moved or changed, but it also has a somewhat permanent look. Examples would be seminar rooms, conference rooms, and boardrooms. Thus, before choosing a physical setting for adult learning, you must first understand how different settings function and how the people that occupy a space define its boundaries.

Osmond (1959) has described two distinct kinds of settings, which he calls *sociofugal* and *sociopetal* settings, that have relevance in considering proxemic arrangements for adult learners. Sociofugal patterns are designed to discourage interaction among people; an example would be an auditorium or classroom where the chairs are arranged in rows. This kind of setting is used when instructors wish to create a focal point at the front of the room where they are standing and usually lecturing.

In contrast, the sociopetal setting orients learners toward a focal point. Usually people will be facing each other (for example, sitting in a large circle), so that interaction and conversation are facilitated. In a typical sociopetal learning pattern, chairs are arranged in a circular pattern or tables are joined together in a large square with chairs for learners around the outside edges. The sociopetal setting is often preferred for adult learning activities. However, Hall (1966) urges us to remember that "what is sociofugal in one culture may be sociopetal in another. . . . What is desirable is flexibility and congruence between design and function so that there is a variety of spaces, and people can be involved or not, as the occasion and mood demand" (p. 110). Canter (1977) notes, too, that in sociopetal settings discussion is encouraged, whereas in sociofugal settings the people in the front rows are more likely to interact with the instructor than are those in rows further back.

Sommer (1967) points out that most learning sites are "still designed with long, straight rows facing the instructor's desk" (p. 489), even though much of the literature supports square or U-shaped seating arrangements. He suggests that there "is no single best arrangement for all classroom tasks. For individual study, a sociofugal arrangement that minimizes eye contact may be preferred, while in small-group discussions a circular or sociopetal arrangement may be best" (p. 502).

Proxemic studies have also examined the location of occupants in space, including such features as distance, crowding, privacy, and territoriality (Aiello, 1976; Altman, 1977; Ashcraft, 1976; Haber, 1980; Insel & Lindgren, 1978; Pastalan, 1970; Vosko, 1985). For example, in adult learning activities where emphasis is placed on group interaction, the distance between participants or their notions about what is their own "territory" could influence the nature of human interactions (Edney, 1976; Henley, 1977). We have observed this in the "herd" instincts of most learners, who return to the very same seats meeting after meeting and may become frustrated or angry if someone intrudes on this "personal" space or territory. Of course, some of these learners simply wish to join friends from prior courses, so the instructor must be sensitive to this in that rearrangements of groups or seating orders could have negative effects.

Even though some learners do select seats because of a herd instinct, the desire to be with friends, or, perhaps more simply, out of habit (Jones, 1975), Steele (1973) suggests that certain settings create status distinctions among occupants: "The structure of a classroom in which the teacher's desk faces the students speaks clearly about how the system expects the student to see [himself or herself]—one of the herd, nonspecial, and having no identity when compared with the teacher, who has a unique, and often raised, place at the front of the room" (p. 51).

Fisher and Byrne (1975) even believe that there are gender differences in the way space is defended. Levanthal, Lipshultz, and Chiodo (1978) also found that "in social settings, opposite-sex pairs selected a side-by-side seating arrangement while [same] sex pairs, especially males, preferred to sit across from one another. In nonsocial settings, individuals selected the side-by-side seating arrangements regardless of sex" (p. 21).

It is important to understand how distance can be influenced by cultural and social expectations. Vosko (1984) provides some guidelines on how important the actual distance between people is in facilitating or inhibiting interaction between the instructor and learners or between learners themselves. He describes eight distance zones and their impact on interaction, ranging from "intimate close" to "public far" (pp. 4–6).

Some adults also will select their location in the physical environment according to how they initially want to interact: "The specific distance chosen depends on the transaction: the relationships of the interacting individuals, how they feel and what they are doing" (Hall, 1966, p. 128). Thus, adults who wish to participate actively in the learning experience will choose locations that allow this. Sommer (1969) believes this suggests that "the relationship between location and participation must take individual choice (environmental preference) into account" (p. 115). Willis (1966) provides an example of the distance zones people establish according to various personal characteristics: "Speakers tend to stand [closer] to women than to men. Compared with men, women stand [closer] to good friends but further from those they describe as friends. Perhaps women tend to be more cautious until close relationships are established. Peers stand closer than do persons older than the listener. Strangers begin conversations at distances greater than that of acquaintances" (p. 222).

An instructor's sensitivity to the preferred location of various learners in educational settings is important for encouraging social contact and interaction. However, these same spaces can enable individuals to disengage themselves from the group if they wish. Altman (1975) offers some related suggestions for instructors: "We should attempt to design responsive environments which permit easy alteration between a state of separateness and a state of togetherness. If privacy has a shifting dialectic quality, we should offer people environments that can be responsive to their shifting desires for contact or absence of contact with others" (p. 107).

Birdwhistell (1970) believes that it is important that the physical setting facilitate a certain amount of mobility or body movement. Such mobility has important implications: "A facility which permits easy movement and a diffuse structure may promote the development of a positive self-concept" and a "freedom of mobility to avoid threatening situations" (Knirk, 1979, p. 23). Proshansky, Ittelson, and Rivlin (1976) also discuss the importance of freedom of choice in physical settings: "(a) A human being, in almost all instances and situations, is a knowledgeable and goal-directed organism; (b) a human being's attempts at need satisfaction always involve . . . [personal] interactions and exchanges with the physical environment; (c) in any situational context, the individual attempts to organize . . . [personal] physical environment so that it maximizes . . . freedom of choice" (pp. 171–172).

A distinction also needs to be made between so-called soft spaces and hard spaces. Hard architectural spaces are impermeable and do not encourage individual mobility or social contact. The sociofugal auditorium or training setting with chairs in rows, sometimes even anchored at the base to some structural support, is an example. Sommer (1974) thinks that such spaces are not very desirable for most adult learning activities. Soft settings are those that have considerable flexibility and allow furnishings to be moved around. Most sociopetal arrangements are "soft." One study of soft settings found that flexible furnishings and permeable surroundings enabled people to move from one location to another as desired or if the learning requirements, such as a small-group discussion, warranted it (Sommer & Olsen, 1980). This type of setting also produces a more relaxed social context for learning experiences.

The ability to move seats and to move freely within seats also has important implications for social interaction. Knirk (1979) encourages planners to "consider wheel and swivels, as they permit some shifting about—especially for high school students and adults" (p. 130). Steele (1973) believes that fixed furniture inhibits social interaction and suggests that rooms with seats "bolted to the floor" are good for maintenance but are "not very good for learning activities other than lectures" (p. 64). We are not suggesting that learners should be brought together just to enhance their social lives, but we agree with Steele and Jenks (1977) that personal growth can be stimulated in important ways other than intellectual if the movement of people in space is considered.

Synaesthetics

The physical setting affects human senses in a variety of ways. Colors can influence a person's mood; a room that is too warm can shorten one's attention span or reduce one's ability to focus. In addition, several senses may be simultaneously involved in our learning efforts, even though we may not be aware of it. The field of synaesthetics helps us to understand how the physical environment is perceived in a polysensory manner and how such perceptions affect learning (Andrews & Giordano, 1980; Marks, 1975; Merleau-Ponty, 1962). Synaesthetics is concerned with determining how learners can be helped to integrate several sensory experiences simultaneously.

Noise, for example, is an environmental factor that can adversely affect our auditory well-being. Wells (1981) talks about our living today in a much noisier world than our auditory system was ever designed to handle. At one time or another, most instructors have been assigned to training sites or classrooms that were next to a construction project, near a noisy lounge, or close to some other source of unwelcome sounds.

Knirk (1979) suggests that there are at least four components of noise in the learning situation that are worthy of our concern: (1) noise reduction (sound insulation qualities); (2) reverberation (liveliness or prolonged reflection of sound); (3) speech interference level (background or conflicting sounds); and (4) an articulation index (ability to recognize speech components).

We use several techniques for controlling internal sounds and preventing intrusive noise. One is to make sure that any learners with hearing difficulties are given their choice of seats. Another is to ensure that there are enough breakout rooms or areas available so that the conversations of one group do not impinge on those of another group. Closing windows and doors, moving in sound barriers, and using audio amplification are other means of coping with noise problems.

Appropriate lighting is also important. If a classroom or nearby exterior space is inadequately lighted, a person's feeling of well-being and ability to read learning materials or to take appropriate notes can be affected. When audiovisual aids are used, it usually is necessary to adjust the level of light so that any screen, monitor, or primary area of focus can be adequately observed from all parts of the room. The main point here is for instructors to ensure that the "quantity of illumination is sufficient for the task" (Murrell, 1965, p. 339) or to make any necessary adjustments if possible.

There also has been research aimed at understanding the differences between artificial and natural light sources. Some people believe that natural lighting (daylight) is better because it enhances color, texture, and even the atmosphere of a room (Caudill, Pena, & Kennon, 1978; Lam, 1977). Others believe that artificial lighting can be better controlled, reduces distractions, and usually is necessary for maximum usage of a space (Rasmussen, 1959; Sommer, 1974).

The problems created by glare have also been examined: "Two types of effect of overly bright and/or contrasting light sources are disability glare and discomfort glare. If a light source has sufficient illumination and is sufficiently close to the direction in which one is looking, it may reduce one's ability to see (disability). It may also produce a discomfort effect" (Bennett, 1977, p. 98). Huchingson (1981) cautions that direct lighting sources can create more glare, contrast problems, and debilitating shadows than indirect lighting sources that can be controlled.

We suggest that an instructor arrive at the training site or classroom early to check out the lighting both within and outside the setting, become acquainted with the means for adding or reducing lighting, check electrical outlets for audiovisual equipment, practice with audiovisual devices before using them, and even ask participants if any of them have special lighting needs.

The thermal conditions of a physical environment are also important. A room that is too warm or too cold will create various kinds of barriers for learners. Humans are in general highly adaptive creatures, but they cannot attend, perceive, or process information easily when the physical environment is too uncomfortable. Huchingson (1981) suggests that there are four major environmental factors that affect personal comfort: (1) temperature, (2) humidity, (3) air velocity, and (4) radiation from the sun or other sources. Most instructors can exert some control over these elements.

Personal comfort concerns can also affect learners in various ways. The cushioning and support provided by chairs can be crucial, especially if the learning session extends beyond forty or fifty minutes. The availability of refreshments in the room or proximity to refreshments outside the room is an important consideration for most learners, especially if they are to be involved in a learning activity for a long period of time. Allowing adequate time for breaks is usually necessary.

Colors, too, can affect the human senses, convey meaning, and produce a pleasant atmosphere (Albers, 1968; Birren, 1978; Itten, 1970). Murrell (1965) suggests that blues, greens, and greys (the cooler colors) encourage passivity and create a sense of coldness. But warm colors or light pastels, such as reds and yellows, "tend to give a sense of warmth and an advancing effect" (p. 337). Some researchers also believe that the presence or absence of decorations is important to polysensory learning (Croney, 1981; Henley, 1977).

Instructors may initially seem powerless to affect such things as the lavatory's location, the type of room decorations available, or the color scheme chosen for a room. However, if such features become barriers to learning, then it may be mandatory for the instructor to attempt to make changes that might improve the physical environment.

Analyzing the Physical Environment

There are a number of questions that can be raised in thinking about the physical setting. What is the optimal physical environment for effective adult learning? What kinds of characteristics should such a setting possess? What kinds of decisions about the environment should be the responsibility of an instructor? What steps can administrators and even learners take to ensure that the environment for learning is as effective as possible?

The preceding material has suggested some answers to these and related questions. Learners also should be asked if they have any special needs related to the environment. Is it possible to satisfy everyone's needs? Probably not! But it is possible to honor adults as sources of information, to learn about some of their needs, and then to try to fill these needs as fully as possible.

Another important practice is to conduct formative evaluation throughout a learning experience. For example, a continual assessment of the environment might reveal that some seats are simply too small or uncomfortable for the type of learning activities being pursued, and efforts could be made to find alternative seats. Again, if certain people are having problems hearing the instructor or other learners, then they could be moved to more appropriate locations in the room.

Such suggestions are not the final answers to questions about the physical environment, nor do they necessarily provide the best possible advice for managing the physical components within the learning environment. Each instructor's personality, preferred instructional techniques, and institutional constraints need to be matched with the unique characteristics of each group of learners to ensure success in the individualized setting.

References

Adult Education Association of the U.S.A. (1956). *Architecture for adult education.* Washington, DC: Adult Education Association of the U.S.A., Commission on Architecture.

Aiello, J. R. (1976). *Effects of episodic crowding: A developmental perspective.* Paper read at the annual meeting of the Eastern Psychological Association, New York. (ERIC Document Reproduction Service No. ED 128 239)

Aker, G. F. (1976). *The learning facilitator.* Paper presented at the World Conference on Adult Education and Development, Dar es Salaam, Tanzania.

Albers, J. (1968). *Interaction of color.* New Haven, CT: Yale University Press.

Alpaugh, P. K., Renner, V. J., & Birren, J. E. (1976). Age and creativity: Implications for education and teachers. *Educational Gerontology, 1,* 17–40.

Altman, I. (1975). *The environment and social behavior.* Pacific Grove, CA: Brooks/Cole.

Altman, I. (1977). *Human behavior and environment: Advances in theory and research.* New York: Plenum.

American Medical Association. (1971). *Peer review manual.* New York: American Medical Association.

Anderson, M. L., & Lindeman, E. C. (1927). *Education through experience.* New York: Workers Education Bureau.

Andrews, M., & Giordano, O. C. (1980). *Sensory learning at Syracuse University.* Syracuse, NY: Syracuse University Press.

Apps, J. W. (1979). *Problems in continuing education.* New York: McGraw-Hill.

Apps, J. W. (1981). *The adult learner on campus.* Chicago: Follett.

Arenberg, D. (1976). *Changes with age in learning and memory.* Paper presented at annual convention of the American Psychological Association, Washington, DC. (ERIC Document Reproduction Service No. ED 137 665)

Arenberg, D. (1977). The effects of auditory augmentation on visual retention of young and old subjects. *Journal of Gerontology, 32,* 192-195.

Arenberg, D., & Robertson-Tchabo, E. A. (1977). Learning and aging. In J. E. Birren & K. W. Schaie (Eds.), *Handbook of the psychology of aging.* New York: Van Nostrand Reinhold.

Ashcraft, N. (1976). *People space: The making and breaking of human boundaries.* New York: Anchor Press.

Atwood, H. M. (1967). Diagnostic procedure in adult education. *Community Teamwork, 19,* 2-4.

Avakian, A. N. (1974). Writing a learning contract. In D. W. Vermilye (Ed.), *Lifelong learners—A new clientele for higher education: Current Issues in Higher Education* (pp. 50-56). San Francisco: Jossey-Bass.

Bauer, B. A. (1985). Self-directed learning in a graduate adult education program. In S. Brookfield (Ed.), *Self-directed learning: From theory to practice* (New Directions for Continuing Education, no. 25, pp. 41-50). San Francisco: Jossey-Bass.

Baum, J. (1978). *An exploration of widowhood: Implications for adult educators.* (ERIC Document Reproduction Service No. ED 157 989)

Becker, F., Sommer, R., Bee, J., & Oxley, B. (1973). College classroom ecology. *Sociometry, 36,* 514-525.

Becker, J. (1960). Architecture for Adult Education. In M. S. Knowles (Ed.), *Handbook of adult education in the United States.* Washington, DC: Adult Education Association of the U.S.A.

Bennett, C. (1977). *Spaces for people.* Englewood Cliffs, NJ: Prentice-Hall.

Bennett, E. S., & Eklund, S. J. (1983a). Vision changes, intelligence, and aging: Part 1. *Educational Gerontology, 9,* 255-278.

Bennett, E. S., & Eklund, S. J. (1983b). Vision changes, intelligence, and aging: Part 2. *Educational Gerontology, 9,* 435-442.

Birdwhistell, R. (1970). *Kinesics and context.* Philadelphia: University of Pennsylvania Press.

Birren, F. (1978). *Color and human response.* New York: Van Nostrand.

Blanchard-Fields, F. (1986). Attributional processes in adult development. *Educational Gerontology, 12,* 291-300.

Bolton, E. B. (1978). Cognitive and noncognitive factors that affect learning in older adults and their implications for instruction. *Educational Gerontology, 3,* 331-344.

Bonham, L. A. (1988a). Learning style use: In need of perspective. *Lifelong Learning: An Omnibus of Practice and Research, 11* (5), 14-17, 19.

Bonham, L. A. (1988b). Learning style instruments: Let the buyer beware. *Lifelong Learning: An Omnibus of Practice and Research, 11* (6), 12-16.

Botwinick, J. (1973). *Aging and behavior: A comprehensive integration of research findings.* New York: Springer.

Botwinick, J. (1978). *Aging and behavior* (2nd ed.). New York: Springer.

Brackhaus, B. (1984). Needs assessment in adult education: Its problems and prospects. *Adult Education Quarterly, 34,* 233-239.

Branton, P. (1969). Behavior, body mechanics, and discomfort. *Ergonomics, 12,* 316-327.

Brightman, S. (1984). Adult education town, USA. *Adult and Continuing Education Today, 14,* 1-2.

Brockett, R. (1983). Facilitator roles and skills. *Lifelong Learning: The Adult Years, 6* (5), 7-9.

Brockett, R. G. (1984). Self-directed learning readiness and life satisfaction among older adults. (Doctoral dissertation, Syracuse University, 1982.) *Dissertation Abstracts International, 44,* 42A.

Brockett, R. G. (1985a). Methodological and substantive issues in the measurement of self-directed learning readiness. *Adult Education Quarterly, 36,* 15-24.

Brockett, R. G. (1985b). The relationship between self-directed learning readiness and life satisfaction among older adults. *Adult Education Quarterly, 35,* 210–219.

Brockett, R. G. (1988). Ethics and the adult educator. In R. G. Brockett (Ed.), *Ethical issues in adult education* (pp. 1–16). New York: Teachers College Press.

Brockett, R. G., & Hiemstra, R. (1985). Bridging the theory-practice gap in self-directed learning. In S. Brookfield (Ed.), *Self-directed learning: From theory to practice* (New Directions for Continuing Education, no. 25, pp. 31–40). San Francisco: Jossey-Bass.

Brockett, R. G., & Hiemstra, R. (forthcoming). *Self-direction in adult learning: Perspectives on theory, research, and practice.* London: Routledge.

Brookfield, S. (1984a). *Adult learners, adult education and the community.* New York: Teachers College Press.

Brookfield, S. (1984b). The contribution of Eduard Lindeman to the development of theory and philosophy in adult education. *Adult Education, 34,* 185–196.

Brookfield, S. (Ed.). (1985). *Self-directed learning: From theory to practice* (New Directions for Continuing Education, no. 25). San Francisco: Jossey-Bass.

Brookfield, S. (1986). *Understanding and facilitating adult learning: A comprehensive analysis of principles and effective practices.* San Francisco: Jossey-Bass.

Brookfield, S. D. (1987). *Developing critical thinkers: Challenging adults to explore alternative ways of thinking and acting.* San Francisco: Jossey-Bass.

Brookfield, S. (1988). Conceptual, methodological and practical ambiguities in self-directed learning. In H. B. Long & Associates, *Self-directed learning: Application & theory* (pp. 11–38). Athens: University of Georgia, Adult Education Department.

Brown, D. (1982). Rehabilitating the learning disabled adult. *American Rehabilitation, 20,* 189–192.

Brundage, D. H., & MacKeracher, D. (1980). *Adult learning principles and their application to program planning.* Toronto: Ministry of Education, Ontario.

Burgess, J. H. (1981). *Human factors in built environments.* Newtonville, MA: Environmental and Design Research Center.

Cabell, H. W. (1986). Learning contracts and the personal computer. In B. Heermann (Ed.), *Personal computers and the adult learner* (New Directions for Continuing Education, no. 29, pp. 57-65). San Francisco: Jossey-Bass.

Caffarella, R. S. (1982). The learning plan format: A technique for incorporating the concept of learning how to learn into formal courses and workshops. *Proceedings of the Lifelong Learning Research Conference* (pp. 45-49). University of Maryland, College Park.

Caffarella, R. S. (1983). Fostering self-directed learning in post-secondary education: The use of learning contracts. *Lifelong Learning: An Omnibus of Practice and Research, 7* (3), 7-10, 25, 26.

Caffarella, R. S. (1988). Ethical dilemmas in the teaching of adults. In R. G. Brockett (Ed.), *Ethical issues in adult education* (pp. 103-117). New York: Teachers College Press.

Caffarella, R. S., & Caffarella, E. P. (1986). Self-directedness and learning contracts in adult education. *Adult Education Quarterly, 36,* 226-234.

Caffarella, R., & O'Donnell, J. M. (1988). Research in self-directed learning: Past, present and future trends. In H. B. Long & Associates, *Self-directed learning: Application & theory* (pp. 39-61). Athens: University of Georgia, Adult Education Department.

Calhoun, R. D., & Gounard, B. R. (1979). Meaningfulness, presentation rate, list length, and age in elderly adults' paired-associate learning. *Educational Gerontology, 4,* 49-56.

Camp, C. J. (Ed.). (1986). Social and personality aspects of adult cognitive development (Special issue). *Educational Gerontology, 12.*

Camp, C. J., Markley, R. P., & Kramer, J. J. (1983). Spontaneous use of mnemonics by elderly individuals. *Educational Gerontology, 9,* 57-72.

Canestrari, R. E., Jr. (1963). Paced and self-paced learning in young and elderly adults. *Journal of Gerontology, 18,* 165-168.

Canestrari, R. E., Jr. (1968). Age changes in acquisition. In G. A. Talland (Ed.), *Human aging and behavior.* New York: Academic Press.

Canfield, A. A., & Lafferty, J. C. (1974). *Learning styles inventory.* Birmingham, MI: Humanics Media.

Canter, D. (1975). *Psychology for architects.* New York: Wiley.

Canter, D. (1977). *The psychology of place.* New York: St. Martin's Press.

Carpenter, W. L. (1967). *The relationship between age and information-processing capacity and age and channel capacity of adults.* Unpublished doctoral dissertation, Florida State University, Tallahassee.

Carrier, C. A. (1987). Computers in adult learning outside the classroom. In J. A. Niemi & D. D. Gooler (Eds.), *Technologies for learning outside the classroom* (New Directions for Continuing Education, no. 34, pp. 51–62). San Francisco: Jossey-Bass.

Cattell, R. B. (1963). Theory of fluid and crystallized intelligence: A critical experiment. *Journal of Educational Psychology, 54,* 1–22.

Cattell, R. B. (1968). Fluid and crystallized intelligence. *Psychology Today, 3,* 56–62.

Caudill, W. W., Pena, W. M., & Kennon, P. (1978). *Architecture and you.* New York: Watson-Guptill.

Cavanaugh, J. C., & Murphy, N. Z. (1986). Personality and metamemory correlates of memory performance in younger and older adults. *Educational Gerontology, 12,* 385–394.

Centra, J. A. (1979). *Determining faculty effectiveness: Assessing teaching, research, and service for personnel decisions and improvements.* San Francisco: Jossey-Bass.

Cervero, R. M. (1988). *Effective continuing education for professionals.* San Francisco: Jossey-Bass.

Charles, D. C. (1983). Adapting materials use to physical and psychological changes in older learners. In J. P. Wilson (Ed.), *Materials for teaching adults: Selection, development, and use* (New Directions for Continuing Education, no. 17, pp. 77–84). San Francisco: Jossey-Bass.

Chene, A. (1983). The concept of autonomy in adult education: A philosophical discussion. *Adult Education Quarterly, 1,* 38–47.

Cheren, M. (1983). Helping learners achieve greater self-direction. In R. M. Smith (Ed.), *Helping adults learn how to learn* (New Directions for Continuing Education, no. 19, pp. 23–38). San Francisco: Jossey-Bass.

Chickering, A. W. (1977). Evaluation in the context of contract learning. *Journal of Personalized Instruction, 2* (2), 96–100.

Christensen, R. S. (1981). Dear diary—a learning tool for adults. *Lifelong Learning: The Adult Years, 5* (2), 4–5, 23.

Clark, C. H. (1980). *Idea management.* New York: Amacon.

Clark, H. E. (1958). *Summary of a survey report on physical facilities for adult education.* Lafayette, IN: Purdue University, Division of Adult Education.

Cole, J. W., & Glass, J. C., Jr. (1977). The effects of adult student participation in program planning on achievement, retention, and attitudes. *Adult Education, 27,* 75–88.

Conti, G. J., & Welborn, R. B. (1987). The interaction of teaching style and learning style on traditional and nontraditional learners. *Proceedings of the 28th Annual Adult Education Research Conference* (pp. 49–54). University of Wyoming, Conferences and Institutes, Laramie.

Cooper, S. S. (1980). *Self-directed learning in nursing.* Wakefield, MA: Nursing Resources.

Council of Educational Facility Planners International. (1976). *Guide for planning educational facilities.* Columbus, OH: Council of Educational Facility Planners International.

Craik, F.I.M. (1977). Age differences in human memory. In J. E. Birren & K. W. Schaie (Eds.), *Handbook of the psychology of aging.* New York: Van Nostrand Reinhold.

Croney, J. (1981). *Anthropometry for designers.* New York: Van Nostrand Reinhold.

Cropley, A. J. (1980). *Towards a system of lifelong education.* Oxford: Pergamon Press.

Cross, K. P. (1977). *A critical review of state and national studies of the needs and interests of adult learners.* Paper presented at the NIE Invitational Conference, Reston, VA. (ERIC Document Reproduction Service No. ED 169 394)

Cross, K. P. (1981). *Adults as learners: Increasing participation and facilitating learning.* San Francisco: Jossey-Bass.

Cunningham, W. R., Clayton, V., & Overton, W. (1975). Fluid and crystallized intelligence in young adulthood and old age. *Journal of Gerontology, 30* (2), 53–55.

Curtis, J. A. (1979). Instructional television fixed service: A most valuable educational resource. In J. A. Curtis & J. M. Biedenback (Eds.), *Educational tele-communications delivery systems*. Washington, DC: American Society for Engineering Education.

Daily, A. (1982). The community college as a resource for retarded adults: A working model. *Lifelong Learning: The Adult Years, 6* (2), 10-11, 3.

Daloz, L. A. (1986). *Effective teaching and mentoring: Realizing the transformational power of adult learning experiences*. San Francisco: Jossey-Bass.

Damon, A., Stoudt, H., & McFarland, R. (1966). *The human body in equipment design*. Cambridge, MA: Harvard University Press.

Darkenwald, G. G., & Merriam, S. B. (1982). *Adult education: Foundations of practice*. New York: Harper & Row.

Davenport, J., & Davenport, J. A. (1985). A chronology and analysis of the andragogy debate. *Adult Education Quarterly, 35,* 152-159.

Davis, B.R.H., & Marlowe, C. L. (1986). The computer as a networking and information resource for adult learners. In B. Heermann (Ed.), *Personal computers and the adult learner* (New Directions for Continuing Education, no. 29, pp. 89-94). San Francisco: Jossey-Bass.

Davis, R. H., & Miller, R. V. (1983). The acquisition of specialized information by older adults through utilization of new telecommunications technology. *Educational Gerontology, 9,* 217-232.

Dean, G. J. (1988). Providing effective career counseling for adult learners. *Lifelong Learning: An Omnibus of Practice and Research, 12* (1), 4-7.

Delbecq, A. (1975). *Group techniques for program planning: A guide to nominal groups*. Glenview, IL: Scott Foresman.

Dewey, J. (1938). *Experience and education*. New York: Macmillan.

Dewey, J. (1956). *Philosophy of education*. Paterson, NJ: Littlefield, Adams.

Dickinson, G. (1973). *Teaching adults: A handbook for instructors*. Toronto: New Press.

DiSilvestro, F. R. (Ed.). (1981). *Advising and counseling adult learners* (New Directions for Continuing Education, no. 10). San Francisco: Jossey-Bass.

Dorsey, O. L., & Pierson, M. J. (1984). A descriptive study of adult learning styles in a nontraditional education program. *Lifelong Learning: An Omnibus of Practice and Research, 7* (8), 8.

Draves, W. A. (1984). *How to teach adults.* Manhattan, KS: Learning Resources Network.

Dressel, P. L., & Thompson, M. M. (1973). *Independent study: A new interpretation of concepts, practices, and problems.* San Francisco: Jossey-Bass.

Drucker, P. F. (1974). *Management.* New York: Harper & Row.

Dunn, R., Dunn, K., & Price, G. E. (1981). *Learning style inventory manual.* Lawrence, KS: Price Systems.

Eble, K. E. (1979). *The craft of teaching: A guide to mastering the professor's art.* San Francisco: Jossey-Bass.

Eble, K. E. (1983). *The aims of college teaching.* San Francisco: Jossey-Bass.

Edney, J. (1976). Human territories comment on functional properties. *Environment and Behavior, 8,* 31–47.

Educational Facilities Laboratories. (1979). *Facility issues in community school centers* (Booklet no. 4). New York: Educational Facilities Laboratories.

Eisdorfer, C. (1965). Verbal learning and response time in the aged. *Journal of Genetic Psychology, 107,* 15–22.

Elbow, P. (1973). *Writing without teachers.* London: Oxford University Press.

Elbow, P. (1981). *Writing with power: Techniques for mastering the writing process.* New York: Oxford University Press.

Elias, J. L., & Merriam, S. (1980). *Philosophical foundations of adult education.* Huntington, NY: Krieger.

Ericksen, S. C. (1984). *The essence of good teaching: Helping students learn and remember what they learn.* San Francisco: Jossey-Bass.

Estrin, H. R. (1986). Life satisfaction and participation in learning activities among widows. (Doctoral dissertation, Syracuse University, 1985.) *Dissertation Abstracts International, 46,* 3852A.

Evans, N. (1985). *Post-education society: Recognizing adults as learners.* London: Croom Helm.

Eysenck, M. W. (1975). Retrieval from semantic memory as a function of age. *Journal of Gerontology, 30,* 174–180.

Farbstein, J., & Kantrowitz, M. (1978). *People in places: Experienc-*

ing, using, and changing the built environment. Englewood Cliffs, NJ: Prentice-Hall.

Fettgather, R. (1989). "Be an adult!": A hidden curriculum in life skills instruction for retarded students? *Lifelong Learning: An Omnibus of Practice and Research, 12* (5), 4-5, 10.

Field, L. (1989). An investigation into the structure, validity, and reliability of Guglielmino's Self-Directed Learning Scale. *Adult Education Quarterly, 39,* 125-139.

Fisher, J. C. (1986). Participation in educational activities by active older adults. *Adult Education Quarterly, 36,* 202-210.

Fisher, J. D., & Byrne, D. (1975). Too close for comfort: Sex differences in response to invasions of personal space. *Journal of Personality and Social Psychology, 33,* 15-21.

Florini, B. M. (1989). *Computer conferencing: A technology for adult education* (Technical Report no. 1). Syracuse, NY: Syracuse University Kellogg Project.

Fluke, D. W. (Ed.). (1988, February). The learning disabled adult learner and adult basic education. *What's the Buzz?* (Pennsylvania's Adult Basic Education Dissemination Newsletter), *7* (6), 1-2.

Fowles, D. G. (Compiler). (1984). *A profile of older Americans.* Washington, DC: American Association of Retired Persons, Program Resources Department.

Fox, R. D. (1984). Learning styles and instructional preferences in continuing education for professionals: A validity study of the LSI. *Adult Education Quarterly, 35,* 72-85.

Fozard, J. L., & Nuttall, R. L. (1971). GATB scores for men differing in age and socio-economic status. *Journal of Applied Psychology, 55* (4), 372-379.

Franz, J. B. (1983). Cognitive development and career retraining in older adults. *Educational Gerontology, 9,* 443-462.

Freire, P. (1970). *Pedagogy of the oppressed.* New York: Herder and Herder.

Freund, J. S., & Witte, K. L. (1976). Paired-associate transfer: Age of subjects, anticipation interval, association value, and paradigm. *American Journal of Psychology, 89,* 695-705.

Fulton, R. D. (1988a, August). *An overview of the research on phys-*

ical learning environments. Paper presented at annual meeting of the Montana State University Kellogg Fellows, Big Sky, MT.

Fulton, R. D. (1988b). The physical environment in adult learning. *Adult Literacy and Basic Education, 12* (1), 48–55.

Galbraith, M. W., & James, W. B. (1984). Assessment of dominant perceptual learning styles of older adults. *Educational Gerontology, 10,* 449–458.

George, L. (1986). Life satisfaction in later life. *Generations, 10* (3), 5–8.

Gibbons, M., Bailey, A., Comeau, P., Schmuck, J., Seymour, S., & Wallace, D. (1980). Toward a theory of self-directed learning: A study of experts without formal training. *Journal of Humanistic Psychology, 20* (2), 41–45.

Glynn, S. M., & Muth, K. D. (1979). Text-learning capabilities of older adults. *Educational Gerontology, 4,* 253–269.

Goldberg, J. C. (1980). Counseling the adult learner: A selected review of the literature. *Adult Education, 30,* 67–81.

Gonda, J., Quayhagen, M., & Schaie, K. W. (1981). Education, task meaningfulness, and cognitive performance in young-old and old-old adults. *Educational Gerontology, 7,* 151, 158.

Goodrow, B. A. (1975). Limiting factors in reducing participation in older adult learning opportunities. *Gerontologist, 15,* 418–422.

Gordon, R. D. (1974). *Learning process in aging and adult education.* (ERIC Document Reproduction Service No. ED 106 734)

Goulet, L. R. (1970). *General and specific interference factors in retention.* Paper presented at the American Psychological Association Convention, Miami Beach, FL. (ERIC Document Reproduction Service No. ED 044 710)

Gounard, B. R., & Hulicka, I. M. (1977). Maximizing learning efficiency in later adulthood: A cognitive problem-solving approach. *Educational Gerontology, 2,* 417–427.

Graney, M. J., & Hays, W. C. (1976). Senior students: Higher education after age 62. *Educational Gerontology, 1,* 343–360.

Gregorc, A. F. (1979). Learning/teaching styles: Their nature and effects. In J. Keefe (Ed.), *Student learning styles: Diagnosing and prescribing programs* (pp. 19–26). Reston, VA: National Association of Secondary School Principals.

Griffin, C. (1983). *Curriculum theory in adult and lifelong education.* London: Croom Helm.

Gross, R. (1977). *The lifelong learner.* New York: Simon & Schuster.

Gross, R. (1979). *Future directions for open learning.* Washington, DC: U.S. Government Printing Office.

Gross, R. (1982a). *The independent scholar's handbook.* Reading, MA: Addison-Wesley.

Gross, R. (1982b). *Invitation to lifelong learning.* Chicago: Follett.

Gueulette, D. G. (1982). Learning in a wired school: Home telecommunications-computer centers. In D. G. Gueulette (Ed.), *Microcomputers for adult learning: Potentials and perils* (pp. 172–186). Chicago: Follett.

Guglielmino, L. M. (1977). Development of the self-directed learning readiness scale. (Doctoral dissertation, University of Georgia, 1977). *Dissertation Abstracts International, 38,* 6467A.

Guglielmino, L. M., & Guglielmino, P. J. (1988). Self-directed learning in business and industry: An information age imperative. In H. B. Long & Associates, *Self-directed learning: Application & theory* (pp. 125–148). Athens: University of Georgia, Adult Education Department.

Guttman, R. (1984). Performance on eight spatial ability tests as a function of age and education. *Educational Gerontology, 10,* 1–12.

Haase, A.M.B., Robinson, R. D., & Beach, R. (1979). Teaching the aged reader: Issues and strategies. *Educational Gerontology, 4,* 229–238.

Haber, G. M. (1980). Territorial invasion in the classroom: Invadee response. *Environment and Behavior, 12,* 17–31.

Hadley, H. N. (1975). *Development of an instrument to determine adult educators' orientation: Andragogical or pedagogical.* Unpublished doctoral dissertation, Boston University, Boston.

Hall, E. (1966). *The hidden dimension.* Garden City, NY: Doubleday.

Hall, E. (1974). *Handbook for proxemic research.* Washington, DC: Society for the Anthropology of Visual Communications.

Harasim, L. M. (1988). *On-line group learning/training method* (Technical Paper Number 7). Toronto: Educational Evaluation Centre, Ontario Institute for Studies in Education.

Harrison, A. F., & Bramson, R. M. (1982). *Styles of thinking*. New York: Doubleday.

Hauwiller, J. G., & Jennings, R. (1981). Counteracting age stereotyping with young school children. *Educational Gerontology, 7,* 183–190.

Havighurst, R. J. (1972). *Developmental tasks and education* (3rd ed.). New York: McKay.

Havighurst, R. J. (1976). Education through the adult life span. *Educational Gerontology, 1,* 41–51.

Hayslip, B., Jr., & Kennelly, K. J. (1985). Cognitive and noncognitive factors affecting learning among older adults. In D. B. Lumsden (Ed.), *The older adult as learner* (pp. 73–98). Washington, DC: Hemisphere Publishing.

Hebert, J. P., Jr. (Project Director). (1988). *Project Upgrade: Working with adults who have learning disabilities*. Manhattan, KS: Manhattan Adult Learning and Resource Center.

Heimsath, C. (1977). *Behavioral architecture*. New York: McGraw-Hill.

Heisel, M. A. (1985). Assessment of learning activity level in a group of black aged. *Adult Education Quarterly, 36,* 1–14.

Henley, N. M. (1977). *Body politics: Power, sex, and nonverbal communication*. Englewood Cliffs, NJ: Prentice-Hall.

Henry, N. J. (1989). *A qualitative study about perceptions of lifestyle and life satisfaction among older adults*. Unpublished doctoral dissertation, Syracuse University, Syracuse, NY.

Hiemstra, R. (1975). *The older adult and learning*. (ERIC Document Reproduction Service No. ED 117 371)

Hiemstra, R. (1976a). *Lifelong learning*. Lincoln, NE: Professional Educators Publications. (Reprinted in 1984 by HiTree Press, Baldwinsville, NY.)

Hiemstra, R. (1976b). The older adult's learning projects. *Educational Gerontology, 1,* 331–341.

Hiemstra, R. (1977-78). Instrumental and expressive learning: Some comparisons. *International Journal of Aging and Human Development, 8,* 161–168.

Hiemstra, R. (1979, March). *The older adult's learning needs*. Poster session presented at the Annual Adult Education Research Conference, Ann Arbor, MI.

Hiemstra, R. (1980a) Howard Yale McClusky: Adult education pioneer and statesman. *Lifelong Learning: The Adult Years, 4* (2), 5-7, 25.

Hiemstra, R. (1980b). *Policy recommendations related to self-directed adult learners* (CEP 1). Syracuse, New York: Syracuse University Printing Service. (ERIC Document Reproduction Service No. ED 193 529)

Hiemstra, R. (1980c). *Preparing human service practitioners to teach older adults* (Information Series No. 209). Columbus: Ohio State University, ERIC Clearinghouse for Adult, Career, and Vocational Education. (ERIC Document Reproduction Service No. ED 193 529)

Heimstra, R. (1981a). Adults as learners. In Z. W. Collins (Ed.), *Museums, adults and the humanities* (pp. 61-72). Washington, DC: American Association of Museums.

Hiemstra, R. (1981b). The contributions of Howard Yale McClusky to an evolving discipline of educational gerontology. *Educational Gerontology, 6,* 209-226.

Hiemstra, R. (1982a). The elderly learner: A naturalistic inquiry. *Proceedings of the 23rd Annual Adult Education Research Conference* (pp. 103-107). Adult and Continuing Education, University of Nebraska, Lincoln.

Hiemstra, R. (1982b). *Self-directed learning: Some implications for practice* (CEP 2). Syracuse, NY: Syracuse University Printing Service. (ERIC Document Reproduction Service No. ED 262 259)

Hiemstra, R. (1985a). *The educative community: Linking the community, education, and family.* Baldwinsville, NY: HiTree Press.

Hiemstra, R. (1985b). The older adult's learning projects. In D. B. Lumsden (Ed.), *The older adult as learner* (pp. 165-196). Washington, DC: Hemisphere Publishing.

Hiemstra, R. (1985c). *Self-directed adult learning: Some implications for facilitators* (CEP 3). Syracuse, NY: Syracuse University Printing Service (ERIC Document Reproduction Service No. ED 262 260)

Hiemstra, R. (1987a). Creating the future. In R. G. Brockett (Ed.), *Continuing education in the year 2000* (New Directions for Continuing Education, no. 36, pp. 3-14). San Francisco: Jossey-Bass.

Hiemstra, R. (1987b). Turning research on older persons into daily practice. *Perspectives on Aging, 16* (1), 17–19.

Hiemstra, R. (1988a). Self-directed learning: Individualizing instruction. In H. B. Long & Associates, *Self-directed learning: Application & theory* (pp. 99–124). Athens: University of Georgia, Adult Education Department.

Hiemstra, R. (1988b). Translating personal values and philosophy into practical action. In R. G. Brockett (Ed.), *Ethical issues in adult education* (pp. 178–194). New York: Teachers College Press.

Hiemstra, R., Goodman, M., Middlemiss, M. A., Vosko, R., & Ziegler, N. (1983). How older persons are portrayed in television advertising: Implications for educators. *Educational Gerontology, 9,* 111–122.

Hiemstra, R., & Long, R. (1974). A survey of "felt" versus "real" needs of physical therapists. *Adult Education, 24,* 270–279.

Highet, G. (1950). *The art of teaching.* New York: Vintage Books.

Highet, G. (1976). *The immortal profession.* New York: Weybright and Talley.

Hixson, L. E. (1968). *Formula for success: A step-by-step procedure for organizing a local institute of lifetime learning.* Washington, DC: National Retired Teachers Association. (ERIC Document Reproduction Service No. ED 028 366)

Holsti, O. R. (1968). Content analysis. In B. Lindsey & E. Aronson (Eds.), *The handbook of social psychology* (2nd ed.). Reading, MA: Addison-Wesley.

Holtzclaw, L. R. (1985). Adult learners' preferred learning styles, choice of courses, and subject areas for prior experiential learning credit. *Lifelong Learning: An Omnibus of Practice and Research, 8* (6) 23–27.

Hopkins, K. D., & Stanley, J. C. (1981). *Educational and psychological measurement and evaluation* (6th ed.). Englewood Cliffs, NJ: Prentice-Hall.

Horn, J. L. (1967). Intelligence: Why it grows, why it declines. *Transaction, 4,* 23–31.

Horn, J. L. (1970). Organization of data on life-span development of human abilities. In L. R. Goulet & P. B. Baltes (Eds.), *Life-*

span developmental psychology: Research and theory. New York: Academic Press.

Horn, J. L., & Cattell, R. B. (1966a). Age differences in primary mental ability factors. *Journal of Gerontology, 21,* 210–220.

Horn, J. L., & Cattell, R. B. (1966b). Refinement and test of the theory of fluid and crystallized intelligence. *Journal of Educational Psychology, 57,* 253–270.

Horn, R. E., & Cleaves, A. (Eds.). (1980). *The guide to simulation/ games for education and training* (4th ed.). Newbury Park, CA: Sage Publications.

Houle, C. O. (1961). *The inquiring mind.* Madison: University of Wisconsin Press.

Hruska, S. R., & Grasha, A. F. (1982). The Grasha-Reichmann Student Learning Style Scales 1982. In National Association of Secondary School Principals, *Student learning styles and brain behavior* (pp. 81–86). Reston, VA: National Association of Secondary School Principals.

Huchingson, R. D. (1981). *New horizons for human factors in design.* New York: McGraw-Hill.

Hulicka, I. M. (1967). Age difference in retention as a function of interference. *Journal of Gerontology, 22,* 180–184.

Hulicka, I. M., & Grossman, J. L. (1967). Age-group comparisons for the use of mediators in paired associate learning. *Journal of Gerontology, 22,* 46–51.

Hultsch, D. F. (1971). Adult age difference in free classification and free recall. *Developmental psychology, 4,* 338–342.

Hultsch, D. F. (1975). Adult age differences in retrieval: Trace-dependent and cue-dependent forgetting. *Developmental Psychology, 11,* 197–201.

Hultsch, D. F. (1977). Changing perspectives on basic research in adult learning and memory. *Educational Gerontology, 2,* 367–382.

Hunsaker, H. C., & Pierce, R. (Eds.). (1958). *Creating a climate for adult learning.* Washington, DC: The Commission on Architecture of the Adult Education Association of the U.S.A.

Hyman, H. (1970). *Interviewing in social research.* Chicago: University of Chicago Press.

Imel, S. (1986). *Adult education for the handicapped: Overview*

(ERIC Fact Sheet No. 23). Columbus: National Center for Research in Vocational Education, Ohio State University.

Insel, P. M., & Lindgren, H. C. (1978). *Too close for comfort: The psychology of crowding.* Englewood Cliffs, NJ: Prentice-Hall.

Itten, J. (1970). *The elements of color* (E. Van Hagen, Trans.). New York: Van Nostrand Reinhold.

James, J. M. (1986). *Instructor-generated load: An inquiry based on McClusky's concept of margin.* Unpublished doctoral dissertation, University of Wyoming, Laramie.

James, W. B., & Galbraith, M. W. (1985). Perceptual learning styles: Implications and techniques for the practitioner. *Lifelong Learning: An Omnibus of Practice and Research, 8* (4), 20–23.

Jarvis, P. (1984). Andragogy—a sign of the times. *Studies in the education of adults, 16* (October), 32–38.

Jarvis, P. (1985). *The sociology of adult & continuing education.* London: Croom Helm.

Johnson, K. A. (1987). Interactive video: The present and the promise. In J. A. Niemi & D. D. Gooler (Eds.), *Technologies for learning outside the classroom* (New Directions for Continuing Education, no. 34, pp. 29–40). San Francisco: Jossey-Bass.

Johnstone, J., & Rivera, R. (1965). *Volunteers for learning, a study of the educational pursuits of American adults.* National Opinion Research Center report. Hawthorne, NY: Aldine.

Jones, E. E. (1979). Adult education and the older adult. *Educational Gerontology, 4,* 349–354.

Jones, H. E., & Conrad, H. S. (1933). The growth and decline of intelligence: A study of a homogeneous group between the ages of ten and sixty. *Genetic Psychology Monographs, 13,* 223–298.

Jones, J. (1975). *Seating choice, status and impact on self-concept.* (ERIC Document Reproduction Service No. ED 143 047)

Jones, J. E. (1980). Teaching art to the elderly: Research and practice. *Educational Gerontology, 5,* 17–31.

Jordan, D. R. (1977). *Dyslexia in the classroom.* Columbus, OH: Merrill.

Jordan, D. R. (1988, February). Learning disabilities in adults. *What's the Buzz?* (Pennsylvania's Adult Basic Education Dissemination Newsletter), 7 (6), 3.

Joyce, B., & Weil, M. (1972). *Models of teaching.* Englewood Cliffs, NJ: Prentice-Hall.

Kasworm, C. E. (1978). Old dogs, children, and watermelon wine. *Educational Horizons, 56,* 200–205.

Kasworm, C. E. (1982). An exploratory study of the development of self-directed learning as an instructional/curriculum strategy. *Proceedings of the Lifelong Learning Research Conference* (pp. 125–129). University of Maryland, College Park.

Kasworm, C. E. (1983). An examination of self-directed learning contracts as an instructional strategy. *Innovative Higher Education, 8,* (1), 45–54.

Keefe, J. W. (Ed.). (1979). *Student learning styles: diagnosing and prescribing programs.* Reston, VA: National Association of Secondary School Principals.

Keinholz, A. (1984). *Styles of thinking: Towards a synthesis of the cognitive and neuropsychological research and its application for comparing students in architecture and medicine.* Unpublished master's thesis, Department of Educational Psychology, University of Calgary, Calgary, Alberta.

Kidd, J. R. (1973). *How adults learn.* Chicago: Association Press.

Kidd, J. R. (1976). Adult learning in the 1970s. In R. M. Smith (Ed.), *Adult learning: Issues and innovations.* Dekalb: Northern Illinois University, ERIC Clearinghouse in Career Education. Northern Illinois University.

Kidd, J. R. (1979). A nation of learners. *Convergence, 12* (1–2), 25–37.

Kinney, M. B. (1989). Elderhostel: Can it work at your institution? *Adult Learning, 1* (3), 21–24.

Knirk, F. (1979). *Designing productive learning environments.* Englewood Cliffs, NJ: Prentice-Hall.

Knoll, J. H. (1981). Professionalization in adult education in the Federal Republic of Germany, and the German Democratic Republic. In A. N. Charters & Associates, *Comparing adult education worldwide* (pp. 90–108). San Francisco: Jossey-Bass.

Knowles, M. S. (1960). Historical development of the adult education movement in the United States. In M. S. Knowles (Ed.), *Handbook of adult education in the United States* (pp. 7–28). Washington, DC: Adult Education Association of the U.S.A.

Knowles, M. S. (1975). *Self-directed learning*. New York: Association Press.

Knowles, M. S. (1980). *The modern practice of adult education* (rev. ed.). Chicago: Association Press.

Knowles, M. S. (1984). *The adult learner: A neglected species* (3rd ed.). Houston: Gulf Publishing.

Knowles, M. S. (1986). *Using learning contracts: Practical approaches to individualizing and structuring learning*. San Francisco: Jossey-Bass.

Knowles, M. S. (1989). *The making of an adult educator: An autobiographical journey*. San Francisco: Jossey-Bass.

Knowles, M. S., & Associates. (1984). *Andragogy in action: Applying modern principles of adult learning*. San Francisco: Jossey-Bass.

Knowlton, M. P. (1977). Liberal arts: The elderhostel plan for survival. *Educational Gerontology, 2*, 87–94.

Knox, A. B. (1968). *Critical appraisal of the needs of adults for educational experiences as a basis for program development* (mimeographed). New York: Teachers College, Columbia University.

Knox, A. B. (1977). *Adult development and learning: A handbook on individual growth and competence in the adult years*. San Francisco: Jossey-Bass.

Knox, A. B. (1980). Helping teachers help adults learn. In A. B. Knox (Ed.), *Teaching adults effectively* (New Directions for Continuing Education, no. 6, pp. 73–100). San Francisco: Jossey-Bass.

Knox, A. B. (1981). Emerging issues in counseling adult learners. In F. R. DiSilvestro (Ed.), *Advising and counseling adult learners* (New Directions for Continuing Education, no. 10, pp. 103–108). San Francisco: Jossey-Bass.

Knox, A. B. (1986). *Helping adults learn: A guide to planning, implementing, and conducting programs*. San Francisco: Jossey-Bass.

Kolb, D. A. (1976). *The Learning Style Inventory: Technical manual*. Boston: McBer.

Kolb, D. A. (1984). *Experiential learning: Experience as the source of learning and development.* Englewood Cliffs, NJ: Prentice-Hall.

Koneya, M. (1976). Location and interaction in row and column seating descriptors. *Environment and Behavior, 8,* 265–282.

Kooken, R. A., & Hayslip, B., Jr. (1984). The use of stress inoculation in the treatment of test anxiety in older students. *Educational Gerontology, 10,* 39–58.

Korhonen, L. J., & McCall, R. J. (1986). The interaction of learning style and learning environment on adult achievement. *Lifelong Learning: An Omnibus of Practice and Research, 10* (2), 21–23.

Kozol, J. (1985). *Illiterate America.* New York: Anchor-Doubleday.

Krasner, L. (Ed.). (1980). *Environmental design and human behavior: A psychology of the individual in society.* New York: Pergamon Press.

Kreitlow, B. W., & Associates. (1981). *Examining controversies in adult education.* San Francisco: Jossey-Bass.

Kuhlen, R. G. (1970). *Motivational changes during the adult years: Psychological background of adult education.* Syracuse, NY: Publications in Continuing Education.

Kulich, J. (1970). *An historical overview of the adult self-learner.* Paper presented at the Northwest Institute on Independent Study, University of British Columbia, Vancouver.

Labouvie-Vief, G. (1976). Toward optimizing cognitive competence in later life. *Educational Gerontology, 1,* 75–92.

Labouvie-Vief, G. (1977). Adult cognitive development: In search of alternative interpretations. *Merrill-Palmer Quarterly, 23,* 227–263.

Lam, W. (1977). *Perception and lighting as forgivers for architecture.* New York: McGraw-Hill.

Landers, K. (1989). *The Oddi Continuing Learning Inventory: An alternate measure of self-direction in learning.* Unpublished doctoral dissertation, Syracuse University, Syracuse, NY.

Langner, W. R. (Compiler). (1987). *Directory of resources for adults with disabilities.* Washington, DC: U.S. Department of Education, Office of Vocational and Adult Education, Division of Adult Education, U.S. Department of Education.

Lean, E. (1983, September). Learning disabled trainees: Finding and helping the "hidden handicapped." *Training and Development Journal*, 56–65.

Leclerc, G. J. (1985). Understanding the educational needs of older adults: A new approach. *Educational Gerontology, 11*, 137–144.

Leean, C., & Sisco, B. (1981). *Learning projects and self-planned learning efforts among undereducated adults in rural Vermont* (Final Report No. 99-1051). Washington, DC: National Institute of Education.

Lersten, K. C. (1974). *Some psychological aspects of aging: Implications for teaching and learning.* Paper presented at the annual conference of the Rocky Mountain Educational Research Association, Albuquerque, NM. (ERIC Document Reproduction Service No. ED 109 093)

Levanthal, G., Lipshultz, M., & Chiodo, A. (1978). Sex and setting effects on seating arrangements. *Journal of Psychology, 100*, 21–26.

Levinson, D. J. (1978). *The seasons of a man's life.* New York: Ballantine Books.

Lindeman, E. C. (1926). *The meaning of adult education.* New York: New Republic.

Lindquist, J. (1975). Strategies for contract learning. In D. W. Vermilye (Ed.), *Learner-centered reform* (pp. 75–89). San Francisco: Jossey-Bass.

Loesch, T., & Foley, R. (1988). Learning preference differences among adults in traditional and nontraditional baccalaureate programs. *Adult Education Quarterly, 38*, 224–233.

Loewenthal, N. H., Blackwelder, J., & Broomall, J. K. (1980). Correspondence instruction and the adult student. In A. B. Knox (Ed.), *Teaching adults effectively* (New Directions for Continuing Education, no. 6, pp. 33–41). San Francisco: Jossey-Bass.

Long, H. (1976). *Continuing education of adults in colonial America.* Syracuse, NY: Syracuse University Publications in Continuing Education.

Long, H. B. (1983). *Adult learning: Research and practice.* New York: Cambridge.

Long, H. B., & Associates. (1988). *Self-directed learning: Application & theory.* Athens: University of Georgia, Adult Education Department.

Long, R. W. (1972). *Continuing education for physical therapists in Nebraska: A survey of current practices and self-expressed needs with recommendations for program development.* Unpublished doctoral dissertation, University of Nebraska, Lincoln.

Lorge, I. (1963). The adult learner. In I. Lorge, H. Y. McClusky, G. E. Jensen, & W. Hallenbeck (Eds.), *Adult education: Theory and method* (pp. 1–9). Washington, DC: Adult Education Association of the U.S.A.

Mager, R. F. (1962). *Preparing instructional objectives.* Belmont, CA: Fearon.

Mager, R. F., & Piper, P. (1970). *Analyzing performance problems.* Belmont, CA: Fearon.

Main, K. (1979). The power-load-margin formula of Howard Y. McClusky as the basis for a model of teaching. *Adult Education, 30,* 19–33.

Marcus, E. E. (1978). Effects of age, sex, and status on perception of the utility of educational participation. *Educational Gerontology, 3,* 295–319.

Marks, L. (1975, June). Synaesthesia: The lucky people with the mixed-up senses. *Psychology Today,* 48–52.

Marton, F., Hounsell, D., & Entwistle, N. (1984). *The experience of learning.* Edinburgh: Scottish Academic Press.

Maxfield, D., & Smith, R. M. (1987). Learning to learn. In C. Klevins (Ed.), *Materials and methods in adult and continuing education* (pp. 278–284). Los Angeles: Klevins.

Mays, F., & Imel, S. (1984). *Adult learning disabilities: Overview* (ERIC Fact Sheet No. 9). Columbus: National Center for Research in Vocational Education, Ohio State University.

McClusky, H. Y. (1963). Course of the adult life span. In W. C. Hallenbeck (Ed.), *Psychology of adults.* Washington, DC: Adult Education Association of the U.S.A.

McClusky, H. Y. (1964). The relevance of psychology for adult education. In G. E. Jensen, A. A. Liveright, & W. Hallenbeck (Eds.), *Adult education: Outlines of an emerging field of university study* (pp. 155–176). Washington, DC: Adult Education Association of the U.S.A.

McClusky, H. Y. (1967). Adventure and the emerging roles of the adult education leader. *N.U.E.A. Spectator, 32* (5), 14–17, 27.

McClusky, H. Y. (1970). A dynamic approach to participation in community development. *Journal of Community Development Society, 1*, 25–32.

McClusky, H. Y. (1974). The coming of age of lifelong learning. *Journal of Research and Development in Education, 7* (4), 97–107.

McCormick, E. (1976). *Human factors in engineering and design.* New York: McGraw-Hill.

McKeachie, W. J. (1965). *Teaching tips: A guidebook for the beginning college teacher.* Ann Arbor, MI: Wahr.

McKeachie, W. J. (1986). *Teaching tips* (8th ed.). Lexington, MA: Heath.

McKinley, J. (1983). Training for effective collaborative learning. In R. M. Smith (Ed.), *Helping adults learn how to learn* (New Directions for Continuing Education, no. 19, pp. 13–22). San Francisco: Jossey-Bass.

McLaughlin, D. (1971). Participation of the adult learner in program planning. *Adult Education, 22*, 30–35.

McMahon, E. E. (1970). *Needs—of people and their communities—and the adult educator.* Washington, DC: Adult Education Association of the U.S.A.

Meierhenry, W. C. (1982). Microcomputers and adult education. In D. G. Gueulette (Ed.), *Microcomputers for adult learning: Potentials and perils* (pp. 11–27). Chicago: Follett.

Mergler, N. L., & Zandi, T. (1983). Adult age differences in speed and accuracy of matching verbal and pictorial signs. *Educational Gerontology, 9*, 73-86.

Merleau-Ponty, M. (1962). *The phenomenology of perception* (C. Smith, Trans.). London: Routledge & Kegan Paul.

Merriam, S. (1977). Interviewing the aged: Some considerations for the adult educator. *Adult Leadership, 25* (7), 215–216.

Merriam, S., & Lumsden, D. B. (1985). Educational needs and interests of older learners. In D. B. Lumsden (Ed.), *The older adult as learner* (pp. 51-72). Washington, DC: Hemisphere Publishing.

Messick, S., & Associates. (1976). *Individuality in learning: Implications of cognitive styles and creativity for human development.* San Francisco: Jossey-Bass.

Miller, B. W., & Hotes, R. W. (1982). Almost everything you always wanted to know about individualized instruction. *Lifelong Learning: The Adult Years, 5* (9), 20-23.

Miller, J. V. (1986). Helping adults balance career and family roles. In J. V. Miller & M. L. Musgrove (Eds.), *Issues in adult career counseling* (New Directions for Continuing Education, no. 32, pp. 95-99). San Francisco: Jossey-Bass.

Monette, M. L. (1977). The concept of educational need: An analysis of selected literature. *Adult Education, 27,* 116-127.

Monette, M. L. (1979). Need assessment: A critique of philosophical assumptions. *Adult Education, 29,* 83-95.

Moore, M. G. (1973). Towards a theory of independent learning and teaching. *Journal of Higher Education, 44,* 661-679.

Moore, M. G. (1987). Print media. In J. A. Niemi & D. D. Gooler (Eds.), *Technologies for learning outside the classroom* (New Directions for Continuing Education, no. 34, pp. 41-50). San Francisco: Jossey-Bass.

Morrison, T. R. (1989). Beyond legitimacy: Facing the future in distance education. *International Journal of Lifelong Education, 8,* 3-24.

Mullan, C., & Gorman, L. (1972). Facilitating adaptation to change: A case study in retraining middle-aged and older workers at Aer Lingus. *Industrial Gerontology, 15,* 23-29.

Murrell, K.F.H. (1965). *Ergonomics.* London: Chapman & Hall.

Nadler, L. (1982). *Designing training programs: The critical events model.* Reading, MA: Addison-Wesley.

New York State Education Department. (1958). *Planning facilities to accommodate adult education.* Albany: State University of New York. (ERIC Document Reproduction Service No. ED 036 982)

Niemi, J. A., & Gooler, D. D. (1987). Themes and issues. In J. A. Niemi & D. D. Gooler (Eds.), *Technologies for learning outside the classroom* (New Directions for Continuing Education, no. 34, pp. 101-108). San Francisco: Jossey-Bass.

Norman, D. A. (1973). *Cognitive organization and learning.* La Jolla: University of California, Center for Human Information Processing. (ERIC Document Reproduction Service no. ED 083 543)

North Carolina Council on Developmental Disabilities. (n.d.). *Peo-*

ple first: A reference guide regarding persons with disabilities. Raleigh: Council on Developmental Disabilities, North Carolina Department of Human Resources.

Oddi, L. F. (1984). Development of an instrument to measure self-directed continuing learning. (Doctoral dissertation, Northern Illinois University, 1984.) *Dissertation Abstracts International, 46,* 49A.

Oddi, L. F. (1985). Development and validation of an instrument to identify self-directed continuing learners. *Proceedings of the 26th Annual Adult Education Research Conference* (pp. 229–235). Arizona State University, Higher and Adult Education, Tempe.

Oddi, L. F. (1986). Development and validation of an instrument to identify self-directed continuing learners. *Adult Education Quarterly, 36,* 97–107.

Ogle, S. E. (1986). Memory and aging: A review and application of current theories. *Lifelong Learning: An Omnibus of Practice and Research, 9* (6), 8–10, 27.

Okun, M. A. (1977). Implications of geropsychological research for the instruction of older adults. *Adult Education, 27,* 139–155.

Okun, M. A., & DiVesta, F. J. (1976). Cautiousness in adulthood as a function of age and instruction. *Journal of Gerontology, 31,* 571–576.

Okun, M. A., & Siegler, I. C. (1977). The perception of outcome-effort covariation in younger and older men. *Educational Gerontology, 2,* 27–32.

Osmond, H. (1959). The relationship between architect and psychiatrist. In C. Goshen (Ed.), *Psychiatric architecture.* Washington, DC: American Psychiatric Association.

Ostwald, S. K., & Williams, H. Y. (1985). Optimizing learning in the elderly: A model. *Lifelong Learning: An Omnibus of Practice and Research, 9* (1), 10–15, 27.

Overstreet, H. (1941). *Leaders for adult education.* New York: American Association for Adult Education.

Pastalan, L. (1970). Privacy as an expression of human territoriality. In L. Pastalan & D. Carson (Eds.), *Spatial behavior of older people.* Ann Arbor: University of Michigan, Institute of Gerontology.

Penland, P. R. (1978). *Self-planned learning in America.* (ERIC Document Reproduction Service No. ED 154 987)

Penland, P. (1979). Self-initiated learning. *Adult Education Quarterly, 29,* 170–179.

Pennington, F. C. (Ed.). (1980). *Assessing educational needs of adults* (New Directions for Continuing Education, no. 7). San Francisco: Jossey-Bass.

Perry, W. (1970). *Forms of intellectual and ethical development in the college years: A scheme.* New York: Holt, Rinehart & Winston.

Peterson, D. A. (1983). *Facilitating education for older learners.* San Francisco: Jossey-Bass.

Peterson, D. A., & Eden, D. Z. (1981). Cognitive style and the older learner. *Educational Gerontology, 7,* 57–66.

Pine, W. S. (1980). The effect of foreign adult student participation in program planning on achievement and attitude. (Doctoral dissertation, Auburn University, 1980.) *Dissertation Abstracts International, 41,* 2405A.

Plopper, M. (1981). Mental health in the elderly. In R. H. Davis (Ed.), *Aging: Prospects and issues.* Los Angeles: University of Southern California Press.

Polloway, E. A., Smith, J. D., & Patton, J. R. (1984). Learning disabilities: An adult development perspective. *Learning Disability Quarterly, 7,* 179–186.

Popham, W. J. (1972). *An evaluation guidebook: A set of practical guidelines for the educational evaluator.* Los Angeles: Instructional Objectives Exchange.

Postman, N., & Weingartner, C. (1969). *Teaching as a subversive activity.* New York: Delacorte Press.

Pratt, D. D. (1984). Teaching adults: A conceptual framework for the first session. *Lifelong Learning: An Omnibus of Practice and Research, 7* (6), 7–9, 28, 31.

Pratt, D. D. (1988). Andragogy as a relational construct. *Adult Education Quarterly, 38,* 160–172.

Price, G. (1983). Diagnosing learning styles. In R. M. Smith (Ed.), *Helping adults learn how to learn* (New Directions for Continuing Education, no. 19, pp. 49–55). San Francisco: Jossey-Bass.

Progoff, I. (1975). *At a journal workshop.* New York: Dialogue House Library.

Proshansky, H. M., Ittelson, W. H., & Rivlin, L. G. (Eds.). (1976). *Environmental psychology: People and their settings.* New York: Holt, Rinehart & Winston.

Rachal, J. R. (1984). The computer in the ABE and GED classroom: A review of the literature. *Adult Education Quarterly, 35,* pp. 86-95.

Rainer, T. (1978). *The new diary.* Los Angeles: Tarcher.

Ralston, P. A. (1981). Educational needs and activities of older adults: Their relationship to senior center programs. *Educational Gerontology, 7,* 231-244.

Rasmussen, S. E. (1959). *Experiencing architecture.* Cambridge, MA: MIT Press.

Rees, P. L. (Compiler). (1988). *Directory of adult-serving programs in the U.S. Department of Education.* Washington, DC: Office of Vocational and Adult Education, Division of Adult Education, Clearinghouse on Adult Education.

Reichmann, S., & Grasha, A. F. (1974). A rational approach to developing and assessing the construct validity of a student learning scale instrument. *Journal of Psychology, 87,* 213-223.

Rigors, P. (1971). *Case methods in human relations: The incident process.* New York: McGraw-Hill.

Ripple, R. E., & Jaquish, G. A. (1981). Fluency, flexibility, and originality in later adulthood. *Educational Gerontology, 7,* 1-10.

Roberts, L. H. (1988, September). Computer conferencing: A classroom for distance learning. *International Council for Distance Education, 18,* 35-40.

Robertson, R., & Grant, G. (1982). Teaching and ethics: An epilogue. *Journal of Higher Education, 53,* 345-357.

Robinson, J. P., Athanasiou, R., & Head, K. B. (1969). *Measures of occupational attitudes and occupational characteristics.* Ann Arbor: University of Michigan, Institute for Social Research.

Robinson, J. P., & Shaver, P. R. (1969). *Measures of social psychological attitudes.* Ann Arbor: University of Michigan, Institute for Social Research.

Rodgers, W., & Herzog, R. (1987). Interviewing older adults: The accuracy of factual information. *Journal of Gerontology, 42,* 387–394.

Rogers, C. R. (1983). *Freedom to learn for the eighties.* Columbus, OH: Merrill.

Rossman, M. H. (1982). Self-assessment. In C. Klevins (Ed.), *Materials and methods in adult and continuing education* (pp. 346–359). Los Angeles: Klevins.

Savicevic, D. M. (1981). Adult education systems in European socialist countries: Similarities and differences. In A. N. Charters & Associates, *Comparing adult education worldwide* (pp. 37–89). San Francisco: Jossey-Bass.

Schaie, K. W., Labouvie, G. V., & Buech, B. U. (1973). Generational and cohort-specific differences in adult cognitive functioning: A fourteen-year study of independent samples. *Developmental Psychology, 9,* 151–166.

Schaie, K. W., & Strother, F. (1968). *Human aging and behavior.* New York: Academic Press.

Schaie, K. W., & Willis, S. L. (1986). *Adult development and aging* (2nd ed.). Boston: Little, Brown.

Scheflen, A. E., & Ashcraft, N. (1976). *Human territories: How we behave in space-time.* Englewood Cliffs, NJ: Prentice-Hall.

Schön, D. A. (1987). *Educating the reflective practitioner: Toward a new design for teaching and learning in the professions.* San Francisco: Jossey-Bass.

Schroeder, W. L. (1980). Typology of adult learning systems. In J. M. Peters & Associates. *Building an effective adult education enterprise.* San Francisco: Jossey-Bass.

Shadden, B. B., & Raiford, C. A. (1984). The communication education of older persons: Prior training and utilization of information sources. *Educational Gerontology, 10,* 83–97.

Sheckley, B. G. (1986). Microcomputers and adult learning: Maximizing potentials. In B. Heermann (Ed.) *Personal computers and the adult learner* (New Directions for Continuing Education, no. 29, 94–104). San Francisco: Jossey-Bass.

Sheehy, G. (1976). *Passages: Predictable crises of adult life.* New York: Dutton.

Sheppard, N. A. (1979). *Educational opportunities for older persons: A review* (Information Series No. 170). Columbus: Ohio

State University, ERIC Clearinghouse for Adult, Career, and Vocational Education.

Siebles, M. W. (Compiler). (1988). *Older persons: Directory of resources for older persons.* Washington, DC: U.S. Department of Education, Office of Vocational and Adult Education, Division of Adult Education.

Sisco, B. R. (1986). New approaches to graduate study in adult education. *MPAEA Journal of Adult Education, 14* (2), 1-9.

Sisco, B. R. (1987). An analysis of the cognitive profiles of selected university adult students. *Proceedings of the 28th Annual Adult Education Research Conference* (pp. 226-232). University of Wyoming, Laramie.

Sisco, B. R. (1988). A study of the teaching strategies used to promote self-directed learning among graduate students in adult education. *Proceedings of the 29th Annual Adult Education Research Conference* (pp. 276-281). University of Calgary, Faculty of Continuing Education, Calgary, Alberta.

Six, J. E. (1987). *Measuring the performance properties of the Oddi continuing learning inventory.* Unpublished doctoral dissertation, Syracuse University, Syracuse, NY.

Six, J. E., & Hiemstra, R. (1987). The classroom learning scale: A criterion measure of the Oddi continuing learning inventory. *Proceedings of the 28th Annual Adult Education Research Conference* (pp. 233-238). University of Wyoming, Laramie.

Smith, R. M. (1982). *Learning how to learn.* Chicago: Follett.

Smith, R. M. (Ed.). (1983). *Helping adults learn how to learn* (New Directions for Continuing Education, no. 19). San Francisco: Jossey-Bass.

Smith, R. M., & Cunningham, P. M. (1987). *The independent learner's sourcebook.* Chicago: American Library Association.

Smith, R. M., & Haverkamp, K. K. (1977). Toward a theory of learning how to learn. *Adult Education, 2,* 3-21.

Sommer, R. (1967). Classroom ecology. *Journal of Applied Behavioral Science, 3,* 489-503.

Sommer, R. (1969). *Personal space.* Englewood Cliffs, NJ: Prentice-Hall.

Sommer, R. (1970). The ecology of study areas. *Environment and Behavior, 2,* 271-280.

Sommer, R. (1974). *Tight spaces.* Englewood Cliffs, NJ: Prentice-Hall.

Sommer, R., & Olsen, H. (1980). The soft classroom. *Environment and Behavior, 12,* 3–16.

Steele, F. (1973). *Physical settings and organizational development.* Reading, MA: Addison-Wesley.

Steele, F., & Jenks, S. (1977). *The feel of the work place.* Reading, MA: Addison-Wesley.

Steele, S. M., & Brack, R. E. (1973). *Evaluating the attainment of objectives in adult education: Process, properties, problems, prospects.* Syracuse, NY: Publications in Continuing Education.

Sternberg, R. J. (1986). *Intelligence applied: Understanding and increasing your intellectual skills.* Orlando, FL: Harcourt Brace Jovanovich.

Stewart, D. W. (1986a). *Adult learning in America: Eduard Lindeman and his agenda for lifelong learning.* Malabar, FL: Krieger.

Stewart, D. W. (1986b). Perspectives. *Lifelong Learning: An Omnibus of Practice and Research, 9* (5), 2.

Stires, L. (1980). Classroom seating, location, student grades, and attitudes: Environment or self-selection? *Environment and Behavior, 12,* 241–254.

Sudman, S., & Bradburn, N. M. (1982). *Asking questions: A practical guide to questionnaire design.* San Francisco: Jossey-Bass.

Symposium on adult learning psychology: Implications for higher education. (1973). Buffalo: State University of New York, Division of Continuing Education. (ERIC Document Reproduction Service No. ED 094 173)

Tager, R. M. (1981). Physical health realities—a medical view. In R. H. Davis (Ed.), *Aging: Prospects and issues.* Los Angeles: University of Southern California Press.

Tagiuri, R. (1968). The concept of organizational climate. In R. Tagiuri & G. H. Litwin (Eds.), *Organizational climate: Explanation of a concept* (pp. 11–31). Boston: Harvard University, Division of Research, Graduate School of Business Administration.

Takemoto, P. A. (1987). Exploring the educational potential of audio. In J. A. Niemi & D. D. Gooler (Eds.), *Technologies for learning outside the classroom* (New Directions for Continuing Education, no. 34, pp. 19–28). San Francisco: Jossey-Bass.

Taub, H. A. (1977). Free and ordered recall: Coding as a function of age. *Journal of Genetic Psychology, 131,* 75–81.

Tennant, M. (1986). An evaluation of Knowles' theory of adult learning. *International Journal of Lifelong Learning, 5,* 113–122.

Thorndike, E. L. (1928). *Adult learning.* New York: Macmillan.

Tough, A. (1967). *Learning without a teacher: A study of tasks and assistance during adult self-teaching projects.* Toronto: Ontario Institute for Studies in Education.

Tough, A. (1978). Major learning efforts: Recent research and future directions. *Adult Education, 28,* 250–263.

Tough, A. M. (1979). *The adult's learning projects* (2nd ed.). Austin, TX: Learning Concepts.

Trent, J. W., & Cohen, A. M. (1973). Research on teaching in higher education. In R.M.W. Travers (Ed.), *Second handbook on research on teaching.* Chicago: Rand McNally.

Tyler, R. (1949). *Basic principles of curriculum and instruction.* Chicago: University of Chicago Press.

Verdros, K., & Pankowski, M. L. (1980). Participatory planning in lifelong learning. In G. C. Whaples & D. M. Ewert (Eds.), *Proceedings of the Lifelong Learning Research Conference.* College Park,University of Maryland, Department of Agriculture and Extension Education.

Verner, C. (1964). *Adult education.* Washington, DC: Center for Applied Research in Education.

Vosko, R. S. (1984). Shaping spaces for lifelong learning. *Lifelong Learning: An Omnibus of Practice and Research, 9* (1), 4–7, 28.

Vosko, R. S. (1985). The reactions of adult learners to selected instructional environments. (Doctoral dissertation, Syracuse University, 1984.) *Dissertation Abstracts International, 45,* 3519A.

Vosko, R. S., & Hiemstra, R. (1988). The adult learning environment: Importance of physical features. *International Journal of Lifelong Education, 7,* 185–196.

Wald, R. (1978). Confronting the learning contract. *Alternative Higher Education, 2* (3), 223–231.

Wass, H., & Olejnik, S. F. (1983). An analysis and evaluation of research in cognition and learning among older adults. *Educational Gerontology, 9,* 323–338.

Wass, H., & West, C. A. (1977). A humanistic approach to education of older persons. *Educational Gerontology, 2,* 407–416.

Wechsler, D. (1958). *The measurement and appraisal of adult intelligence* (3rd ed.). Baltimore, MD: Williams and Wilkins.

Weisenburg, T., Roe, A., & McBride, K. E. (1936). *Adult intelligence.* New York: Commonwealth Fund.

Wells, M. (1981). *Gentle architecture.* New York: McGraw-Hill.

White, M. A., & Hansen, M. D. (1976). Guidelines for achievement of learner satisfaction in gerontological short-term training. *Educational Gerontology, 1,* 193–197.

White, S. (1972). *Physical criteria for adult learning environments.* Washington, DC: Adult Education Association of the U.S.A., Commission on Planning Adult Learning Systems, Facilities, and Environments. (ERIC Document Reproduction Service No. ED 080 882)

Wiesner, P. (1983). Some observations on telecourse research and practice. *Adult Education Quarterly, 33,* pp. 215–221.

Wiesner, P. (1987). Utilizing television. In J. A. Niemi & D. D. Gooler (Eds.), *Technology for learning outside the classroom* (New Directions for Continuing Education, no. 34, pp. 9–18). San Francisco: Jossey-Bass.

Will, P. (1958). Environment for learning. In H. Hunsaker & R. Pierce (Eds.), *Creating a climate for adult learning.* Washington, DC: Commission on Architecture for Adult Education, Adult Education Association of the U.S.A.

Willis, F. N. (1966). Initial speaking distance as a function of the speaker's relationship. *Psychonomic Science, 5,* 221–222.

Winn, F. J., Jr., Elias, J. W., & Marshall, P. H. (1976). Meaningfulness, interference, and age. *Educational Gerontology, 1,* 297–306.

Witte, K. L., & Freund, J. S. (1976). Paired-associate learning in young and old adults as related to stimulus concreteness and presentation methods. *Journal of Gerontology, 31,* 186–192.

Wlodkowski, R. J. (1985). *Enhancing adult motivation to learn: A guide to improving instruction and increasing learner achievement.* San Francisco: Jossey-Bass.

Worthen, B. R., & Sanders, J. R. (1973). *Educational evaluation: Theory and practice.* Worthington, OH: Jones.

Name Index

Jones, E. E., 162
Jones, H. E., 22, 23
Jones, J., 254
Jones, J. E., 223, 224, 225, 226, 228
Jordan, D. R., 153, 155
Joyce, B., 36

K

Kantrowitz, M., 251
Kapp, 233
Kasworm, C. E., 107, 160
Keefe, J. W., 239, 241
Keinholz, A., 240
Kennelly, K. J., 228
Kennon, P., 257
Kidd, J. R., 11, 22, 27, 28, 38, 247
Kinney, M. B., 159
Knirk, F., 250, 255, 256, 257
Knoll, J. H., 233
Knowles, M. S., 5, 11, 14, 33, 46, 63,
    65, 95, 96, 105, 106, 108, 109,
    110n, 114, 118, 163, 191, 206, 225,
    231–234, 243, 245, 247
Knowlton, M. P., 159, 160
Knox, A. B., 24, 25, 29, 65–66, 69,
    125, 223, 224, 225, 226, 228, 239,
    243, 244, 245
Kolb, D. A., 239, 240
Koneya, M., 248
Kooken, R. A., 163
Korhonen, L. J., 239
Kozol, J., 7
Kramer, J. J., 225
Krasner, L., 251
Kreitlow, B. W., 220
Kuhlen, R. G., 162
Kulich, J., 236

L

Labouvie, G. V., 23
Labouvie-Vief, G., 163, 227
Lafferty, J. C., 239, 240
Lam, W., 257
Landers, K., 237
Langner, W. R., 155
Lean, E., 153, 154
Leclerc, G. J., 227

Leean, C., 139
Lersten, K. C., 223, 225, 227, 228
Levanthal, G., 254
Levinson, D. J., 227
Lindeman, E. C., 233, 235–236
Lindgren, H. C., 253
Lindquist, J., 105–106
Lipschultz, M., 254
Lockwood, J., 94, 95
Loesch, T., 239
Loewenthal, N. H., 141
Long, H. B., 11, 23, 24, 223, 235, 236,
    243
Long, R., 243
Long, R. W., 190
Lorge, I., 23
Lumsden, D. B., 227
Lyons, M., 94

M

Mager, R. F., 193, 243
Main, K., 218
Marcus, E. E., 227
Markley, R. P., 225
Marks, L., 256
Marlowe, C. L., 142
Marshall, P. H., 164
Marton, F., 239
Mather, C., 236
Maxfield, D., 239
Mays, F., 155
McBride, K. E., 22
McCall, R. J., 239
McClusky, H. Y., 10, 11, 218
McCormick, E., 248
McFarland, R., 249
McKeachie, W. J., 36
MacKeracher, D., 65
McKinley, J., 141
McLaughlin, D., 243
McMahon, E. E., 243
Mergler, N. L., 225
Merleau-Ponty, M., 256
Merriam, S., 9, 10, 227, 228
Merriam, S. B., 22, 26
Messick, S., 241
Middlemiss, M. A., 27, 160
Miller, J. V., 68

Subject Index

A

Activities. *See* Learning activities; Preplanning activities

Adult, concepts of, 31

Adult Education Association of the U.S.A., 246

Adult Education Research Conference, 235

Adult learners: ability of, and ownership, 67–68, 72–73; abuse of freedom by, 70–72; analysis of characteristics of, 20–34; autonomy of, 138; background on, 20–21; barriers for, 30–31; characteristics of, 32–33; comfort level of, 84; confidence building for, 185–186; control possibilities for, 12; emotional characteristics of, 29–31; as experience rich and theory poor, 50, 56–57; individualized instruction for, 1–73; initial contact with, 81–87; instructional process linked with, 5–6; introductory activities for, 85–87, 188; involvement in needs assessment by, 95; with learning disabilities, 152–159; mental characteristics of, 21–26; needs and expectations of, 59–61; needs assessment for, 94–103; older, 159–165, 223–228; ownership for, 63–73; physical characteristics of, 26–29; resistance from, 51–53, 57, 71; role enlarged for, 10–11; self-confidence of, 14–15; and shared responsibility, 62–73; social characteristics of, 31–34; special groups of, 150–166; stimulating, 14–15

Advisory council, for needs assessment, 190

AEDNET (Adult EDucator's NETwork), 145

Agency visits, learning from, 214–215

American Medical Association, 193

American Society for Training and Development, 173

Andragogy, research and theory on, 5, 231–234

Anthropometry, research and theory on, 248–250

Army Alpha test, 22

Assessment, of learning ability, 22–23. *See also* Evaluation; Needs assessment

mative and formative, 123–124, 127–128, 130–132; techniques for, 128–130

F

Facilitative role: attitudes toward, 13; and content expertise, 66–67; evaluation of, 132; impact of, 11, 16–17; and older adults, 226; and open instructional strategy, 42; and stimulation for learners, 14–15

Feedback: and evaluation, 93, 124; and instructional plan, 90–91; on learning contracts, 112–113; role of, 55–56

G

Games, for needs assessment, 189–190

General Educational Development, 32

George Washington University, and learning disabilities, 155

Germany, and andragogy, 233

Grades: criterion-referenced, 126–127; and learning contracts, 109, 116–117; negotiating, 127–128

Graduate courses, developing, 220–222

Graduate Record Examination, 122

Greece, evaluation in ancient, 122

Group interactions, for needs assessment, 189–190

Group learning activities, 212–214

Group size, for adult students, 59, 164

H

Health, of adult learners, 29

Hearing: of adult learners, 28; and instructional needs, 161

Hungary, andragogy in, 233

I

Implementation: checklist for, 172; in model, 47, 92, 170

Individualized instruction: approaches to, 1–73; appropriate situations for, 58–61; assimilating, 49–61; background on, 1–2, 49–50; benefits of, 175–176; checklist for, 172–173; circumstances for, 1–73; concerns about, 183–187; conclusion on, 178; in content areas, 186; content-process balance in, 60–61; future of, 177–178; group size for, 59, 164; impact of, 15–19; introduction techniques for, 85–87, 188; methods for, 75–132; model for, 44–48, 77–93, 168–171; in nonformal settings, 186–187; in nontraditional settings, 135–149; patience and flexibility for, 54–55; personalizing, 54–58; potential of, 167–178; practical applications for, 181–228; problems with, 176; process of, 6, 77–93; reasons for, 4–7; research and theory for, 229–259; research needed on, 178; resistance to, 51–54; resources for, 179–259; and self-direction, 5, 6–7, 10–11, 60, 105, 107, 162; settings for, 58–59; shared responsibility for, 62–73; for special audiences, 150–166; steps in, 77–93; strategies and techniques for, 35–48; structured approach of, 57–58; success in, 133–178; time needed for, 183–184. *See also* Instruction

Information resources, and computer conferencing, 148–149

Inquiry Mode Questionnaire (InQ), 242

Institutions: bureaucratic resistance from, 53–54, 117–118; and evaluation, 125, 132; future of, 177–178

Instruction: for adults, 35–48; approaches to, 15–16; background on, 35–36; criteria for, 36–39; describing process of, 87; evaluating, 124–125; learners linked with process of, 5–6; learning linked with, 39–40; in literature, 36;

N

National Adult Education Conference, 235
National Opinion Research Center, 236
Needs assessment: aspects of, 94–103; background on, 94–95; group activities for, 100–102; and instructional plan, 90; instruments for, 95–100, 191–192; in nontraditional education, 141; for older adults, 226–227; as on-going, 102–103; research and theory for, 243–244; techniques for, 95–100, 189–195
New Hampshire, intelligence testing in, 22
New York State Education Department, 246–247
Nominal group involvement, for needs assessment, 189–190
Nontraditional education: adapting individualized instruction to, 135–149; background on, 135–136; design issues in, 139–141; examples of, 143–149; future of, 141–143; increase in, 137; individualized instruction in, 59; learner involvement in, 138–139, 146–148; open learning systems for, 138; technology for, 136–139, 141, 142–143, 144–148
North Carolina Council on Developmental Disabilities, 156

O

Older adults: approaches for, 159–166; barriers for, 227–228; evaluation for, 163, 223–224; increase of, 159–160; instructional needs of, 160–165; involvement of, 224; meaningfulness for, 164, 224–225; needs assessment for, 226–227; resources for, 162, 223–228
On-line computer conferencing, for nontraditional education, 145–148

Ownership: approaches to shared, 62–73; and attitudes, 14; background on, 62–63; and informal environment, 88; and instructional planning, 89; and learning contracts, 107–108; and needs assessment, 97, 100, 103; obstacles to, 70–73; promoting, 63–70; self-discipline and self-confidence for, 65–66

P

Participate (Parti) program, 146–148, 196–201
Peer evaluation, for needs assessment, 193
Performance appraisal, for needs assessment, 193–194
Physical environment. See Environment, physical
Planning: checklist for, 172; in model, 40–44, 46, 89–91, 170; overall, 78–81; and the unexpected, 174
Poland, andragogy in, 233
Posteducation society, 4–5
Preplanning activities: checklist for, 172; in model, 45–46, 78–81, 169; and overall planning, 78–81
Progressivism, and adult learning, 9
Proxemics, research and theory on, 252–256
Public Law 94-142, 152

Q

Questionnaire, for needs assessment, 192

R

Reaction time: of adult learners, 28; and instructional pace, 163, 223
Reading log, interactive, 205–208
Records analysis, for needs assessment, 194
Research: on andragogy, 5, 231–234; on environment, 245–259; on learning styles, 239–242; on needs

assessment, 243–244; on self-directed learning, 5, 235–238

Resources: information, 148–149; in learning contracts, 109, 111; for learning disabilities, 155–159; for older adults, 162, 223–228; planning for, 80; for practical applications, 181–228; on research findings, 229–259; variety of, and ownership, 64–65

Responsibility. *See* Ownership

Role modeling, 55

Rossman's self-assessment inventory, 37

S

Scholastic Aptitude Test, 122

Self-confidence: of adult learners, 14–15; for older adults, 162–163; for ownership, 65–66

Self-directed learning: impact of, 6–7, 60; and learning contracts, 105, 107; and learning theories, 10–11; and older adults, 162; research on, 5, 235–238

Self-Directed Learning Competencies Self Appraisal Form, 107

Simulations, for needs assessment, 189

Society: changing, and educational change, 7–8; posteducation, 4–5

South Carolina, University of, learning contracts at, 105

Study groups, learning activities in, 212–214

Study guide: for computer conferencing, 146; for nontraditional education, 141, 146; and workbooks, 80–81, 87, 91, 112, 116, 221

Supervisory rating, for needs assessment, 193–194

Symposium on Adult Learning Psychology, 162, 223, 227, 228

Synaesthetics, research and theory on, 256–259

Syracuse University: adult education at, 143–146; computer technology at, 136, 146–148; Kellogg Project at, 144–146

Syracuse University Resources for Educators of Adults (SUREA), 144

Systematic devices, for needs assessment, 192–194

T

Task analysis, for needs assessment, 192–193

Team teaching, learning activities in, 214

Technology: and learning disabilities, 159; for nontraditional education, 136–139, 141–148

Testing: and evaluation, 126–128; for needs assessment, 194

Theory log, interactive, 209–211

Type Indicator, 240

U

Union of Soviet Socialist Republics, autodidactic learning in, 233

United Kingdom: andragogy in, 232; ergonomics in, 252

U.S. Department of Education, 155

V

Vision: of adult learners, 27–28; and instructional needs, 161

W

Wechsler Adult Intelligence Scale, 26

Workbook: in graduate course, 221; and learning contracts, 112, 116; uses of, 80–81, 87, 91, 141, 146

Y

Yugoslavia, andragogy in, 233